# the graduate
# career handbook

"A comprehensive and practical guide – an invaluable tool for graduates seeking work."

*Graduate Gateway Team, the University of Salford*

"Finding the right graduate job may well be the biggest challenge that students at university face. *The Graduate Career Handbook* provides a real insight into today's workplace and a step-by-step guide to surviving the graduate recruitment process. It is an invaluable reference that students and graduates should not be without."

*Martin Birchall, Managing Director, High Fliers Research Ltd*

"Shirley Jenner's *The Graduate Career Handbook* is a MUST for university students and recent graduates. It is a comprehensive guide on career options, as well as offering practical advice on CVs, applications, interviews, realistic salary expectations and how generally to cope with a new job. An excellent addition to the literature."

*Professor Cary L. Cooper, BUPA Professor of Organizational Psychology and Health, UMIST*

"It is often said that 'those who know what they want, get what they want'. Shirley Jenner's highly readable and informative book seems a valuable resource to help students clarify career aspirations and, most importantly, seek a good organizational fit with their values and beliefs. For completeness, it also includes the usual approaches of checking career alignment with knowledge and skill bases.

With its comprehensive descriptions, this volume should also help to demystify modern recruitment and selection processes and allow individuals to prepare for these effectively. Ultimately, being both well informed about the latter and more confident about career and employer choice can only help ensure a better outcome for both job seekers and managers alike.

A particular strength of this text is its focus on 'self-development', a highly valued attribute in today's workforce. It is extensive in its referencing and suggestions for obtaining further information, much of it 'on-line'. This, coupled with numerous examples and exercises, can only enhance its credibility as a useful self-development resource."

*Vicki Garson, HR Director (Training & Development/Graduate Recruitment), AstraZeneca*

"At a time when graduates are faced with an ever-increasing range of jobs, this handbook should be essential reading for undergraduates and graduates. It combines the best elements of a reference textbook on graduate jobhunting and a practical, problem-solving workbook."

*Alistair Grant, Senior Vice-President – Human Resources, Avecia Limited*

"This is a monumental work, comprehensive and very useful for potential and recent graduates. I think that the strengths are the clear signposting, the student reflective activities, the breadth of coverage, and the inclusion of empirical data to provide a context for the well-structured advice. I think this is an excellent aid for reflective career development."

*Professor Lee Harvey, Director of the Centre for Research into Quality, University of Central England in Birmingham*

"One of the most important elements of Shirley's book has been to highlight the fact that if graduate recruitment is to be successful for both parties, then the graduate must try to align his/her personal wants, needs, knowledge, skills, background and personality to the multitude of graduate schemes in the market place. This book goes through the correct process by which graduates, of whatever discipline, should approach applying for quality graduate schemes, and aim to maximize what they will also get out of it.

This book illustrates to graduates, irrespective of academic discipline, that they should consider all options open to them, and aim to harness their personal skills, knowledge, background and experience, to enable them to find the 'best fit' graduate scheme."

*Gareth Jarman, HR Scheduling, Andersen Consulting*

"This is a most comprehensive, thorough and up-to-date handbook to career planning and job-seeking which will be of great benefit not only to those about to graduate – or recently graduated – but to anyone facing a major decision point in their career. Whilst signposting lots of resources and sources of help, it nevertheless places the individual at the centre of the process. Through exercises and activities the reader is encouraged to take ownership of the management of their own career, and the conceptual material is always illuminated by real case histories. Ms Jenner has pulled off the difficult trick of combining encouragement and hopefulness with pragmatic realism. This book will be a valuable reference, too, for career guidance practitioners working both in higher education and elsewhere, as well as for university tutors and parents."

*Martin E. Thorne, President of the Association of Graduate Careers Advisory Services (AGCAS) and Director of the Careers Advisory Service, University of Nottingham*

"In my view this book will be very useful for new graduates and undergraduates seeking their first career-related jobs. It is authoritative and comprehensive, while also being highly accessible and readable."

*Stephen Taylor, Senior Lecturer in Human Resource Management, Manchester Metropolitan University*

# the graduate career handbook

---

## making the right start for a bright future

**Shirley Jenner**

*An imprint of* **Pearson Education**

London · New York · San Francisco · Toronto · Sydney · Tokyo · Singapore
Hong Kong · Cape Town · Madrid · Paris · Milan · Munich · Amsterdam

**Pearson Education Limited**

Edinburgh Gate
Harlow CM20 2JE
Tel: +44 (0)1279 623623
Fax: +44 (0)1279 431059
www.pearsoned.co.uk

First published in Great Britain 2000

© Pearson Education Limited 2000

The right of Shirley Jenner to be identified as Author of this Work has been asserted by her in accordance with the Copyright, Designs and Patents Act 1988.

ISBN 978 - 0 - 273 - 64428 - 6

*British Library Cataloguing in Publication Data*
A CIP catalogue record for this book can be obtained from the British Library.

10  9  8  7  6

Typeset by Pantek Arts, Maidstone, Kent
Printed and bound in Great Britain by Ashford Colour Press Ltd, Gosport, Hants

*The Publishers' policy is to use paper manufactured from sustainable forests.*

# ABOUT THE AUTHOR

You may be wondering what experiences and knowledge qualify me to write a book about jobhunting. Why trust my advice?

I graduated from the University of Durham with a BA (Hons) in Geography, then gained professional training as a chartered town planner. After working in both local government and private consultancy, I decided that a long-term career in planning was not right for me.

I became a trainer and personal development specialist, working with large and small companies in the private sector as well as the Civil Service, education and not-for-profit organizations. This has involved careers counselling, stress management and providing interpersonal communication skills training. I am also a lecturer in human resource management and international business, appointed as a visiting lecturer to Manchester School of Management, UMIST, in 1998.

As a result of my research, teaching and work experience, I have developed a specialist knowledge of graduate labour markets, the recruitment and selection process and career development pathways.

I lead interactive seminars on career planning, jobhunting and careers development and have produced information and guidance materials for university careers advisory services' web sites. Finally, I have also advised UK graduate recruiters about best practice career development and am co-author of *Recruiting, Retaining and Developing Graduate Talent* (Pearson Education, 2000).

# contents

# acknowledgements

I am grateful for having the opportunity to research and write this book. It represents a very exciting and challenging phase in my life.

Thanks to my students at the universities of Salford and UMIST – especially for entrusting me with your stories of struggle and success in the jobhunting arena. My thanks go also to the thousands of students who completed questionnaires anonymously as your answers have greatly aided research in this area.

Thanks to my academic colleagues for their support, advice and guidance, especially Jill Earnshaw and Mike Smith – your comments have improved and clarified the advice and information contained here.

I am indebted to those thinkers in the field whose ideas have helped me structure this book and given me confidence that my recommendations stand on a firm foundation, particularly John Arnold, Peter Herriot, John Holland and Denise Rousseau, and many more listed in the Bibliography.

This book is full of data that are available only as a result of the hard work and research activities of other people. In particular, I would like to thank Lee Harvey, Sue Moon and Vicki Geall (University of Central England); Kate Purcell and Jane Pitcher (Warwick University) and consultants at High Flyers; Saratoga and Universum.

My thanks go also to Martin Thorne, President of AgCAS, and the many staff of various UK careers advisory services who have contributed to my research by means of interviews, providing information and ideas and granting permission to use some of their materials. Thanks to CSU – publishers of the *Prospects* directory – for its help.

ASE – NFER Nelson is one of the leading producers of psychometric and aptitude or ability tests for graduates. Many thanks for providing the sample tests that make this book so helpful for anyone facing such tests or questionnaires.

Grateful thanks to the graduate recruiters who have contributed to my research, by answering my questionnaires, being interviewed and providing so much information. I trust you will all benefit enormously as students make better choices about careers and employers! I hope we have made the playing field a little more level. Carl Gilleard, Chief Executive of the Association of Graduate Recruiters (AGR), thank you for offering helpful insights into current recruitment trends and issues.

I have a deep appreciation for all my husband, Ian, has done – without his love and patience this book would never have been written. Thanks also to Lucy and Matthew, our wonderful children, who help me keep hold of the important things in life.

I should also thank so many friends among the congregation at Holy Trinity Platt, Rusholme, my local church. Your love, prayers and encouragement have been greatly valued.

# preface

*The graduate employment market is increasingly crowded, competition is fierce and selection techniques are becoming more sophisticated ...*

*Jobhunters need to be well informed and high skilled to get to the front of the queue.*

---

**Did you know?**

► Over 400,000 students graduate every year.

► Only around 7000 vacancies are advertised in leading graduate job directories.

► Around 50 per cent of all first degree students leave university with either a first or an upper second class degree.

► Relatively few students enter graduate jobs in the first few months after leaving university. Many continue with postgraduate study, take time out or find work in non-graduate jobs.

► The best known graduate recruiters receive, on average, 68 applications for every job, but only 10 per cent of applicants are asked to come to an interview.

► Every year, employers have hundreds of unfilled vacancies because they cannot find graduates with the right skills and experience.

---

## JOBHUNTING – FEELING UNDER PRESSURE?

Maybe you are painfully aware that your time at university is drawing to a close – finals loom on the horizon and you have little space to even think about planning your career! There are so many careers to choose from, deciding which way to go is very difficult.

Perhaps you already know the direction you would like to take, but are finding it hard to get down to applying for jobs. Jobhunting is a very time-hungry activity, especially when you are under pressure to complete assignments, write essays and prepare for exams.

How much success are you having? Disappointed? If so, how can you work out what is going wrong and get it right next time? Perhaps you have abandoned thoughts of getting a job before you graduate and are waiting until after finals – this is an increasingly popular strategy.

In writing this book, I understand that you are under pressure – under pressure to make decisions and under pressure to perform.

## MAKE THE RIGHT START

This book is here to help you as you make the exciting, difficult and challenging transition from university to work.

► Make the right career decision based on your unique career shape.

► Find out how employers think and behave.

► Develop all the jobhunting skills you need: writing applications, designing winning CVs, interview techniques, passing aptitude or ability tests and handling assessment centres.

Working through the information and activities in this book will itself enhance your attractiveness to prospective employers. You will know yourself and what you want, develop greater self-confidence, communication skills, understand teamworking and much more.

# introduction

In this book, you will find:

► everything you need for successful jobhunting during or after university;

► inside information about recruitment practices;

► practical advice and exercises to develop the skills you need;

► opportunities to practise taking aptitude or ability tests and improve your results;

► advice on how to build brilliant CVs, make stunning applications and interview well;

► details of a web site companion where you can download exercises and resources to help build your own career portfolio and find all the key links to jobhunting and information sites worldwide.

## THE PURPOSE OF THIS BOOK

This book is intended to be your key resource for each of the stages you will go through as you set about securing a graduate job. The contents will challenge you and invite you to think deeply and honestly about yourself. Contained here are the most influential theories, models and information currently available, so the book will inform you as well. Go at your own pace, dipping into the sections you need, when you need them.

The information and activities contained in this book are all designed to help you on to the right career path and then find an employer who can meet your expectations. It has been written following discussions, questionnaires and focus groups with undergraduates, postgraduates and a large number of those already established in their first job. The issues I address in this book are the ones everyone's talking about and wrestling with.

The book is also based on major research findings from the leading organizations involved in graduate recruitment, from interviews with graduate recruiters in both the private and public sectors, interviews with staff in university careers advisory services and from my own experiences as counsellor, lecturer, recruiter and researcher. In short, it is a summary of information and guidance from the people who know what is happening across the UK, Europe and beyond.

# PART I YOUR CAREER CHOICE

▶ What direction do you want your life to take?

▶ What are the influences on your choice of career destination?

▶ Overcoming the obstacles, coping with the pressure.

The book is written in three parts, each one covering an important stage in choosing and securing the right career and the right employer. Part 1 helps you decide on the right career direction for you, offering opportunities to explore and understand yourself, identify your personal strengths, weaknesses and clarify your aspirations. By reading through Chapters 1 to 5, you will gain a deeper understanding of yourself, your relationships and your career ambitions. You will be given an opportunity to discover your own personal profile, or career **SHAPE** by looking at your:

**S**kills

**H**opes and

**A**mbitions

**P**ersonality

**E**xperience of work

The focus here is on helping you clarify your career aims, but the activities will also provide you with excellent material for making applications, writing a CV and preparing for interviews.

Chapter 6 helps you to identify and overcome obstacles in your career path and offers a range of problem-solving skills, such as force field analysis and highlights the **SMART** goal-setting strategy. Chapter 7 helps you to handle the pressures of jobhunting now and provides a foundation for avoiding burnout once you start work.

# PART II LOOKING AT GRADUATE JOBS
# AND EMPLOYERS

▶ What are the good and bad points about the job you are considering?

▶ Are there options you have overlooked?

▶ How can you find out what a particular organization is really like to work for?

In Chapter 8, you can find out about current trends in graduate jobs. This will be especially useful to anyone who has studied the arts, humanities or sciences and will help you understand your prospective employers' perspective on graduate recruitment. This will help you when filling in application forms and preparing for interviews.

Chapter 9 provides a job classification and a framework to assess the good and bad points about the type of job you are considering. There are lots of suggestions about the new job opportunities that are opening up, those beyond the traditional milk round.

Chapter 10 looks at cultures and climates that exist within organizations and shows you how to cut through the image management of glossy recruitment brochures and get to the truth. Read this and you will find out what your prospective employer is really like to work for! I even provide a workplace health check so you can compare employers and pick the one you are most suited to. Chapter 11 provides more ideas for choosing your first employer, with information about top employers and careers.

Chapter 12 summarizes your employment rights at work – essential reading for anyone holding down a part-time job or in full-time employment. It is also good preparation for those applying for jobs as you'll know what to expect when you are offered a job and start work.

## PART III KEY STEPS TOWARDS GETTING THE JOB YOU WANT

- ▶ Get the job you want.
- ▶ Want the job you get!
- ▶ Jobhunting.
- ▶ Making applications.
- ▶ Interview techniques.
- ▶ Aptitude or ability tests.
- ▶ Assessment centres.
- ▶ Job offer!

Part III helps you through the whole selection process, highlighting the skills you need for successful jobhunting. Chapter 13 gives an overview of the selection process as seen by your prospective employer, providing you will valuable inside information. Reading this will really put you at an advantage over other candidates – you will have seen into the mind of the recruiter! Find out how recruiters think, discover the inside secrets of person specifications and get to grips with competences. Empower yourself!

Chapter 14 gives practical jobhunting advice and includes reference points to the major UK and international job vacancy web sites. Prepare stunning application forms by following the guidelines in Chapter 15, which includes special sections on the standard application form and tailor-made employer forms.

You have an opportunity to build a brilliant CV in Chapter 16 and write winning covering letters. Get yourself invited for an interview and, when you do, read Chapter 17, which contains key information about interview techniques used by employers.

Chapter 18 provides all the information and skill-development training you need to face assessment centre challenges such as second interviews, presentations, teamwork and problem-solving exercises. Some of the information in this section rarely comes into graduate hands, so read it to be 100 per cent ready to excel.

Chapter 19 explains psychometric tests and includes an opportunity to take several different aptitude or ability tests, with tips on how to improve your performance. You can also prepare for personality and career interest tests. Accepting a job offer is a big step, so Chapter 20 highlights the pitfalls and suggests practical ways to negotiate a fair deal. The last chapter offers practical help as you prepare for a successful beginning as you start work – you don't get a second chance to make a first impression!

## WHO IS THIS BOOK FOR?

▶ Undergraduates.

▶ Postgraduates.

▶ Recent graduates.

If you have turned to this section, be assured, this book is for you! Undergraduates, postgraduates and for everyone during the first few years after graduation.

The information and skills contained here will be of use in your first, second, third or fourth year of college or university. This applies to full-time, part-time and sandwich students, those who are young, mature or in between. I have written this book to reflect the needs and aspirations of men and women, for UK residents, international students from Europe and further afield – irrespective of differences in age, gender, sexual orientation, disability, race, ethnicity.

This book will help with career decision making for any and all destinations – my own experience of working in the private sector, local government, the Civil Service, education and not-for-profit organizations give it a broad perspective! The activities throughout aim to get you thinking about your own agenda and aims and help you identify the issues that affect you.

As well as undergraduates, this book is of use to postgraduates and anyone struggling in their present job and thinking of leaving or changing career direction. It could also be of use to parents – either those, like mine, who didn't go to university themselves, or those who are aware of the speed of change and complexity of the graduate job scene and want up-to-date information so they can help rather than hinder!

This book can also be of use and interest, even before university, to teachers, career advisers, those who support students and those who lecture to them. Graduate recruiters would also gain a great deal from the case studies – stories of the pleasure and pain involved in the whole process!

## WHAT DO YOU WANT TO GAIN FROM THIS BOOK NOW?

Here you will have an opportunity to look closely at yourself and your career aspirations. Over time, you may work through all the relevant chapters or just focus on a particular issue or improve a specific skill. You may find it helpful to *write down your starting point in the space provided*. You may have one main issue to wrestle with or a career-related event, such as an interview, coming up soon.

As well as using the contents pages, refer to the index, which is designed to help you find your way to the information, advice and skill development activities when you need them.

## SOMETHING TO DO

If you haven't already started one, I suggest that you create your very own 'career development' portfolio now. Invest in a substantial A4 folder. This is the place to record your learning, because everything you do as you work through this book will contribute towards building your CV, handling interviews and securing the job you hope for.

It is also worth noting that many of the activities and record sheets from this book can be downloaded from the following web site:

www.business-minds.com/gradcareers

Use these to learn about yourself and find out which career is right for you. Good luck!

# Part I

## your career choice

# The Shape of Things to Come

H. G. WELLS (1866–1946), BRITISH WRITER, BOOK TITLE

**In this chapter, you will:**

❑ become clearer about the future shape of your career;

❑ locate yourself on the career thinking cycle;

❑ find out how to build a positive career strategy;

❑ understand the factors affecting your career choice;

❑ identify and begin clearing obstacles;

❑ consider alternatives to work ... further study or time out.

**In the activities:**

**1.1** Where are you on this career decision-making continuum?

**1.2** What factors affect your career choice?

# CAREERS DECISIONS – HOW ARE YOU DOING?

What comes into your mind when the word 'career' is mentioned?

Perhaps you are trying to find the *right* career, but don't yet know what that is. Maybe you will be taking your finals soon, you know the sort of job you want, but work pressures and exams loom and you just can't face a full-blown jobhunting strategy right now. You may be a graduate, suddenly the weeks and months since leaving university are slipping by without your having made much progress.

Decision making is a complicated process and many students and graduates find it hard to find the right direction. Whatever your personal circumstances, this chapter offers you an opportunity to think about your own career plans and the influences on your career choice. You can consider the options and begin building your own personalized jobhunting strategy.

The idea of having just one career or profession that you choose at graduation and stay with for life is increasingly rare. You will come back and review your choice many times during your life, you may come to different conclusions and take new directions as your life unfolds. Some people reading this book will have had prior work experience, others very little. The case studies throughout this book demonstrate that career decision making is an ongoing activity – this is just the beginning of a life-long process. Be encouraged, though, as the Chinese proverb says, 'the journey of a thousand miles begins with one small step'.

## HOW CLEAR ARE YOU ABOUT YOUR FUTURE CAREER?

You may be one of those rare undergraduates who started thinking about your future career early on, perhaps during your first or second year. You may be taking your finals this year and feel you ought to at least make a start on planning your future. Perhaps you are one of the thousands of people who have already graduated and are getting down to career planning.

You may find yourself following the typical thinking cycle shown in Figure 1.1.

You may enter and leave the thinking cycle many times, hitting complete dead-ends or feeling you are just going round in circles. This is quite normal! How decided do you feel right now? I invite you to place yourself along this career decision-making line as shown in Activity 1.1. Your answer is important as it will help you know how to use this book.

If your answer to Activity 1.1 is one of the lower numbers, you should find the rest of Part I of the book useful, especially the self-evaluation chapters and Chapter 6. If you are clear about your career choice, the self-assessment chapters will help you prepare a successful jobhunting strategy and develop the material you need for a great CV.

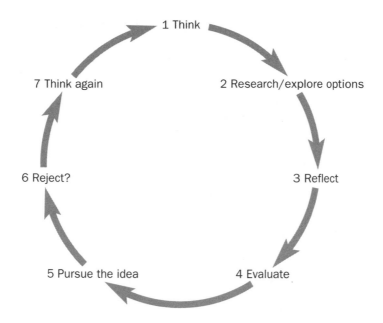

FIGURE 1.1  Thinking about careers

ACTIVITY 1.1    Where are you on this career decision-making continuum?

Circle the comment below that most accurately describes how you feel now.

| Utterly stuck | No idea | Vague idea | Many options | Almost decided | Clear goals |
|---|---|---|---|---|---|
| 1 | 2 | 3 | 4 | 5 | 6 |

# CHOOSING THE RIGHT CAREER

There is a bewildering array of careers-counselling models and decision-making exercises available. You may already have tried some of them, at school or at your university careers advisory service. Underpinning most of them is a fundamental belief that you can assess yourself and match this profile to a job.

## WHAT MAKES CHOOSING THE RIGHT PATH SO DIFFICULT?

Effective career decisions require:

▶ a clear understanding of yourself – skills, hopes, ambitions, personality and limitations;

- ▶ a good understanding of the range of careers/occupations available, the work done, prospects and so on;
- ▶ the ability to link these two domains together logically;
- ▶ recognition of the broader personal, social and economic factors that affect you personally.

If only life were that straightforward! The information and activities in this section are designed to help you unravel some of the complexity. Self-understanding is a tricky business – we don't always know ourselves. Self-analysis is a 'road less travelled' for many, except in times of crisis or change.

You may also question the possibility of there being one stable, certain self to be known – we are complicated individuals. Much of the career decision-making process is actually about working out who we are, whether or not we like what we see and what to do about it if we don't.

There are aspects of yourself and your interests that you can choose to emphasize; others you may want to minimize, conceal or avoid facing. The balance between these can fluctuate enormously. Most of us can imagine ourselves doing many quite different things. The good news is that most people are suited to many categories of jobs, have considerable flexibility and can adapt.

However, to create a convincing CV and handle job applications and interviews, accurate self-assessment is an essential skill – one you will go on using and developing for the rest of your life. There will be no escape … for anyone accepting a job will experience the pleasure and pain of enforced annual appraisals and evaluations of your performance. This is not just about getting a job, it involves skills you will need the whole of your working life.

## FACTORS AFFECTING YOUR CHOICE OF CAREER

What are the main influences on your choice of career or, for some, what are the factors that make choosing the right job and career so difficult?

Activity 1.2 helps you to focus on the key issues that affect you. It will help you identify strengths, uncover concerns and worries if you have any and help you feel more confident in your choice of career direction.

You may wish to look at the range of problem-solving/decision-making methods in Chapter 6 if you are feeling blocked or unsure as to how to make progress.

Take a blank piece of A4 paper and write your name on it, as shown.

**Step 1**

Think about all the various things that influence your decision about the sort of career or job you want. This may include your degree subject, personal interests, family, previous work experience. Certain influences will be positive, while others, perhaps, are restricting you. You could try this exercise alone or with friends in a café or pub. They might find it helpful too!

Take at least 10 minutes to do this. When you think you have finished, don't stop. Think of at least five more items. Then, turn the page and look at Figure 1.2. Does this list provide any more ideas about what factors affect you?

> **Name**
>
> **Factors affecting my career choice**

**Step 2**

Look at the list you have written.

Which are the three main factors influencing your career choice? Write them in the box or make a note in your career portfolio (if you are creating one).

> 1. _____
>
> 2. _____
>
> 3. _____

Is there an area where you are facing a particular problem? If so, write it here.

_____

Identify three factors that are strengths or resources you can build on, then write them in the box.

> 1. _____
>
> 2. _____
>
> 3. _____

**FIGURE 1.2  Possible factors affecting your career choice**

## ARE YOU ON THE RIGHT PATH?

We have considered the many things that combine to influence your career decision. Examples of two very different career decisions are given in the case studies of Andrew and Melissa.

**CASE STUDY   Andrew – the accountant who would rather be a GP**

When I was at school, my father owned and ran a family business involving the whole-sale supply of fruit and vegetables to retail shops throughout Wales. The business had been started by his father and had developed into a thriving concern, employing some 40 people. Being the only son (I have two sisters), I always had one eye on taking over from Dad. No pressure at all was exerted, but I always felt within myself that I would be letting my family down if I did not go into the business. I spent holidays working there, making deliveries and accompanying Dad to the Liverpool Wholesale Market to learn the ropes of buying produce. Dad used to leave the house at 3.30am every morning!!

My own expectation of entering the business led to a lot of conflict within myself. I am not a forceful person, whereas my father and grandfather thrived in the rough and tumble of the small business environment. I therefore felt torn: I wanted to fulfil the role of owner–manager of a successful business, but was concerned that I would not have what it takes to make a success of it.

Looking back from where I am now, I can see that the decision point that resulted in my entering accountancy was my choice of A levels. At that stage, I could have chosen science A levels and gone on to do medicine. With hindsight, this is what I should have done. However, I was not, at that stage, sufficiently free of the expectation of going into the family firm. I chose to do arts subjects, which I enjoyed (history, geography and economics), instead of making the decision to go for medicine.

In the event, the decision concerning the family firm was taken away from me. My father died while I was at university studying Management Sciences. The business was sold to support my mother and other family members. I considered doing medicine as a second degree, but decided that it would take too long. I made the decision to train as an accountant.

**CASE STUDY   Melissa – on air**

Melissa was in her first year as a media student. In the long term, she hoped to get a job as a broadcast journalist with the BBC or another large media organization.

Aware of the huge competition for scarce jobs Melissa decided to start early and negotiated a part-time role at the local hospital radio. This gave her great experience, learning from experienced broadcasters, using the equipment, handling problems and working under pressure.

In addition, this work experience convinced Melissa that she had chosen a career she really enjoyed and could be good at. She loved the work and knew she was on the right path.

## What lessons can you draw from Melissa's and Andrew's career decisions?

Career decisions are complicated and can often be heavily laden with family expect-ations, even when no direct pressure is exerted.

If there is a career path you are thinking about, explore it early, get some work experience to help you know what it would really be like and whether or not you could be successful at it.

# FURTHER STUDY OR TIME OUT BEFORE STARTING WORK?

Not all undergraduates decide to work straightaway, many decide they need either further qualifications or some experience of work first. Lots of students see the time immediately after graduating as the once-in-a-lifetime opportunity to travel and see the world.

You may be interested to see the results of a survey of students' plans after graduation shown in Table 1.1.

**TABLE 1.1  Plans after graduation – class of 1999**

| Plans | Percentages |
|---|---|
| Expecting to start a graduate job | 29 |
| Intending to do a postgraduate course | 20 |
| Taking time off/travelling | 18 |
| Expecting to look for a graduate job | 14 |
| Expecting to take other work | 9 |
| No definite plans | 9 |

Source: Graduate Careers Survey, 1999, High Fliers Research Ltd

The High Fliers research indicates that it is often the most able and ambitious students who postpone career plans and jobhunting because they are focused on achieving the best degree result possible. Graduate employers are becoming aware of this trend to delay career decisions and are no longer depending so heavily on the traditional milk round. Graduate recruitment is slowly becoming more of an all-year-round activity. Take care though – many still run the traditional recruitment drives with an annual intake. Many employers offer undergraduates summer vacation places at the end of the second year that can lead to jobs after graduation.

## CONSIDERING THE OPTIONS

### Further study

The reasons for doing further study vary. The main ones usually cited by postgraduates themselves are:

▶ 'It was an essential requirement for my intended career (for example, teaching, law or for many arts and humanities students)';

▶ 'I always wanted a doctorate', etc.;

▶ 'I was offered a place and a grant, so I accepted';

▶ 'I wasn't sure what I wanted to do, I hoped more study would give me the direction I wanted'.

For many students, though, further study is not an option because of financial limitations and worries about getting into more debt. According to some studies (*Working Out?*, 1999), 10 per cent of students with debts had not been able to fund further postgraduate study and had gone straight into jobs instead and 15 per cent of graduates said debts meant they had to take the first job offered.

## Taking time out/travelling

Azure blue sea lapping gently at your feet under a hazy tropical sky ... Who could resist the idea of relaxing after finals?

Taking time out for a holiday or to travel the world can be an excellent idea, but make sure you have thought about:

► what you want to do, achieve, learn;
► what your resources are – what the financial implications will be for you;
► what happens next – think about what you will do when you get back, before you go!

Employers vary enormously in their attitudes to time out. Some will allow you to defer a job for a year to travel if you can demonstrate that it will add value – for example, by learning a language or developing other skills. Some employers will also accept recent graduates who have taken a year out to travel/work if it can be seen as *relevant*. Usually, the more graduates a company employs each year, the more likely it is to allow a deferment.

Time now for a reality check. Most surveys indicate that graduates are leaving university with heavy debts. Only one in ten new graduates left university in 1998 without owing money borrowed during their period of study, while one in four owed in excess of £5000. The average debt in 1999 was between £3200 and £4400; this may rise for students graduating in 2000 and beyond.

## 'Other work' – treading water and fill-in jobs

Many graduates accept fill-in jobs after graduation. Some studies have found the proportion of students expecting to take what is euphemistically termed 'other work' to be as high as 20–25 per cent. Clearly, many students recognize that the first job they take after graduation may not be linked to their idea of a career. This choice may be due to debt or, perhaps, other personal circumstances.

However, no experience is ever wasted and Chapter 5 offers lots of ideas and guidance on using other work as a stepping stone to great career prospects. In addition, Chapter 9 provides a detailed classification of graduate jobs. Chapter 9 also looks at under-employment and fill-in jobs in more detail.

# S U M M A R Y

► Most students do not feel very clear about their future career direction. This emerges slowly, sometimes only after work experience or a year or so in work following graduation.

You will enter and leave the career thinking cycle many times, often feel stuck, lost and confused. This is a normal part of the process. The fog will lift, though.

▶ Choose a career strategy that will work for you – taking a few steps along the way while you are at university will be a big help.

▶ You will be able to use the information, ideas and insights you have gained in this chapter to plan how you will use this book.

## NEXT STEPS

▶ Be aware of the factors that are affecting your career choices. Work to overcome any obstacles and build on your strengths and resources.

▶ The next four chapters offer you an opportunity for further self-assessment, helping you identify the main elements. This will help you find your own unique career **SHAPE**. This mnemonic, you will recall, stands for:

**S**kills, knowledge and abilities (Chapter 3)

**H**opes and

**A**mbitions (Chapter 4)

**P**ersonality (Chapter 5 )

**E**xperience of work (Chapter 6).

▶ Alternatively, you may want to move straight to a specific chapter or section. Use the contents page or index to help you locate the information, skills or activities that are priorities for you.

▶ Start this process sooner rather than later!

## FURTHER INFORMATION

Please note that contact information is included at the ends of chapters throughout this book and in the Appendix.

### KEY WEB SITES

Some careers guidance information for undergraduates/recent graduates:
  www.get.hobsons.com
  www.prospects.csu.ac.uk

Self-assessment/careers guidance/on-line career path tests:
  www.shlgroup.com
  www.prospects.csu.ac.uk

Information about ten leading professions, such as actuaries, IT, accountancy and management consultancy:
  www.insidecareers.co.uk

## YOUR LOCAL HIGHER EDUCATION CAREERS ADVISORY SERVICE

Help in Self-evaluation – career tests such as *Prospects HE*

*Prospects'* Focus series

Occupational advice booklets

Specialist professional information booklets

Higher education careers advisory service publications

Careers advice: some offer psychometric testing, interviews, workshops

Manchester/UMIST's careers advisory service has an excellent web site

www.netwise.ac.uk

or visit the University of London CAS at

www.careers.lon.ac.uk

## FURTHER READING

### GENERAL INFORMATION TO GET YOU STARTED

These should be available from your local careers advisory service:

▶ *Placement and Vacation Work Casebook* (a series of specialist titles, revised annually) Hobsons (also, see the web site www.hobsons.com)

▶ *Focus on Work Experience* (part of *Prospects* series) (also, see the web site www.csu.prospects.co.uk)

▶ T*he A to Z of Work Experience*

Most also offer:

▶ a locally produced vacancies bulletin;

▶ to hold a local work experience careers fair;

▶ a local community service skills exchange.

Placement opportunities and ideas can be found at:

Liverpool  www.business-bridge.org.uk

Manchester  www.workbank.man.ac.uk

There are also specialist schemes, such as the *Workable Graduate Support Scheme*, which provides support to create placements for disabled students with major employers. Find out more from the following web site:

www.workable.org.uk

See also the Appendix for further work experience information.

# your skills and knowledge

If a little knowledge is dangerous, where is the person who has so much as to be out of danger?

T. H. HUXLEY (1825–95), BRITISH BIOLOGIST, ON ELEMENTARY INSTRUCTION IN PHYSIOLOGY

**In this chapter, you will:**
- [ ] learn about the importance of skills;
- [ ] find out what employers are looking for – the top 20 skills and attributes;
- [ ] check out your skills for a successful working life;
- [ ] discover how to improve your skills;
- [ ] be able to gauge your career-related knowledge – how are you doing?

**In the activities:**

**2.1** A thumbnail sketch of your key skills and knowledge base

**2.2** Career skills profile

**2.3** An audit of my knowledge and expertise

# INTRODUCTION

Together, this and the next three self-assessment chapters outline your unique career **SHAPE**:

**S**kills and knowledge (this chapter)

**H**opes
**A**mbitions } (Chapter 3)

**P**ersonality (Chapter 4)

**E**xperience of work (Chapter 5)

These chapters provide you with information and exercises to help you know and understand yourself better. The results can be used in subsequent chapters as the basic raw material for choosing the right job, writing a brilliant CV and handling interviews. Finding out more about your strengths can help you decide what you would be good at. Exercises may help you identify weak spots, in which case you can act now to overcome them. Information in this chapter will also help you compare your skills with those of other students so you can size up the competition!

The notion that you possess distinctive skills, knowledge and abilities is central to the whole process of career success. This is so because, first, you need to know what you are suited to. Second, you will need to market yourself to prospective employers. The field of graduate recruitment and selection increasingly hinges on ensuring a good match between what a prospective employer is looking for and what you have to offer.

---

**ACTIVITY 2.1    A thumbnail sketch of your key skills and knowledge base**

This exercise asks you to describe yourself in terms of your unique blend of skills and knowledge. Give a thumbnail sketch of your key skills, areas of expertise and knowledge and abilities in the space provided below:

My main skills are:


I am knowledgeable about:


---

Was that hard to do … or was the amount of space far too small? It may have been difficult because I gave you just a couple of headings. Like most other aspects of job-hunting, even the process of self-evaluation doesn't occur in a vacuum. No doubt you will be concerned to evaluate your skills in relation to:

how your level of skill and knowledge affect your choice of career;

what employers are looking for;

what other students have got to offer and how you measure up.

# SO, WHAT ARE EMPLOYERS LOOKING FOR?

Many employers have high expectations of the skills and abilities of graduate employees. They view you as motivated, energetic and adaptable. Some may expect you to make an immediate contribution and add value from your first day, while others will be more interested in training you and developing your potential. Some, of course, do both! However, studies have shown repeatedly that most employers of graduates are looking for certain core qualities or attributes. The top 20 are listed in Table 2.1.

**TABLE 2.1  What employers want – the top 20 skills and qualities**

| Rank | Skills and qualities employers want | Rank | Skills and qualities employers want |
|------|-------------------------------------|------|-------------------------------------|
| 1 | Willingness to learn | 11 | Desire to achieve/motivation |
| 2 | Commitment | 12 | Problem-solving ability |
| 3 | Dependability | 13 | Analytical ability |
| 4 | Self-motivation | 14 | Flexibility |
| 5 | Teamwork | 15 | Initiative |
| 6 | Oral communication skills | 16 | Can summarize key issues |
| 7 | Cooperation | 17 | Logical argument |
| 8 | Written communications skills | 18 | Business awareness |
| 9 | Drive/energy | 19 | Numeracy |
| 10 | Self-management | 20 | Adaptability |

Source: Adapted from Harvey, L. *et al.* (1997), *Graduate Work: organisational change and students' attributes*, CRQ, University of Central England.

# UNDERSTANDING EMPLOYERS

You will notice that the attributes listed above include a mixture of skills and other qualities concerned with your drive and ambition as well as your personality. Sometimes it is hard to separate out what is a skill from a personal attribute. This is why many employers now describe their requirements in terms of both skills and personal attributes, dimensions or competences. A competence is defined by its originator as 'an underlying characteristic of a person that results in effective and/or superior performance in a job' (Boyatzis, 1982).

The belief that underpins the competences type of approach is that jobs (usually managerial and professional ones) can be broken down into their essential elements and then described in performance terms. Many recruiters believe that these underlying characteristics or competences are revealed in the way you use your skills. (We will look more closely at the use of person specifications and understanding what employers want in Chapter 13.)

I mention it here at the start of the self-evaluation process because many reading this book will be under pressure to get applications in quickly. Not all employers use a competences approach, but many do. A standard application form (SAF) and many employers' application forms (EAF) ask competence style questions. Even smaller organizations are starting to use this type of language, so your familiarity with the approach should impress most prospective employers.

The next section offers you an opportunity to assess yourself against the top 20 attributes shown in Table 2.1 as well as a few other important ones. After this exercise, I provide a detailed framework of career skills that you can use for self-assessment, improvement and as a guide to making successful applications.

# WHAT ABOUT YOU?

Activity 2.2 offers you a chance to audit your own skills. This is important because an assessment of your own skills can help you find the right career pathway.

Find out how you score against work-related skills. In this exercise many of the areas are specifically work-related but some measure how well you look after yourself. This is important because to be successful and happy at work, you will need to handle the pressures and challenges. In fact, I think this is so important I have included a whole chapter on stress fitness (Chapter 7).

## A CAREER SKILLS PROFILE

Activity 2.2 asks you to rate your skills against five important areas of working life. The list focuses primarily on skills and knowledge – we will look at motivation and career goals in the next chapter. You are invited to assess your own skills – from 1 for excellent to 5 for poor. In addition, you will notice that for some of the items I have included a measure that represents the average mark students at a wide range of universities across the UK gave themselves.

This activity will help you:

► identify your strengths and weaknesses;
► have a basis for further self-development;
► compare your skill rating to those of other UK students.

## ACTIVITY 2.2    Career skills profile

Look at each of the skills in the checklist and rate your own level of ability.

| Thinking/cognitive skills | Excellent | Good | Average | Below average | Poor | UK student average |
|---|---|---|---|---|---|---|
| Logical thinking | 1 | 2 | ③ | 4 | 5 | 2 |
| Critical analysis | 1 | 2 | 3 | ④ | 5 | 1 |
| Problem solving | 1 | 2 | ③ | 4 | 5 | 3 |
| Ability to use numerical data | 1 | 2 | 3 | 4 | ⑤ | 3 |
| Ability to be creative | 1 | ② | 3 | 4 | 5 | 4 |
| Spatial ability | 1 | 2 | 3 | ④ | 5 | – |
| Manual dexterity | 1 | 2 | ③ | 4 | 5 | – |
| Research skills | 1 | 2 | 3 | ④ | 5 | 1 |
| **Knowledge** | | | | | | |
| Specialist subject knowledge | 1 | 2 | ③ | 4 | 5 | 1 |
| Entrepreneurial skills/commercial awareness | 1 | ② | 3 | 4 | 5 | 4/5 |
| **Work/study effectiveness** | | | | | | |
| Ability to prioritize tasks | 1 | ② | 3 | 4 | 5 | 2 |
| Manage time effectively | 1 | 2 | 3 | ④ | 5 | 2 |
| Interpersonal skills | 1 | 2 | ③ | 4 | 5 | 2 |
| Written communication | 1 | 2 | ③ | 4 | ⑤ | 1 |
| Presentation skills | 1 | 2 | 3 | ④ | 5 | 2 |
| Ability to work in teams | 1 | 2 | ③ | 4 | 5 | 3 |
| Leadership skills | 1 | 2 | ③ | 4 | 5 | 4/5 |
| Managing pressure/stress well | 1 | 2 | ③ | 4 | 5 | n/a |
| Keep a good work/rest of life balance | 1 | 2 | ③ | 4 | 5 | n/a |
| **Personal development** | | | | | | |
| Self-confidence | 1 | 2 | 3 | ④ | 5 | 2 |
| Self-discipline | 1 | 2 | 3 | ④ | 5 | 2 |
| Self-reliance | 1 | 2 | 3 | ④ | 5 | 1 |
| Independence | 1 | 2 | 3 | ④ | 5 | 1 |
| Awareness of strengths and weaknesses | 1 | 2 | ③ | 4 | 5 | 2 |
| Desire to go on learning | ① | 2 | 3 | 4 | 5 | 3 |
| **Information technology** | | | | | | |
| Positive attitude to IT applications | 1 | 2 | ③ | 4 | 5 | |
| Internet skills | 1 | 2 | ③ | 4 | 5 | |
| Familiarity with e-mail | 1 | 2 | ③ | 4 | 5 | |
| Understanding of role of IT applications in graduate recruitment | 1 | 2 | ③ | 4 | 5 | |
| Information-gathering skills | 1 | 2 | 3 | ④ | 5 | |
| Awareness of latest IT developments and applications | 1 | 2 | ③ | 4 | 5 | |
| Overall computer literacy | 1 | 2 | ③ | 4 | 5 | 3 |

UK student average results adapted from Figure 7, *Great Expectations: The New Diversity of Graduate Skills and Aspirations*, 1996, Purcell, K. *et al.* CSU–AgCAS–IER.

Conclude the exercise by creating your own 'Working life skills profile' statement. You may find it encouraging to note down your three main strengths. Based on your self-assessment, which are the areas in which you consider you need to develop further? Note these down.

My strengths/resources are:

1. _Creative_
2. _Desire to go on learning_
3. _Entrepreneurial skill_

Skills needing improvement are:

1. _Use numerical data_
2. _Written Communication ( English )_
3. _Research skill_

If you gave yourself a low score for your ability to manage stress or keep a good work/rest of life balance, you should read Chapter 7 on stress fitness as it gives you an opportunity to look more closely at lifestyle and health.

## YOUR KNOWLEDGE BASE

You may also find it useful to finish this section by auditing your knowledge and areas of expertise. This will help you:

▶ identify your current areas of academic/professional expertise;

▶ ensure you draw on all the knowledge you have gained from school, university, hobbies;

▶ notice where you have knowledge gaps and take action to remedy these;

▶ identify further sources of information to help you find out about careers and jobs.

Use Activity 2.3 as a framework for analyzing these areas. You may try working through the topic areas with a friend, perhaps from the same course or someone interested in pursuing the same type of career.

If you are studying a vocational or skill-based course, this will be especially important. Don't forget that many employers are looking for graduates who can hit the ground running, demonstrating how much relevant knowledge you already have. If you are an arts and humanities student and your course has very little direct vocational relevance, this is an important way of discovering more about the career possibilities open to you.

Whatever course you have studied, most employers are keen to find students and graduates who can demonstrate business awareness. You may have noticed from the previous activity that the average UK student does not have very highly developed business knowledge. You need to know about your future work environment and this includes anyone interested in the public and not-for-profit sectors, too. This is one area where you really can stand out from the crowd, so don't miss the opportunity to do so.

## ACTIVITY 2.3    An audit of my knowledge and expertise

Think about what you already know with respect to an intended career or job under the headings given below. Try to identify all the sources of information you have to hand, but note that this is not a definitive list of possibilities, just the start. Keep the list in a safe place – it will be useful when you write your CV or fill in job application forms.

When you get to the interview stage, you can virtually guarantee that you will be asked what you know about the career generally and the organization in particular.

| Formal education | Work experience | Training |
|---|---|---|
| *School:* (A levels, etc.) | *Term time:* | (E.g., attended courses in: |
| *College/university subjects covered:* | *Holidays:* | word processing Internet IT applications languages presentation skills. |
| Year 1 Year 2 Year 3 Year 4 | *Placement/year out:* | For those with work experience, this should include professional or work-based training and any continuing professional development courses you have attended.) |
| *Final year project/ dissertation:* | | |
| *Work-related skills:* (Such as specific techniques, handling equipment.) | | |
| **Self-development** (E.g., using computers, video, TV, books, counselling, advice.) | **Family and friends** (Things you have learned from those around you – work/career roles of parents, brothers, sisters, relations and family/ personal friends.) | **Interests** (Things you have learned from hobbies and interests, such as music, sports, university/college societies and clubs.) |
| **Career/occupation** (Knowledge of the specific career/occupation you are interested in.) | **Organization** (Knowledge of the specific organization you intend to apply to.) | **Industry** (Knowledge of the industry or sector – main competitors, current issues, etc.) |

Based on your knowledge self-assessment, note the following.

Very knowledgeable about:

1. _Documentary film_
2. _Experimental film_

Need to know more about:

1. _Camera_
2. _Editing_
   _English_.

# SUMMARY

▶ This chapter has highlighted the top 20 attributes that many employers want. This list is just the start, of course, many employer describe their own specific requirements.

▶ The idea of competencies has been introduced and some typical thinking style competences have been described.

▶ The notion of working life skills has been outlined, with a chance to assess yourself and identify your strengths and to discover areas for further improvement.

▶ You have thought through the wide areas of knowledge and expertise gained through your background, family network, friends and contacts and studies.

# SIGNPOSTS TO MORE HELP

### Thinking skills and ability tests

Ability testing: see Chapter 19

### Communication

Interview skills: see Chapter 17
Teamwork: see Chapters 4 and 18

### Knowledge

Part II
Chapter 14, the section on networking

### Personal development

Chapter 6

### Looking after yourself

Chapter 7

# your career hopes and ambitions

A man's reach should exceed his grasp, or what's a heaven for?

ROBERT BROWNING

## In this chapter, you will:

- ❏ find out what your career interests say about your future;

- ❏ become clear about your personal values and beliefs;

- ❏ set your career goals;

- ❏ think about your work environment;

- ❏ get some idea as to how much you are worth;

- ❏ take a step nearer to your ideal job.

## In the activities:

**3.1** Identify your work interests

**3.2** Your career goals

**3.3** What do you stand for?

**3.4** Design your ideal job

# INTRODUCTION

In this chapter you will focus on your interests, personal values and career goals. Most approaches to career guidance and career choice are based on the notion of matching your particular skills, abilities and interests to a job so that it will satisfy you. Of course, this is also linked to the idea of finding something that you will be good at. Reading through this chapter will help you match yourself to the right career path and provide rich material to use when filling in application forms or wrestling with difficult interview questions.

# CAREER INTERESTS

## WHAT DO YOUR INTERESTS SAY ABOUT YOUR FUTURE JOB?

Being clear about what interests and what bores you is an important part of jobhunting for two main reasons. First, this can help you find the job or career you are suited to. Second, most employers are very keen to check that you know yourself well and that you are pretty sure you will be happy in the job if they decide to offer it to you. Many of you will have some general idea of the sort of job or career you are heading for, but some will not. Career indecision is very common and even those of you who do have a clue may still be nursing self-doubt.

Many career psychologists believe that your vocations/work can be viewed as belonging to one of three main types: working with people, data or practical/scientific. Many careers guidance tests and questionnaires are based on this approach as shown in more detail in Figure 3.1.

This three-way hierarchy is a very basic, simple structure, but it should at least give you a framework for considering the general areas of work available. Of course, many students and graduates have work interests that fall into more than one of the main divisions. For example, you may be drawn to both caring for people and the practical/creative arts, in which case you could look at occupations that involve both dimensions, such as occupational therapy or teaching art. In a similar vein, you may be a chemist, but are interested in working with people, not just looking at test tubes, so you could explore the marketing and commercial aspects of product development.

Equally, many jobs today require you to integrate aspects of all three – people, data and practical – dimensions. The balance between them will depend on the type of career and on the organizational setting in which you work.

Working out which is the right career for you is not an exact science. Science can help of course, and your local careers advisory service may have several career/personality tests available. The only real drawback with these tests is that they are only as good as the information *you* provide. In order for them to be helpful, your answers to the questions they pose need to be as accurate as possible, and this, I believe, is the tricky bit.

**The world of work – Advanced Occupational Interest Inventory (AOII)**

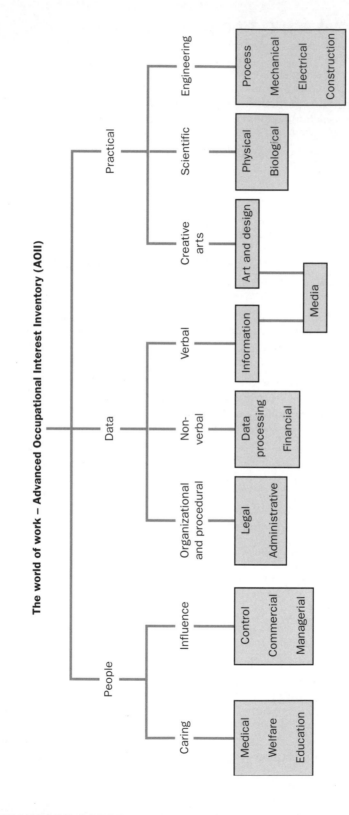

**FIGURE 3.1  The world of work**

Source: Adapted from the SHL© Occupational Interest Inventory and used with kind permission of Saville and Holdsworth (UK) Ltd

This activity has been adapted from SHL's occupational interest inventory and an AgCAS worksheet. Use it to identify your major job interests and what you really want to avoid.

| Consider each of the work dimensions described below. Decide if this is:<br><br>1 a major interest;<br>2 an area you do not feel strongly about;<br>3 one you wish to avoid.<br><br>**Work dimensions** | Major Interest<br><br>I would enjoy this being a large part of my job | Do not feel strongly about<br><br>I would be equally happy with or without this | Wish to avoid<br><br>I do not enjoy this aspect of work and wish to avoid it |
|---|---|---|---|
| **Caring for people**<br>Directly helping and supporting people who are ill, disadvantaged or who suffer in some way. | 1 | 2 ○ | 3 |
| **Being persuasive**<br>Influencing people to accept an opinion or product. Also to persuade people to act or behave in a certain way. | 1 | 2 ○ | 3 |
| **Advising people**<br>Guiding others by using expert knowledge and skills. | 1 ○ | 2 | 3 |
| **Instructing people**<br>Teaching others or passing on knowledge and expertise. | 1 ○ | 2 | 3 |
| **Managing people**<br>Organizing, coordinating and directing a team or group. Being responsible for the output. | 1 ○ | 2 | 3 |
| **Working with data**<br>Collecting and interpreting data, facts, figures or other information. | 1 | 2 | 3 ○ |
| **Organizing and administration**<br>Planning and organizing people, events or circumstances. Supporting others. | 1 ○ | 2 | 3 |
| **Literary and written work**<br>Using written or spoken words in a creative, original or professional manner. | 1 | 2 ○ | 3 |
| **Conceptual work/ideas**<br>Understanding, devising, developing and criticizing theories and ideas. | 1 | 2 | 3 ○ |
| **Scientific work**<br>Observing, evaluating and understanding physical or biological phenomena, processes and systems and their interrelationships. | 1 | 2 | 3 ○ |
| **Being creative/artistic**<br>Creating or designing dramatic, challenging, novel or aesthetically pleasing artefacts. | 1 ○ | 2 | 3 |
| **Being entrepreneurial**<br>Using initiative in a business context, taking an interest in profitability, being involved in business ventures or taking risks. | 1 | 2 ○ | 3 |

Source: Adapted from the SHL© Occupational Interest Inventory and used with kind permission of Saville and Holdsworth (UK) Ltd

# NEXT STEPS IN CAREER PLANNING

Career interest questionnaires can only guide you towards the right job when you know enough about the various jobs out there to fully assess their potential. There are numerous sources you can use to find out about occupations. Some of the main ones are listed below.

## YOUR CAREERS ADVISORY SERVICE

Your local careers advisory service is full of useful information about occupations and offers a range of services. The following are particularly useful.

▶ **Careers advisers**
Most careers advisory services have staff dedicated to supporting students from specific disciplines. Advisers are specially trained to help you through the career decision-making process – for example, by interpreting and discussing career test results and options available. You can use them in a number of different ways – as a source of information, a sounding board for ideas and options. They often keep in touch with recent graduates and can be a fount of useful information about careers and particular employers.

▶ **AgCAS information booklets**
These are very good. They cover a huge range of occupational areas, tell you about the types of work involved, give examples of typical work routines and responsibilities, set out training requirements and some give an idea of pay and promotion possibilities.

▶ **GTI career journals**
A series of ten career publications that cover specific employment areas, such as IT, law, finance, engineering. Highly readable accounts of what people do and who the well-known employers are.

▶ **Occupational files**
Many careers advisory services compile specific occupational files, containing useful cuttings, pamphlets and case studies.

## YOUR DEPARTMENT AND LECTURERS

Many lecturers and tutors have also worked outside academia and have first-hand knowledge of careers or jobs you may be interested in. If not, they are very good at passing you on to someone else who should be able to help. They may have contacts built up over years of student placements and work experience ventures, dissertations and so on. Be ruthless in exploiting your tutors!

## WORK EXPERIENCE

One of the best ways to find out about careers is to test the waters. Look at the options for work experience outlined in Chapter 5 and see where you can fit some in.

### Your network of associations

You can find out a huge amount from your immediate friends, family, neighbours. If you want to start networking, turn ahead to Activity 14.1 on page 164. Identify your network, to make a start.

# YOUR CAREER GOALS

Another way of thinking about your ambitions is to focus on what you hope to achieve after graduation. During the 1990s, the media popularized the notion of Generation X – young people disillusioned with Thatcherism and the excessive career aspirations and materialism that went with it. Graduates in the new millennium are said to have different goals and values – is this true?

The next activity is designed to help you identify your own career goals. As our ambitions don't exist in a vacuum, this exercise is based on a recent survey that asked over 2000 final-year UK university students about their goals.

---

**ACTIVITY 3.2　Your career goals**

Which career goals do you hope to achieve within three years of graduation? This checklist does not include all the alternatives, so if you don't see an option that is important to you, include it in the 'Other' space provided.

Using the list below, rank your priorities first, second and third.

| Career goals | Rank |
|---|---|
| Build a sound financial base. | 2 |
| Reach managerial level or gain professional qualifications. | 1 |
| Attain a balance between personal life and career. | 2 |
| Travel internationally. | 1 |
| Work on increasingly challenging tasks. | 1 |
| Relocate internationally. | 1 |
| Become the owner of my own business. | 1 |
| Create or develop new products or services. | 2 |
| Contribute to the development of society. | 3 |
| Become a specialist in my field. | 1 |
| Influence corporate strategies. | 3 |
| Other | |

---

The media has popularized the notion that the students and graduates wanting jobs in 2000 and beyond are seeking a work/other life balance. The exercise you have just done is designed to help you think about the balance *you* want to achieve.

Are enjoying an active social life, keeping fit, having fun and building strong relationships with family/friends/partner/children important at this time in your life?

If they are, how do these values match with your career goals? Could there be potential conflicts in this area? I address this issue again in Chapter 11.

## YOUR VALUES AND BELIEFS

Thinking about career goals is important, but it does not complete the picture in terms of self-evaluation. You will be most happy in a job that reflects your own values. The next exercise is intended to stimulate thoughts about the issues you may be confronted with at work. These issues may hit you head-on at the outset. Often, though, they emerge more gradually as you are exposed to the realities of working life.

---

**CASE STUDY   We believe it is a necessary evil**

---

A few years ago, I applied for a job working for a leading pharmaceutical company. I was thrilled to get an interview, but was completely thrown when asked about my views on animal testing. The innocuous job in the Human Resources Department was actually supporting the animal testing staff.

All I can recall is spluttering something about it 'being bearable when done to find a cure for cancer, but not for cosmetics' and the interviewer's voice saying 'Yes, we believe it is a necessary evil, but how would you feel telling your friends you work here?'

---

You may feel the answers to some of the questions opposite are predictable, but how does the organization or career you are thinking of stand up to your personal values? One of these issues may be a guiding force for you. Many people still feel called to be involved in a particular problem area of society or wrestle with a tricky issue. If you do have strong religious, political or ethical beliefs, think through the implications for the career path you are considering.

## ACTIVITY 3.3  What do you stand for?

Personal values and beliefs checklist

| Issue | Where do you stand? | | | | |
|---|---|---|---|---|---|
| | Strongly support | Support | Not sure | Oppose | Strongly oppose |
| Abortion | 1 | 2 | 3 | 4 | 5 |
| Animal testing | 1 | 2 | 3 | 4 | 5 |
| Arms trade | 1 | 2 | 3 | 4 | 5 |
| Conservation | 1 | 2 | 3 | 4 | 5 |
| Corruption | 1 | 2 | 3 | 4 | 5 |
| Distinctive personal faith | 1 | 2 | 3 | 4 | 5 |
| Ethical business | 1 | 2 | 3 | 4 | 5 |
| Gay rights | 1 | 2 | 3 | 4 | 5 |
| Glass ceilings | 1 | 2 | 3 | 4 | 5 |
| Global warming | 1 | 2 | 3 | 4 | 5 |
| GM foods | 1 | 2 | 3 | 4 | 5 |
| Green politics | 1 | 2 | 3 | 4 | 5 |
| Human rights | 1 | 2 | 3 | 4 | 5 |
| Integrity | 1 | 2 | 3 | 4 | 5 |
| Landmines | 1 | 2 | 3 | 4 | 5 |
| Not-for-profit organizations | 1 | 2 | 3 | 4 | 5 |
| Nuclear energy | 1 | 2 | 3 | 4 | 5 |
| Overseas aid | 1 | 2 | 3 | 4 | 5 |
| Poverty | 1 | 2 | 3 | 4 | 5 |
| Racism | 1 | 2 | 3 | 4 | 5 |
| Recycling | 1 | 2 | 3 | 4 | 5 |
| Renewable energy | 1 | 2 | 3 | 4 | 5 |
| Sexism | 1 | 2 | 3 | 4 | 5 |
| Spiritual life | 1 | 2 | 3 | 4 | 5 |
| Trade unions | 1 | 2 | 3 | 4 | 5 |
| Working long hours | 1 | 2 | 3 | 4 | 5 |
| Other | 1 | 2 | 3 | 4 | 5 |
| Other | 1 | 2 | 3 | 4 | 5 |

What you will be doing at work is important, but so are other factors. You need to think about the location, work environment, relationships, organizational culture and the rewards. The exercise below will help you focus on your ideal job. You may feel you already know – well, try the exercise anyway, make sure you know what you are looking for. In this activity, you design your own ideal job. This will help you identify everything that's really important.

| Ideal job features | Your preferences |
| --- | --- |
| What salary are you hoping for? Does the thought of earning a large salary motivate and drive you? | high better |
| Are you hoping to obtain a well-recognized professional training and/or further qualifications or do you prefer a job that leaves your options open? | I wanna be professional. |
| Is it important that you are given substantial additional training and opportunities for personal development? | I want to have extra training. |
| Do you like to be inside/outside? Do you have any special preferences or needs? | I can endure both, but inside all times fsd |
| Do you value predictability and routine ways of doing things? | I love this boring type. |
| Is it important that you do not have someone 'breathing down your neck'? Do you need freedom and flexibility in what you do? | I love freedom. |
| Many people value power – what sort of power do you want? Do you want to have responsibility early on or is a training position preferable? | I can have responsibility early |
| Is it important that you can use your imagination or express yourself in a creative way? | I really hope so. |
| Do you want to put something back into society? Is there a specific group of people or issue you want to get involved with? | no. I wanna keep private. |
| Some of us want to work alone or in one-to-one situations; others are only happy in large offices where they can talk to lots of other people. Which suits you best? | I think I can take both. |
| How important is location to you? Do you want a job in London, another big city or is the role more important than the location? | I think role is imp. but I like ab road |
| So, my ideal job would be ... | |

This is not an exhaustive list, but it should give you some ideas. You also need to consider the structure of your ideal organization. What sort of goals does it have? Is it small or large? Does it have a complicated hierarchy or no hierarchy at all? What opportunities are there? Can you travel? Can you work in different countries? These issues are discussed in more detail in Chapters 9 and 11.

What sorts of relationships do you want at work? How would the boss manage you? What would your work colleagues be like? What sorts of customers or clients would you like to deal with? To address these issues, you could turn to Chapter 10.

# SALARY EXPECTATIONS

We have looked at a range of issues concerning career goals and motives. Salary is not always the key thing about a job – you want the work itself to be interesting and rewarding, too. However, most of you will be starting out with substantial debts to pay off, so I include a short section about salaries here for information and to help you compare jobs if you are fortunate enough to have more than one job offer!

## Starting salary

The importance of starting salary varies enormously for different individuals. For some it is a key factor in choice of career, for others salary may be less important than, for example, the opportunity to travel, challenging work or feeling socially useful. However, it is an important factor for many people in both choosing a particular career path and when it comes to deciding between different job opportunities.

Figures regarding both expectations and reality concerning salary are problematical as the graduate labour market is very complicated and fragmented. Still, there are some useful statistics, patterns and trends that I outline briefly to help you in your decision making. You may also find this information useful later on when you come to negotiate your own contract of employment.

Several organizations, including the Association of Graduate Recruiters (AGR), Incomes Data Services (IDS), CSU Ltd (publishers of *Prospects Today*) and Industrial Relations Services (IRS) all publish annual surveys that outline the range of starting salaries paid in the year of publication as well as estimates of rates that will apply the following year. These studies give a clear and pretty consistent picture of going rates in any one year.

The AGR survey tends to report higher figures than some of the other pay surveys because its respondents tend to be the larger employers of new graduates. By contrast, the CSU survey, based on large numbers of advertised positions from across all business sectors of the economy, invariably comes out with a lower average than the others.

Table 3.1 shows the range of salaries that well-known, generally large, graduate employers expect to pay for those starting jobs in 2000. So, use the information with caution, as the figures reflect pay in blue-chip organizations and may not apply to the job you are considering.

## TABLE 3.1 Graduates starting salaries, 2000

|  | All organizations | | Industrial sector | | Non-industrial sector | |
|---|---|---|---|---|---|---|
|  | 2000 forecast | % change on 1999 | 2000 forecast | % change on 1999 | 2000 forecast | % change on 1999 |
| Top 10% | 21,500 | 2.4 | 20,100 | 0.5 | 23,800 | 0.8 |
| Median | 18,000 | 2.9 | 18,100 | 3.4 | 18,000 | 5.1 |
| Bottom 10% | 16,000 | 3.2 | 16.500 | 5.1 | 15,882 | 3.7 |

Source: AGR/IES, *Graduate Salaries and Vacancies Survey*, 2000.

Getting to grips with the huge amount of information available about starting salaries can be an awesome task. CSU has created a user-friendly, searchable web site that provides the latest figures and helps with interpreting and applying them. It provides a breakdown of starting salaries by type of employer, type of work, location and subject of study at: http://www.prospects.csu.ac.uk/student/cidd/lmi/index.htm.

## Key points about graduates' starting salaries

▶ Organizations are aware of *going rates* in a particular sector of the economy and for particular jobs. Many appear to keep in line with other employers.

▶ The highest paid jobs are those in consultancies and agencies, such as computer and management consultants.

▶ There is a wider variation between top and bottom levels of starting pay in the non-industrial sector than in the industrial sector. The non-industrial sector includes professional services such as accountancy, training and IT at the top end of the pay spectrum and much lower average salaries, for example, in the public sector at the bottom end.

▶ Salaries vary by location, with the highest average rates in East Anglia and the lowest rates in Scotland, North and North West England. In a survey by *High Fliers* (1999), the average expected salaries in the 25 universities the survey covered ranged from £19,200 in Oxford to £14,400 in Glasgow.

▶ Some jobs abroad attract very high salaries but these often relate to vacancies for technical specialists.

▶ The Inner and Outer London allowance paid by some employers can vary enormously, from a few hundred pounds to over £2000.

▶ Graduates with degrees in mathematical sciences and informatics are likely to obtain jobs with higher starting salaries than graduates in other disciplines. Current research suggests the opening up of a bigger gap between salaries offered for scientific jobs and those that do not require technological expertise. Statistically, graduates in arts and humanities are likely to end up with the lowest starting salaries.

One final trend that needs highlighting is the pattern for new female graduates to be paid less than male graduates. *Labour Force Survey* figures reveal that in 1998 the median figure for new male graduates in full-time employment was £14,768 compared with only £12,584 for new female graduates. This pattern reflects the fact that female graduates accept lower paid jobs and many work in traditionally lower paid occupational areas.

## Expectations of pay progression

Starting pay is an important consideration, but you may also be interested in the speed at which your salary will increase – often called *pay progression*. Studies show considerable variation in the way that pay increases are handled. Think about what you expect and what different jobs or employers offer. If in doubt, ask. Some employers may agree to review your salary after six months while others may wait for a year or more.

As mentioned, one clear trend is the difference between male and female earnings. Women graduates, on average, start on lower salaries than males, they then catch up in the years immediately following graduation before steadily falling behind again thereafter. In 1998 male graduates in full-time jobs were earning an average of £30,000 after 13 years in the workforce, compared with a figure of £21,000 for women.

The extent to which this reflects the operation of discriminatory practices and obstacles preventing women from gaining access to higher paid jobs is unclear. IES suggests that this may be the case in part. Lower and slower pay progression may be explained by the proportion of women taking career breaks in their late twenties and early thirties, thus slowing down or halting longer-term salary progression. Whatever the reasons, the differential between average male and female graduate earnings remains substantial. Chapter 10, 'Organizational culture and climate', includes more information on equal opportunities.

## SUMMARY

▶ You have thought about your work interests.

▶ You now know the key factors and what your ideal job would be.

▶ You know what your ideal work environment would be.

▶ You have a large amount of information available to help match yourself to the right job and employer.

▶ You can use the information about salaries when choosing between job options.

## SIGNPOSTS TO MORE HELP

Summaries of the latest figures about starting salaries and salary projections can be found at: http://www.prospects.csu.ac.uk/student/cidd/lmi/index.htm.

A very useful quarterly publication by CSU called *Graduate Market Trends* may be available for reference at your local university careers service; summaries are often posted on the web site mentioned above.

# personality at work

**Personality is hard to describe, hard to measure and hard to change – but all these can be done!**

**In this chapter, you will:**

☐ consider the importance of personality in career decision making;

☐ understand the concept of personality;

☐ discover how well you know yourself;

☐ find out how your personality affects the way you work;

☐ learn how personality can change;

☐ become aware of how your personality influences your ability to work in a team.

**In the activities:**

**4.1** A thumbnail sketch of your personality

**4.2** How well do you know yourself?

**4.3** Putting Johari window techniques into practice – how well do you know yourself? Part II

**4.4** What sort of team member are you?

# THE IMPORTANCE OF PERSONALITY

A good understanding of your personality is seen by many career advisers and writers as being pretty central to deciding on a suitable career. Personality is hard to describe, hard to measure and even harder to match to jobs. Knowing your general personality characteristics may help suggest broad areas of suitability for certain jobs or can highlight roles that you may be very unsuited to.

Most writers acknowledge that any given type of work or job tolerates different personality characteristics. John Arnold, a contemporary expert writer on careers advised that you 'should not get too carried away with personality – other aspects of the self are more applicable'. In particular, he suggests that values may be a better indicator.

However, understanding personality is important for four key reasons:

▶ you can develop greater self-awareness;

▶ you need to describe yourself on application forms;

▶ you need to understand the attributes employers are looking for;

▶ it is important to check out the extent to which your personality, values and attitudes are compatible with the type of job you do and the company culture you become part of.


# WHAT IS PERSONALITY?

Personality can be used as a universal term to encompass all the psychological, intellectual, emotional and physical characteristics of an individual, especially as they are presented to other people. We say that someone has a 'big personality' or 'no personality' or is a 'sports personality'.

Personality is also reflected in our behaviour. When we act out of character we often say 'It just wasn't like me …', 'I wasn't myself'. This indicates a key aspect of personality – it's a relatively stable and permanent aspect of you as a person. You may have mood swings, be up or down according to specific circumstances, tiredness and so on, but your basic personality remains constant despite these changes.

The whole notion of personality is, of course, hugely complicated, with widely different schools of thought. Personality overlaps all the other aspects of your **SHAPE** (see page 12 if you need to recap what this stands for) because it is influenced by your values, beliefs, attitudes and motivation.

## THE ORIGINS OF PERSONALITY

Much has been written on this topic alone and, of course, an ideological debate (war?) wages between the different schools of thought. Some of the main approaches to psychology and personality theory are described below.

Some believe personality is a matter of genetics (nature), others that it's about your family, its structure and social setting (nurture). Some extremely sensible people believe it's the result of both, in combination. Others point to the importance of the situation or setting on our personality. You behave differently on a rugby field, in the pub, in lectures, during a tutorial. Well, most of us do!

## PERSONALITY THEORIES

Sigmund Freud was the originator of the 'psychoanalytic' approach. Freud believed that our personalities form early in life, as we wrestle with unconscious drives and instincts. These forces mould our sexual identity and personality. Carl Jung (founder of 'analytical' psychology) also believed in unconscious forces but saw personality as emerging as a result of how we handle life's transitions.

The last few decades have seen the growth of a range of 'neo-Freudian' approaches that reject the emphasis on sexual and aggressive drives and give more emphasis to cultural and environmental factors. Personality assessment is usually made by analyzing a person's life history or by using tests that examine perceptions.

The 'cognitive-social' school considers that the way we understand and interpret the world can explain our behaviour. It measures personality by assessing the skills and abilities people use to solve problems and reach goals.

The 'humanistic' school suggests that all individuals possess a creative tendency towards growth and personal development. Carl Rogers, the best-known theorist of the humanistic school, suggests we have a core self that becomes lost and a false self develops as we comply with the demands of those around us (parents, teachers and so on). The Rogerian view is that personality or self-image is deeply affected by the rules or 'conditions of worth' you grow up with. We all know our family life is a huge source of influence! Personal growth, change and development are possible as we move closer to our core self and away from the false self. (I will return to the question of personality change later in this chapter.)

There are two other main approaches to personality – 'trait' and 'type' theories.

These are not theories at all in the strict sense of the word as they do not really attempt to explain personality or behaviour. The strength and popularity of trait theories in the field of graduate recruitment comes from the fact that they offer a way of describing and assessing behaviour. Type theories and approaches are a close relation to the trait approach, but are seen by some practitioners as being less refined. Let us now look at these approaches in more detail.

# PERSONALITY: TRAIT OR TYPE?

Both type and trait (pronounced 'tray') theories have strengths, weaknesses, advocates and critics.

## THE TYPE APPROACH

The existence of 'types' can be traced back to the ancient Greek philosophers. Hippocrates thought personality was determined biologically by four humours, suggesting four main types of personality, explained by individual physical constitution as follows:

▶ **blood** the *sanguine* person, always full of enthusiasm and energy;

▶ **bile** the *melancholy* person, always sad and pessimistic about life;

▶ **phlegm** the *phlegmatic* person, always slow and apathetic, unemotional;

▶ **choleric** the *choleric* person, always irritable and restless.

Jung also thought there were four main types of people, while other modern psychologists have developed there own typologies with various numbers of categories. The idea of type theory is to group people with others who share similar characteristics. Labels like these are easy to use, but they can be limited. Research shows people don't fit easily into one category – types can be oversimplistic and misleading. Most people are not a pure type, but, rather, complicated blends of attributes and dimensions. This has been increasingly recognized by psychologists. Few approaches now accept that you can be classified as a pure type – especially when there are only four to choose from!

However, one well-known contemporary application of the type approach is Belbin's Team Role inventory, which I discuss below under the heading Personality at work on page 43.

## THE TRAIT APPROACH

Trait approaches recognize the complexity of human attributes and the presence of consistently different patterns of thought, feeling and action. The approach was developed by Gordon Allport, who believed that the trait is the observed tendency to behave in a particular way. Personality underlies this behaviour and can be inferred from it.

Unlike Hippocrates' typology of just four personalities, Allport found there were 18,000 words that could be used to identify differences between people. Such a massive list is not practical to use when assessing individuals. Consequently, theorists and statisticians have worked for over 50 years to produce shorter, more manageable lists of core personality factors. Indeed, new forms of statistical tools, such as factor analysis, were created specially to wrestle with these complicated problems! Raymond Cattell reduced the list to 16 main traits.

## Personality profiles – the five main dimensions

Given the huge market for assessing personality, a plethora of different tests and measures have been devised based on the trait approach. All of them use your answers to a questionnaire to create a detailed profile of your personality as a basis for comparison with other people.

The key point here is that personality is seen as being a complicated thing, comprised of many different aspects that can be measured. Providing tests for use in recruitment and selection is very big business. In the graduate job scene, personality is often seen as an important indicator of whether or not you will be suited to a particular job and fit in with the organizational culture. (More details of personality testing are provided in Chapter 19.)

The strength of trait approaches is their ability to describe and measure aspects of individual personality. It is generally recognized by many occupational psychologists that personality can be described by reference to five key dimensions or global factors that represent a combination of many other individual traits.

This means your answers to a personality questionnaire can be compared to the way other similar people have described themselves. These global factors are often portrayed as a sort of continuum, the most familiar probably being the notion of being an extrovert or an introvert. Most of us lie somewhere between the two extremes for each of the global factors listed below. The big five factors are:

▶ extroversion

▶ anxiety

▶ tough-mindedness

▶ independence

▶ control.

*Extroversion (extroversion ↔ introversion)*
Extroverts are outgoing, warm individuals who enjoy company. They are lively, fun-loving and are often quite open about themselves. They are group-oriented people who naturally join in with others. An introvert is someone who is self-sufficient and prefers their own company. Introverts are careful, serious and self-reliant. They prefer to make their own decisions.

*Anxiety (anxious ↔ confident)*
Anxious people are emotionally changeable and respond quickly to others. They worry a lot and are often tense. They are also impatient people with a lot of nervous energy. They can be very shrewd and hard to fool; they may appear sceptical.

At the other end of the continuum, the confident person is calm in the face of adversity, meets challenges easily, exudes self-assurance. A high degree of stability is also accompanied by a resilient, even, placid manner that can sometimes be too trusting and relaxed.

*Tough-mindedness (objective ↔ subjective)*
Tough-minded people are unsentimental and look at things objectively. They have a no-nonsense attitude and prefer to follow a traditional, established approach. The opposite is the tender-minded person who is more subjective and willing to experiment.

*Independence (assertive ↔ cooperative)*

Independence is characterized by a dominant, forceful person who is competitive. People who score highly on the independence dimension are usually assertive, which means that they can also be rather insensitive to other people. Agreeable people are cooperative, preferring to avoid conflict, and are often described as shy.

*Control (conscientious ↔ flexible)*

The self-controlled person is conscientious and dutiful. They are likely to be tidy, organized and have a commonsense, practical approach to problem solving. They also persevere – some might say they are stubborn. Their friends and work colleagues may describe them as perfectionists. At the opposite end of the spectrum, the flexible personality can tolerate untidiness, may ignore protocol and follow an expedient, often imaginative approach to solving problems.

Very few people will exhibit the extremes described above. Most of us achieve a balance between these aspects and would be positioned somewhere in between the two opposite poles. Trait approaches recognize this and have a very careful, precise way of measuring and describing individuals and your position along the continuum.

# WHAT ABOUT MY PERSONALITY?

Describing your own personality is hard to do, yet it is an important part of the preparation for making career decisions and jobhunting. I recall a very demanding moment at an interview I went to when the Personnel Manager asked me to 'Give a thumbnail sketch of your personality' and I hadn't thought about it before. Try it yourself so you're prepared!

---

### ACTIVITY 4.1    A thumbnail sketch of your personality

Write a couple of sentences below to describe your personality.

> I would describe myself as …

---

How did that exercise go? It may have been difficult, especially if you have not had much experience of self-evaluation. It does get easier with practice, though. Self-assessment is an essential skill in jobhunting, so it's worth doing it.

Look again at your profile. How accurate is it really. Be honest, did you describe yourself as you are or as you would like to be? The next exercise invites you to create a balanced profile of yourself and then see how closely your self-perceptions match those of other people.

Find five words from the list below that you feel describe you most accurately. Write them down on a separate piece of paper. Be totally honest – there's no point kidding yourself you are something you're not. Include aspects you regard as your main strengths and at least one weakness.

| | |
|---|---|
| Active | Quiet |
| Changeable | Confident |
| Even-tempered | Sensitive |
| Unsociable | Reserved |
| Optimistic | Tense |
| Peaceful | Talkative |
| Aggressive | Reliable |
| Carefree | Calm |
| Controlled | Sociable |
| Excitable | Restless |
| Lively | Authoritative |
| Outgoing | Touchy |
| Pessimistic | Responsive |
| Anxious | Sober |
| Careful | Thoughtful |
| Easygoing | Serious |
| Impulsive | Driven |
| Moody | Shy |
| Passive | Patient |

How well does your description of yourself match with the sort of person who would be successful and happy in the job or career you are considering?

## GETTING THE FULL PICTURE: LOOKING THROUGH THE JOHARI WINDOW

Self-assessment can be greatly enhanced by finding out how other people see and experience you. To this end, let me introduce you to the Johari window – a helpful model for thinking about the image we present to the world, how we see ourselves and what others really think (see Figure 4.1).

The Johari window model suggests that our world is made up of various windows through which different aspects of you can be viewed. Some of these are your own private insights about yourself, those you share only with those you know and trust well, if at all. The model also highlights the fact that other people will also have an opinion about you. It may be similar to your selfperception or, importantly, it may be very different. Your self-awareness can grow enormously if you are willing to receive feedback from others.

First, in Window 1 is your 'public face'. This is the public arena of your life. Information is known to you and to others. Your name, what you study, where you were born and so on. If you are a shy or private person, Window 1 may be very small.

Window 2 is your 'blind spot'. This represents the things you don't know about yourself but others do. These may include, for example, other people's opinions and perceptions of you.

If you are an open, approachable person, your blind spot may be quite small. You may ask for, and receive, feedback. This is an invaluable skill in preparation for job-hunting. If you know how you come across to others, this will help you know the sort of impression you make at interview. If you need to change anything and learn from others, now is the time to do it.

Window 3 is 'your private world' – those things that are unknown to others but known to you. You can choose to keep this part of your life large or you can open up and let others get to know you well.

Window 4 is things unknown to you and everyone else. As your self-awareness grows, this window can become smaller.

There is no right Johari window shape, but it is in your favour to reduce the size of your blind spot and become more self-aware. This will help you to have the impact you intend on those recruiting you.

|  | | You | |
| --- | --- | --- | --- |
|  | | Known | Unknown |
| Other people | Known | **1** Your public face | **2** Blind spot |
|  | Unknown | **3** Your private world | **4** Unknown self |

**FIGURE 4.1  The Johari window**

---

**ACTIVITY 4.3    Putting Johari window techniques into practice – how well do you know yourself? Part II**

Now ask someone who knows you well to choose five words from the list provided in Activity 4.2. Ask them to be honest and to include at least one weakness. Receiving feedback from others is an invaluable source of information we need – especially for jobhunting.

Compare notes. Are you surprised at the similarities and/or differences between the two lists?

What was similar? _____

What was different? _____

What does this tell you about the accuracy of your self-assessment? How are you perceived by others?

# SELF-DEVELOPMENT – HOW CAN I CHANGE?

As mentioned above, the growth and development of personality is understood in many different ways by different groups of psychologist. Most agree that a blend of past experiences and biological factors combine to make you the person you are today. You have developed your own individual way of seeing and understanding the world and of moving through it. There is a close relationship between thoughts, feelings and behaviour, as shown in Figure 4.2.

Thoughts, feelings and behaviour are integrated in a special way that is individual to you. You may be aware that you frequently experience certain feelings and thoughts in particular situations. For example, you may feel nervous before giving a presentation or awkward when meeting someone new. It is possible to change the patterns of thinking, feeling and action and develop new ones. Changes are unlikely to lead to a radical change in your personality, but you can learn to develop new patterns of thinking and behaviour. You are unlikely to change, for example, from being shy and passive to being an assertive extrovert, but you can learn to be more assertive and less compliant if you want to.

## EIGHT THINGS PEOPLE WANT TO CHANGE ABOUT THEMSELVES

► 'I get so anxious';
► 'I wish I could be more assertive';
► 'I wish I was more outgoing';
► 'How can I be more organized?';
► 'I just can't get motivated';
► 'I wish I was more sensitive to other people';
► 'How can I be more open?';
► 'I wish I could be more flexible and creative'.

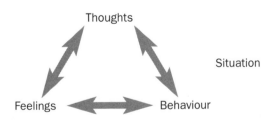

**FIGURE 4.2  The self-development triangle**

## HOW CAN I CHANGE?

There are no easy answers or simple prescriptions, but there are just three pre-conditions:

▶ you must want to change;

▶ you must be willing to get out of your comfort zone;

▶ you need determination.

If you have these, then you can make great strides in self-development. Chapter 6 is provided to give you the framework and tools you need to do just that. Before you rush off to work on your personality and overcome the particular aspect of yourself you wish to change, please read below about teams. Every personality has a part to play in the modern workplace. Focus for a few moments on the great strengths you already have to offer.

# PERSONALITY AT WORK

I have already mentioned that many roles at work can be fulfilled effectively by people with very different personalities. In fact, every organization needs diverse people, not clones. Use the ideas that follow to re-frame your personality positively – see how the very things you may regard as a limitation can actually be viewed as a positive strength.

## TEAM ROLES

Meredith Belbin's work has become well known in management circles – it will certainly raise your kudos if you know of his ideas on team roles. Belbin suggests that effective teams need a range and balance of skills. Working together, different personalities enable a team to complete all the different tasks needed for success. In fact, with a Belbin-style approach, the whole is greater than the sum of its individual parts.

Project- and work-based teams need a leader, but they also need ideas people and critical thinkers. Teams also need people who are good at networking and building relationships and others who pay attention to detail. This is great news for anyone worried about a particular aspect of personality, it clearly demonstrates that what you see as a cloud can be the silver lining to any team you belong to. Belbin's team roles typology is shown in Figure 4.3.

You can use these ideas to help you when completing standard and employers' application forms, building your CV or answering interview questions. As we saw in Chapter 3 teamworking is one skill that most employers are seeking.

**TABLE 4.1    Useful people to have in teams**

| Type | Typical features | Positive qualities | Allowable weaknesses |
|------|------------------|--------------------|-----------------------|
| Plant | Individualistic, serious-minded, unorthodox | Genius, imagination, intellect, knowledge | Up in the clouds, inclined to disregard practical details or protocol |
| Implementer | Conservative, dutiful, predictable | Organizing ability, practical, common sense, hardworking, self-disciplined | Lack of flexibility, unresponsive to unproven ideas |
| Coordinator | Calm, self-confident | A capacity for treating all potential contributors on their merits | Sometimes manipulative, delegates own work to others |
| Shaper | Highly strung, outgoing, dynamic | Drive and readiness to challenge inertia, ineffectiveness, complacency or self-deception | Proneness to provocation, irritation and impatience |
| Resource investigator | Extrovert, enthusiastic, curious, communicator | A capacity for contacting people and exploring anything new, an ability to respond to a challenge | Liable to lose interest once the initial fascination has passed |
| Monitor evaluator | Sober, strategic, discerning | Judgement, discretion, hard-headedness | Lacks inspiration or the ability to motivate others |
| Teamworker | Socially oriented, mild, sensitive | Ability to respond to people and situations, promote team spirit | Indecisiveness at moments of crisis |
| Specialist | Single-minded, dedicated | Provides specialist knowledge and skills | Contributes only on narrow front, dwells on technicalities, overlooks the big picture |
| Completer | Painstaking, orderly, conscientious | A capacity for follow through, attention to detail, perfectionism | Can worry about small things, be reluctant to let go |

Source: adapted from R. M. Belbin, *Team Roles at Work*, 1993, Butterworth-Heinemann. Used with kind permission.

Very few people fit one type perfectly – most of us will have characteristics from two or three of these team roles. Perhaps you can see yourself here?

Think about times at university or at work when you have been part of a team. This could be your experience as part of an academic/tutorial group or socially. Consider the list of 'Useful people to have in teams' in Table 4.1.

**1.** Which one most closely reflects you?

_____

**2.** How will you use your strengths in a team?

_____

**3.** Is there anything about your natural style you might need to restrain?

_____

**4.** What about other members of teams or groups you belong to – does the Belbin framework help you to understand how different personalities can work together?

_____

Hopefully, the team role ideas have encouraged you to see your personality in a new light. Everything about you can be framed in a positive light if you know how. There may be aspects that you do not feel happy to just live with. If so, move on to Chapter 6 where you can create your own self-development plan.

# SUMMARY

▶ In this chapter, we have considered the importance of personality to developing greater self-awareness, as a basis for completing application forms, CV building and in order to understand what employers are looking for.

▶ The concept of personality has been discussed and some of the problems associated with this slippery subject have been explored.

▶ The origins of personality theories and the purpose of personality testing have been reviewed, very briefly.

▶ You have been introduced to a well-known management model called the Johari window.

▶ You have discovered just how well (or how little) you know yourself.

▶ You have looked at ways of making your personality work for you with a particular focus on teamworking.

# SIGNPOSTS TO MORE HELP

For ideas on self-development: Chapter 6.
For how to succeed at selection tests: Chapter 19.

## 'The only place where success comes before work is in a dictionary.'

VIDAL SASSOON QUOTING ONE OF HIS TEACHERS IN A BBC RADIO BROADCAST.

**In this chapter, you will:**

❏ find out why students work;

❏ find information about different placements and internships;

❏ consider the benefits and problems associated with term-time working;

❏ become familiar with the Students at Work factfile;

❏ learn about the pleasure and the pain of work from case studies;

❏ discover how to get the most out of work;

❏ know what to do if it doesn't work out – review your skills and experience.

**In the activities:**

**5.1** Work experience action planner for undergraduates

**5.2** How to get the most out of your term-time work experience

**5.3** Create your own work experience portfolio

# WORK EXPERIENCE CAN HELP YOU STAND OUT FROM THE CROWD

Experience of work is increasingly important in the world of graduate employment. Holiday work and placement or sandwich years can offer you a marvellous opportunity to build up marketable skills and experience. These experiences can also be very helpful in the process of discovering more about a job or career that suits you. You can gain an inside picture of a particular employer, career and see how this fits in with your hopes and expectations.

## WHY WORK?

Work experience can be a real help in making career choices or, as many of the case studies below reveal, can help you know what to definitely avoid doing again in the future.

The reality for a large proportion of undergraduates is that work experience is also an essential way of keeping down debts or even supporting family and dependants of their own. This can mean pressure on study time, stress and also the worry of poor working conditions and low-paid insecure work.

NUS figures in the *Students at Work* survey indicate that 40 per cent of students are employed during term time and over 75 per cent of these work through holidays as well. Some reading this book will be all too aware of personal responsibilities, maybe to family members, young and/or old. It may be that you are expected to help out in practical, unpaid ways at home or in a family business. Some students want to work to supplement income from 'other sources' and to have a better lifestyle, pay for hobbies or travel that they could not do otherwise.

Many graduates take first jobs that do not work out. You may be feeling let down by your current employer – the job just is not what you were promised. On the other hand you may be one of the many graduates who take a job quickly after finals knowing it does not have long-term prospects and you are ready for change. Short-term work experience can:

► help you clarify your career goals;
► improve your employability;
► earn you some cash;
► put you ahead of the competition.

## WHAT SORT OF WORK EXPERIENCE?

There are many types of work opportunities available in the average three to four years of an undergraduate's degree course. There are similar opportunities open to many at postgraduate level as well. The next few pages outline the main types of work opportunity available. The information will help you plan a strategy to suit your own personal career ambitions or to explore the possibilities if you are still uncertain.

## TYPES OF WORK EXPERIENCE

There are so many different work experience opportunities available. It is helpful to think about work experience as being one of the four following types:

▶ undergraduate work that is part of your course;

▶ self-directed summer holiday work experience;

▶ paid term-time work;

▶ ad hoc voluntary work.

### Undergraduate work experience as part of your course

Many university courses now include an element of work experience as part of the course. This can range from really useful opportunities to learn about different careers and develop skills to superficial token efforts at involvement. Look at Table 5.1 and see what sort of work experiences your course offers.

**TABLE 5.1  Types of undergraduate work experience**

| Types of work experience | Duration | Objectives | Income? |
|---|---|---|---|
| Sandwich course/placements | 40–48 weeks | Structured programme of relevant work in appropriate setting | Usually |
| Work experience element | 2–15 weeks | Opportunity to experience real-life setting as a context for study or associated professional qualification | Unlikely |
| Overseas placement | 12–48 weeks | To widen experience of cross-cultural skills and/or language development | Some |
| Work-linked individual or group-based project | 1–14 weeks | Problem-solving, research and teamworking skills | Rarely |
| Workplace visit | 1–5 days | To raise student awareness of workplace practices, career taster | Rarely |
| Workplace tour | 1 day | Raise student awareness of workplace environments | Rarely |
| Case studies | Seminars | To help understand application of theory to practice | Rarely |

Source: adapted from Harvey, L., Geall, V. and Moon, S. (1998) *Work Experience: Expanding opportunities for undergraduates*. Birmingham, CRQ.

*Sandwich year/industrial placements*

There is a wide range of courses, many including a sandwich or placement year – part of the attraction is the high proportion of students who are offered a job afterwards. Students are usually given help and guidance in finding a suitable employer for a year. Watch out, though, you are not eligible to be paid the minimum wage on an industrial or teaching placement (see Chapter 12 for more on this).

A number of well-known, popular graduate recruiters offer structured programmes of relevant work, and competition for these is usually intense. Applying for many such placements is very similar to applying for a graduate job, often using a structured application form. Screening, interviews and even assessment centres are used in the selection process. Between 50 and 70 per cent of students who succeed in obtaining such placements go on to be employed by the organization on graduation, so they can create a genuine win–win situation.

Many departments will have built up links with local employers, large and small, and may be able to offer help and guidance in seeking a year placement. If it is part of the course requirement, there will be a staff member responsible for guiding and advising students.

Many courses now allow students to take a year out from a traditional three-year degree to study or work in a relevant area at home or overseas. If you are thinking of doing this, you need to first contact the year tutor in your department for permission.

---

**CASE STUDY   Danny's sandwich course placement**

---

Danny was studying for a BSc in Business and Management Studies at Salford University. This was a sandwich course and Danny applied for, and accepted, a year placement as an Accounts Executive with a firm producing a wide range of domestic and personal healthcare products.

'Since my GSCEs, I always felt I wanted a business-based career. I chose a placement to help me develop the skills I needed. Work experience taught me a lot. At first I felt disorientated and wondered if I was in the wrong job. Quickly, though, I found my feet and soon felt more competent in my role. At the end of my placement, I knew exactly which career direction I wanted to work towards achieving.'

---

*Workplace projects, visits and tours*

Course-based trips and projects can offer genuine insight and experience. All too often, however, they can end up as dislocated, tedious affairs that appear burdensome to the host employer and useless to the student.

You can avoid these pitfalls by influencing the work experience episode to your advantage. You can try to get the maximum benefit from these enforced opportunities by:

▶ deciding on your own goals and interests and then trying to tailor the experience to suit you;

▶ where you do have discretion and choice, make the most of it;

▶ use every opportunity to make a good impression;

▶ create networks, follow up visits with a thank you and say what you learned from the experience.

## Working during summer holidays

What are holidays for? Anyone involved in university life knows this is the period when lecturers escape their teaching workload and write conference papers, articles or research. What about the students? The holidays are a key time to build your career.

How do you view them? A chance to rest, relax, earn some cash or get the sort of work experience that will put you ahead of the rest when it comes to getting a real job after graduation?

### ACTIVITY 5.1  Work experience action planner for undergraduates

Look at the table below. Which types of holiday work have you already experienced? Given the time you have left, what scope is there for using your holiday to maximum benefit. You need to plan ahead as some of the employer- and agency-based opportunities have set closing dates or fill up very quickly.

| Main types of work experience | Duration | Objectives |
| --- | --- | --- |
| Structured work/training scheme | 6–10 weeks | To gain relevant work experience and insight |
| Short holiday courses | 1–3 days | Career tasters – some are used by potential employers as a form of screening/assessment |
| Work experience during summer | 6–10 weeks | Career taster, often used by potential employers as a form of screening/assessment |
| Work shadowing | 1–2 weeks | First-hand observation of senior manager or professional at work |
| Organized international programme | 6–10 weeks | Gain knowledge of another culture, improve language skills – fun! |
| Voluntary | 6–10 weeks | Gain understanding of, and show interest in, particular client groups; social issues |

Source: adapted from Harvey, L., Geall, V. and Moon, S. (1998) *Work Experience: Expanding opportunities for undergraduates*. Birmingham, CRQ.

### Action planner

Answer the following questions

**1.** What are your personal goals for the next short holiday?

_____

**2.** What practical steps will you take now to ensure you reach your goal successfully?

_____

**3.** What are your personal goals for the next long/summer holiday?

_____

**4.** What can you do now to make some progress with your plans?

_____

Over the three or four years of a degree course, you will have many opportunities to pick and mix the way you spend your holidays, so think through your strategy as early as you can. Now is not too early!

---

**CASE STUDY  STEP**

---

The Shell Technology Enterprise Programme (STEP) offers an eight-week work placement opportunity in the small business and voluntary sector. It is open to second/penultimate year undergraduates. Students follow a specific programme, which is intended to be of real use to a business or organization, and receive a minimum training allowance of £120 per week. All STEP programme students have to write an account of their experiences.

Applications are accepted from January and close at the end of May. See www.shell-step.org,uk for more details

---

**CASE STUDY  Rebecca's experience of management shadowing in the NHS**

---

'I spent several days with a large NHS Healthcare Trust on a management shadowing scheme. This involved me attending meetings all around the UK as well as at the Trust's HQ. These experiences were brilliant. They helped me understand the role of a manager and the skills needed.

My time in the NHS Trust helped me become much more focused on the type of management I am interested in.

*Getting the best from your holiday work experience*

▶ Set your goals.
▶ Think ahead – check deadlines and closing dates for applications so you don't miss the boat!
▶ Budget wisely – check out the costs and try to be just a little bit realistic!
▶ Check the practical things – health, vaccinations, insurance, visas …

## Paid term-time work

Money is a key factor and motivator for almost every student in paid term-time work. Research shows that the majority of students are working to pay for basic living and study costs and pay back or reduce debts. All well and good, but the bad news is that this can affect your studies, the quality of your assessed work and your degree result. Therefore, it can affect your long-term career prospects.

Most students work in retail and the hotels/pubs/catering industries that are known for low pay, long, 'unsociable' hours, job insecurity and low levels of employee protection trade union activity.

**CASE STUDY**   NUS *Students at Work* survey – factfile

▶ In 1999 full-time students were working an average of 13.5 hours a week plus 6.5 hours overtime … well above the limits recommended by most universities.

▶ Of students interviewed in the NUS survey, 34 per cent reported health and safety problems. These included injuries such as cuts and burns, muscle strain and coping with abuse and threats from pub, bar and club fighting.

▶ Of full-time students who work part-time, 38 per cent had missed lectures or failed to hand work in on time because of demands of their employment.

▶ Of those working, 21 per cent failed to submit coursework because of demands of their employment.

▶ Of full-time students who worked. 48 per cent believed they would have got higher grades if they had not been employed.

▶ Many students have poor pay and working conditions, get no sick pay, no holiday pay and no meal breaks … no wonder 27 per cent felt working while studying affected their health.

Source: Labour Research Department, NUS, *Students at Work* Survey, 1999

---

**CASE STUDY**   Linda – 'How working part-time almost ruined my chance of getting a degree'

'I came to study in London in September 1998. I took a part-time job at a local supermarket. At first I just worked two shifts a week, but as the bills mounted I increased this. The course was hard work, though. I just didn't have the time to study properly. I found myself missing lectures, handing in work late. Working long hours (often I worked 20–30 hours a week) were grinding me down. I could not ask my parents for financial help – anyway, I didn't want to.

I decided to see one of the student counsellors and get some financial advice from the Student Union before going to a bank. I reduced my hours back to just two shifts a week, learned to budget better, to be less anxious about getting into debt and to keep a longer-term view … that getting a good degree would be much better for my career prospects than all those hours on the checkout.'

Apart from the financial rewards, there are many positive benefits to working part-time. You can develop key work skills, such as communication, handling money, numeracy, customer care, working with others, handling difficult clients/colleagues/bosses. You can gain insights into the types of work you are suited to and which ones to avoid.

Your work experiences will enhance your future employability, especially if you reflect on and record your learning in an appropriate way. Think about the specific job-related skills, but also about your understanding of the bigger picture. Where did your job fit in with those of the other members of the work team or group? How were you organized? What organizational procedures were in place to make it all happen?

If you are on good terms with your boss or manager, you could ask to shadow him or her for part of a day, go to head office. You could talk to other senior managers and staff, find out what they do and how everything fits together.

You can demonstrate the development of greater business awareness, take an interest in the organization's business strategy, read the company newsletter or paper, if it has one. If it's a smaller operation, ask to talk to the managers about their marketing strategy and their intentions to make the place operate efficiently.

---

**CASE STUDY  Hannah – business awareness gained while working in a teashop**

Hannah was in her first year of a Media Studies and Language degree at the University of Salford, working weekends and two evenings in a local teashop. The teashop was part of a UK-based chain of some 34 other outlets. Hannah described her work as 'waitressing'. I discussed with her the career skills and understanding she was gaining. Hannah's first reaction was 'minimal', but on investigation …

Hannah described a new policy that had been introduced to create a sort of career progression in the tearoom. This was only available to staff with several weeks' tenure in the job. It involved a trip to London to take part in a customer service training day and wearing a red apron that you were entitled to wear afterwards – a sign of promotion.

Clearly Hannah had identified that the emerging business strategy was to promote customer care, better training and an internal career structure for waitresses. This was seen by the business as a key part of its goal to build a strong base of return clientele who received excellent service.

Thus, Hannah can now say that she:

▶ has direct experience of the links between customer service and business success;

▶ understands the rationale behind corporate policies and practices in recruiting and keeping waitresses;

▶ highly developed interpersonal and teamworking skills.

Why not follow Hannah's example and try this approach to reframing your work experiences ready for inclusion in a CV?

---

Hopefully, you will find that paid work does enhance your finances or at least limits the size of future debt.

In summary, there are five key benefits to be gained from paid term-time work:

▶ the development of key work skills;

▶ insights into what you want and don't want from your eventual career;

▶ enhanced employability;

▶ business awareness;

▶ healthy – or, at least, healthier – finances.

There can be a number of pitfalls to term-time work, so look at the checklists and see if you need to improve your experience now.

| Do | Avoid |
|---|---|
| **Think** about how what you do fits into the bigger picture of the organization.<br><br>**Reflect** on, and note down, what skills you have used, learned or developed (why not produce a work experience portfolio? See Activity 5.3).<br><br>Reflect on, and **note down**, what personal aptitudes you have needed to do the job – trustworthiness, patience, attention to detail …<br><br>**Do the job** as well as possible and see what you can learn from others.<br><br>**Ask penetrating questions** about how the organization works – try to really understand it.<br><br>See if you can do more than one job – **move** to different sections or departments.<br><br>Make sure it goes in **your CV**.<br><br>Know **your employment rights** (see Chapter 12). | **Working long hours** – many universities recommend you don't work more than 15 hours a week during term time.<br><br>**Cutting down on study time** – you can't make up time by cramming.<br><br>**All work and no play** – you need to ensure that you have a balanced lifestyle. Do it now – it doesn't get easier if you leave it!<br><br>**Working in unsafe conditions** or without proper protection and training.<br><br>Don't accept **pay below the minimum wage**.<br><br>**Worrying** about money. If you don't feel in control of your financial position, find someone professionally trained to help you, such as a student adviser or an independent counsellor. Most local authorities have specially trained debt counsellors. Banks may not be totally independent. |

*Overcoming term-time work problems*
If you have a problem or difficulty regarding your employment – such as pay or working conditions – then turn to Chapter 12, which sets out some basic information about employment rights and gives details of local and national agencies that can help you.

## Voluntary work

Many students gain a great sense of satisfaction from doing unpaid/voluntary work during term time or the holidays. The range of work is, of course, massive. You can do something close to your career interests or escape into a completely different and unfamiliar world.

Most university careers advisory services operate some sort of voluntary work directory. Local authorities usually have schemes for students to help with school-children or young people in a number of ways. There are schemes for visiting the elderly or housebound at home, offering practical help, such as doing some gardening or shopping for or with them. You can get involved on a regular term-time basis – say, one afternoon or evening a week. Another alternative is to be involved in a summer or short holiday project. The world is your oyster when it comes to volunteer opportunities.

## ACTIVITY 5.3 Create your own work experience portfolio

Maximize the benefits you gain from your work experience by creating your own personal portfolio using the checklist. Take some hole-punched A4 paper and work through the ten topic areas to produce a valuable record of what you have learned.

This can be used to help you when you are creating your CV and preparing for Interviews and assessment centres.

| 1 | Company details | Name, address, your work location. |
|---|---|---|
| 2 | Employment details | Your role, terms and conditions (full-time, part-time, paid, voluntary). Date you started and duration of employment. |
| 3 | Your role | Details of your job (job description and personnel specification, if you can obtain them). Highlight your skills and abilities, but also demonstrate how your role added value to the organization. |
| 4 | About the company | Is it large, small, local or multinational? How does the company make money, what were its plans and objectives, what are its main products or services, organizational culture, departmental or professional subcultures? |
| 5 | Business strategy | If it is a large organization, there may be a business strategy for each of the different parts. What were the key issues for the part of the organization you worked for? |
| 6 | Organizational structures, policies and procedures | What did you learn about the organization's structure, policy framework and procedures, such as marketing, customer care, human resource management policies, health and safety issues? Could you assess the strengths and weaknesses of the organization? Did you recommend or suggest any changes? |
| 7 | Skills and abilities | Employers attach particular importance to:<br>▶ interpersonal skills;  ▶ research;<br>▶ IT and communication skills;  ▶ problem solving;<br>▶ teamworking and influencing;  ▶ self-development. |
| 8 | Achievements | Highlight any specific contributions you made to the organization — be as specific as possible. Keep records of compliments made, feedback received or written appraisals. Emphasize what you did and how you did it. |
| 9 | Personal development | Highlight areas where your work experience helped you develop personally – in terms of, say, self-confidence, giving presentations, handling IT applications, clearer career direction. |
| 10 | Reflections | Note down how your understanding of the organization and your role changed over time. Emphasize the transferability of lessons learned to future workplaces. |

Collect as much information as you can during your period of employment. If you have left, you can use your network of contacts to glean some useful information. You can always visit the organization's web site or use the ideas on information sources listed in Chapter 11.

## SUMMARY

This chapter has outlined the wide variety of work experience opportunities open to you.

You need to plan a strategy to suit your own personal career ambitions. This will involve:

▶ setting yourself some work experience goals;

▶ exploring the options and considering doing something really different;

▶ gaining experience, skill and insights;

▶ reflecting on your learning;

▶ using the local network of tutors, careers staff, students;

▶ taking care when working during term time;

▶ building bridges between the past and the future to enhance your employability;

▶ not panicking – you can draw learning from any and every situation and experience.

## FURTHER INFORMATION

### GENERAL INFORMATION TO GET YOU STARTED

These should be available from your local careers advisory service:

▶ Placement and Vacation Work Casebook (a series of specialist titles, revised annually), Hobsons (also www.hobsons.com)

▶ Focus on Work Experience (part of *Prospects* series) (www.csu.prospects.co.uk)

▶ The A to Z of Work Experience

Most also offer:

▶ a locally produced vacancies bulletin;

▶ a local work experience careers fair;

▶ a local community service skills exchange.

Placement opportunities and ideas can be found at:

Liverpool  www.business-bridge.org.uk

Manchester  www.workbank.man.ac.uk

There are also specialist schemes, such as the Workable Graduate Support Scheme, which provides support to create placements for disabled students with major employers. Find out more from the following web site:

www.workable.org.uk


# USEFUL CONTACTS

## FOR WORK EXPERIENCE INFORMATION

National Centre for Work Experience
344–354 Grays Inn Road
London WCIX 8BP
Tel: 020 7833 9723
Web site: www.ncwe.com


## OVERSEAS WORK AND INDUSTRIAL EXCHANGE SCHEMES

International Exchange Programme (AIESEC)
Web site: www.aiesec.org
Voluntary Service Overseas (VSO)
Web site: www.oneworld.org
BUNAC Camp America
Web site: www.bunac.org.uk

See also the **Appendix** for further work experience information.

# Two thirds of what we see is behind our eyes.

ANCIENT CHINESE PROVERB

## In this chapter, you will:

- ☐ discover a six-step model to help overcome obstacles to your career:

- ☐ **E**xplore and identify the problem;

- ☐ **N**ew understanding and insight;

- ☐ **G**oal setting;

- ☐ **A**ction;

- ☐ **G**et results;

- ☐ **E**valuate and review progress.

## In the activities:

**6.1** Identify the obstacle

**6.2** My lifeline

**6.3** Get **SMART**

**6.4** Putting force field analysis into action

**6.5** Create your own positive thinking code

**6.6** Your support network

# THE ENGAGE MODEL

This chapter sets out a six-step model to help you overcome the obstacles you encounter in deciding on your career direction and in securing the job you want. This is not a simple 'off the peg' tactic, but a framework to apply to any situation that requires a problem-solving technique. The model gives you a sequence of steps to help you manage problems and make decisions in a way that reflects your values and personality.

I use the acronym **ENGAGE** because I think it's easy to remember and so easier to use!

**ENGAGE** provides a sequence of logical steps to achieve your goals. The length of time and amount of energy needed at each stage will differ with each individual situation.

**TABLE 6.1    The ENGAGE model for overcoming problems**

| Stage | Problem-solving tasks | Techniques and activities |
|---|---|---|
| 1 **E**xplore and identify the problem | Identify the main problem areas or concerns, specify details and be aware of feelings | Personal reflection<br>Activity 6.1: Identify the obstacle |
| 2 **N**ew understanding and insight | Develop fresh insights and perceptions about yourself | Activity 6.2: My lifeline |
| 3 **G**oal setting | Translate problems identified into 'goal statements' | Activity 6.3: Get **SMART** |
| 4 **A**ction | Work to strengthen resources, minimize deficits and 'inhibitors' and overcome negative self-talk | Activity 6.4: Putting force field analysis into action<br>Activity 6.5: Create your own positive thinking code |
| 5 **G**et results | Implement self-help and problem-solving skills, persevere to consolidate and maintain change and progress | Activity 6.6: Your support network |
| 6 **E**valuate and review progress | Review progress made against goals set | Assess learning so far |

Let us look at each of the six stages in turn.

## STAGE 1 EXPLORE AND IDENTIFY THE PROBLEM

In any problem-solving process, the essential first step is to identify the exact nature of the problem.

You may be painfully aware of a particular problem or issue that you are wrestling with. Perhaps reading the earlier chapters has helped you identify a need for personal development in a specific area. Is there something about yourself that you are struggling with and wanting to change, such as shyness or nerves? Perhaps you face financial problems or see your good degree result slipping away because of poor time management.

Below is a list of some common problems that many undergraduates and recent graduates experience.

► 'I just can't decide which job I am suited to';
► 'Employers all want you to get a 2:1 and I just don't think I will get one';
► 'What good is [your subject] if you want to get into [career]?';
► 'I just don't know what my skills are';
► 'I wish I was more confident';
► 'I am so shy, I could never give a presentation';
► 'I wish I didn't get so nervous';
► 'If only I was more organized';
► 'My parents really want me to go into X, but I am more interested in Y'.

## Identify the obstacle

The first step to overcoming an obstacle is to admit that it is there. It is very important to try to define the problem as you see it. What does it affect, when and where does it happen?

You may find it particularly helpful to explore the problem with a friend, preferably someone who is a good listener. Set aside a short, but substantial (30–45-minute), slot in private.

Find a few quiet moments to write down the problem as you see it. I suggest writing it down so you can refer to it later – seeing how much progress you have made will be an enormous encouragement.

Write it down in the box provided in Activity 6.1, or in a safe place.

---

**ACTIVITY 6.1    Identify the obstacle**

My main problem at the moment is ...

---

## STAGE 2 NEW UNDERSTANDING AND INSIGHT

The changes you want to make can be achieved. First, you will need to gain deeper understanding of the problem or the way you respond to it. Over time, we all develop patterns of thinking, feeling and responding.

For most obstacles, there is considerable scope for self-help. You can do this in three ways:

- ▶ learn from the past;
- ▶ learn from other people;
- ▶ learn by listening to yourself.

### Learning from the past

You can gain new insights into your personality, emotions, responses and career goals by looking back. Your family/step-family and past experiences have laid down an important foundation for your personal development and sense of identity. Past periods of your life are likely to have involved both positive, supportive experiences as well as difficult ones.

Your early years hold the key to development of self-image, personality and emotional well-being. Looking back can be a rewarding opportunity to see yourself in the context of your family, school, hobbies, social life, achievements and disappointments. The next exercise comes with a warning. Looking back can be positive; it can also be painful. It can be a springboard to facing and overcoming aspects of your life or relationships you know need attention.

| ACTIVITY 6.2 My lifeline |
| --- |

Take a blank piece of lined A4 paper and draw a small dot at the bottom. Underneath the dot write your name and date of birth.

*My lifeline*

My birth 0———5———10———15———20———25———30——— …

Next, think back and record significant events or memories. In particular, try to think about:

- ▶ major changes or events in the family;
- ▶ relationships with parents, siblings;
- ▶ school experiences;
- ▶ friendships;
- ▶ achievements and disappointments.

Note down here the following:

- ▶ *insights* into your strengths and resources:

    In the past I have succeeded at _____

- ▶ Do you have any new insights into your fears or self-doubts? Has this exercise helped you to identify and understand why you tackle certain situations or problems in the way you do?

    Past hurts, failures or disappointments still affect me _____

If you have found this exercise helpful and identified area of strength as well as doubts, you can add these to your notes at the end of the activity.

## Learn from other people

Another helpful source of fresh insights and ideas about yourself is other people. If you really want to know, you can ask. If you did not do it earlier, you could refer back to Activity 4.3, which offers an opportunity to obtain a picture of the way someone else sees you.

Receiving feedback from others is an invaluable source of information. It may help you discover that what you see as a problem, others see as a very valuable asset. Many folk say that shy people are very good listeners and are more sensitive than extrovert types.

Other people may even help you see your 'obstacle' in a completely new light!

## Learn by listening to yourself

We often allow negative thoughts and feelings to influence our behaviour and limit our achievements. We all have an inner voice and, even if we may not be particularly aware of it, it can have a powerful effect. It might say, for example:

▶ 'I never do anything well';

▶ 'It will probably go wrong';

▶ 'Everyone can do it better than me';

▶ 'I am bound to make a mistake';

▶ 'I'm no good in a large group'.

Do you recognize any of these? Many obstacles exist because we have allowed these sorts of negative patterns of thinking to take root. We believe what the negative inner voice is whispering to us. The good news is that negative thought patterns can be replaced by more positive ones. Changes in the way you feel and behave often follow a change in the way you think.

If you are prone to negative or self-defeating thought patterns, you can overcome them by:

▶ recognizing them;

▶ counteracting them;

▶ creating your own positive thinking code;

▶ building on success.

First, though, you need to set yourself some goals.

## STAGE 3 GOAL SETTING

The next stage of any problem-solving technique is to give yourself clear, achievable goals. If you are aiming towards an imprecise and unclear target, how will you know when you hit a bull's-eye? The mnemonic **SMART** may help you. See Activity 6.3 for what it stands for.

Set **SMART** goals, **SMART** meaning:

**S** pecific
**M** easurable
**A** chievable
**R** ealistic
**T** ime-limited

**TABLE 6.2    SMART goals are ...**

| | |
|---|---|
| **S**pecific | Try to be specific. What exactly is the nature of your problem or concern? |
| **M**easureable | Think about the solution you are seeking. |
| **A**chievable | Make sure your request is within the realms of possibility. |
| **R**ealistic | Don't set yourself up to fail. Be realistic about what you are asking for – a sequence of small improvements will be more productive than one huge leap. |
| **T**ime-limited | Decide what you think is a reasonable time-scale, then follow through. |

Set yourself a **SMART** goal now. It could relate to anything you have identified as needing to be achieved. For example, you may have recognized that academic work pressures and lack of time prevent you looking into jobs, even though you want to. An unrealistic goal at this stage would be 'Get a job by the end of next week' or 'get all my essays written in the next fortnight'. Instead, break down your objectives into smaller, achievable goals.

**SMART** goals could be:

▶ to complete the two specific assignments due for this term and hand them in on time.
▶ set aside 1 hour on Thursday evening between 6 and 7pm to complete a career skills audit (see Activity 2.3).

Note here the goal you have identified as needing to be achieved next.

_____
_____
_____
_____

## STAGE 4 ACTION

You must now strengthen your resources and, at the same time, minimize the factors that are inhibiting your progress. The notion of progress towards your objectives taking place in a 'force field' of enabling and inhibiting factors may be helpful. Force field analysis is a really helpful tool in any problem-solving activity. You first identify your goals. Next, you identify those forces or factors that may hinder or restrain you from reaching them. You also identify resources that can help you.

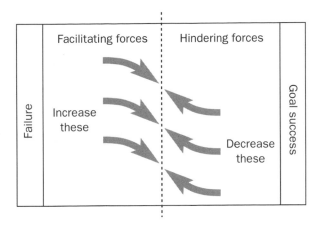

**FIGURE 6.1  Force field analysis**

## Hindering forces – your aim is to decrease these

These can be forces that come from within you – negative beliefs, fears, doubts from university pressures, essays, assignments, family – expectations, demands, limitations and larger socio-environmental forces, such as gender stereotypes, racism and so on.

Hindering forces that you can do something about include unrealistic beliefs about yourself, negative thinking, making excessive demands of yourself and perfectionism. You may also need to develop ways of counteracting any negative thinking you have noticed. Once you have identified your own patterns of negative thinking, you can convert them into positive ones. Win the battle of the mind – use the following ten questions to help you do just that.

► Is this a thought or a fact?

► What is the effect on me of thinking this way?

► Is this the only interpretation available?

► Am I thinking in polar extremes?

► Is everything wrong because of one small mistake I made?

► What can I do to affect the outcome?

► Am I allowing my worries to overshadow the real picture?

► What is the alternative?

► Even if it happened, would it really be a catastrophe?

► What can I learn from this?

## Facilitating forces – your aim is to use and build on these

Force field analysis also requires you to identify all the positive resources available. Again, these can be within you (your drive, tenacity) or come from your family or social network (tutors, careers advice, libraries, counselling services, lecturers, parents and so on).

Obstacles come in all shapes and sizes, so use the next activity to help you to apply the force field approach to the particular issue you have identified.

---

**ACTIVITY 6.4   Putting force field analysis into action**

Thinking of your next career goal, use the table below to identify your own helping and hindering forces.

| What you need to achieve your goal | What might hinder this? | What might help? |
| --- | --- | --- |
| 1. | | |
| 2. | | |
| 3. | | |

---

## Visualize success

Many people find it helpful to visualize themselves accomplishing the task or goal set. Why not try it and see if this helps you. If you have imagined yourself through each step of reaching your own goal, it makes it much easier to do it for real. This also works if you are worried, for example, that a presentation may go wrong. Imagined each scenario and plan what you would do if it did. This is a great way of overcoming performance anxiety.

---

**ACTIVITY 6.5   Create your own positive thinking code**

Particular self-defeating patterns of thought and behaviour will be unique to you. You can create your own personal code to promote greater confidence. Pin this up in your bedroom or study or the kitchen – it will help you to keep making progress towards your goal.

A positive thinking code could include statements such as those shown below. Read through the list and select the ones that suit you, use this list as a basis for your own personal code.

*continued*

---

- ▶ 'I am talented in many things.'
- ▶ 'I can say no when I want to.'
- ▶ 'I can make mistakes – it will not be the end of the world.'
- ▶ 'I am learning all the time.'
- ▶ 'I can admit when I don't know something.'
- ▶ 'I can reward myself for effort as well as achievement.'
- ▶ 'I can get things wrong.'
- ▶ 'I do not have to be perfect.'
- ▶ 'I deserve to have treats and fun.'
- ▶ 'I do not have to live up to other people's expectations of me.'

Can you think of some more, personal to you?

- ▶ _____
- ▶ _____
- ▶ _____

## STAGE 5 GET RESULTS

At this stage, you begin to implement the steps you have identified that will lead you to your **SMART** goals. You may make progress independently, but you can also build support networks and maximize the resources available to help you progress.

The next exercise helps you to identify the people, organizations or sources of information that can offer support and help you achieve your goals. See these as resources that can help you to get results.

### ACTIVITY 6.6    Your support network

Identify who or what:

- ▶ helps you relax _____
- ▶ makes you laugh _____
- ▶ allows you to talk openly about worries _____
- ▶ you can discuss and explore career options with _____
- ▶ can give practical advice about: _____
  - – your studies _____
  - – your money _____
  - – your accommodation _____
  - – your career aspirations _____
  - – your health _____
- ▶ helps you to resolve conflicts _____
- ▶ tells you the truth _____
- ▶ you can cry or be upset with _____
- ▶ celebrates your achievements _____

How does your support network look? Are there any obvious gaps? Make sure you are building yours!

## STAGE 6 EVALUATE

You will need to constantly review progress made against your goals. Build on success and reward yourself when you do make progress.

In evaluating progress, you may find you have grown personally in some unexpected ways. Increased self-esteem can percolate to many other aspects of your life. However, the demands of university life and career choices can take their toll – you may be struggling with problems that need professional help and support. Around 1 in 10 of all students visit their local counselling service at some point during their studies (support services for personal problems are listed in the Appendix).

Don't forget, especially in relation to career decisions, that the goalposts are constantly moving. Even having worked towards the goal set, you may discover that there are yet further goals to achieve. This may be the moment to start work on a fresh self-development project or, perhaps, it may be thrust upon you when your first job interview appointment arrives.

You can use the six steps of the **ENGAGE** model many times over, for any of the challenges life throws your way.

## SUMMARY

- ► Overcome obstacles by first recognizing that you have encountered one.
- ► Try to identify the problem and look at the patterns of thinking that may be reinforcing it.
- ► Set yourself some achievable goals – don't aim for the moon at your first attempt.
- ► Build on your strengths and find ways around weakness or try to see them in a new light.
- ► Review progress and, if it isn't working, move on to Plan B and keep trying.
- ► You may find it helpful to look at the next chapter, on improving your stress fitness.

# under pressure – improve your stress fitness

**Learn how to cope with the demands of university, jobhunting and life at work!**

**In this Chapter, you will:**

- [ ] understand stress;
- [ ] spot signs of healthy stress;
- [ ] know how to identify when you are overstressed;
- [ ] take your own personal stress fitness test;
- [ ] learn **SMART** skills and techniques to improve your own stress fitness.

**In the activities:**

**7.1** Signs of healthy stress

**7.2** Are you overstressed?

**7.3** Recognize your own stressors

**7.4** Stress fitness test

# UNDER PRESSURE?

You don't need me to tell you that being a student can be stressful. You may feel that this is the most demanding phase of your life so far. You are under pressure to perform in assignments and exams, manage your finances, relationships, paid work, cope with flatmates or, worse (if you are at home), living with your parents!

These pressures partly explain why so many students are reluctant to add more stress to their lives and so put off choosing and finding a job until after graduation.

# WHAT IS STRESS?

The process of understanding stress began with Walter Cannon's description of the 'fight or flight response', which describes how we respond to perceived danger. The body releases adrenaline, blood pressure is raised, heartbeat and breathing quicken, ready for action.

Richard Lazarus later developed the most widely used approach to understanding stress during the 1980s. Lazarus distinguished three types of stress:

► **harm** or **loss** such as losing something of great value and bereavement;
► **threat** anticipated harm;
► **challenge** opportunities that may be positive and potentially developmental.

Based on Lazarus' work, most modern interpretations recognize stress is being a blend of external pressures or challenges and an individual's ability to cope with those demands.

# RESPONDING TO STRESS

Each of us is different in the amount of stress we can tolerate. This explains why one person may thrive under certain conditions, seeing the situation as an exciting challenge. However, faced with the same situation, another person may be overwhelmed by fear and anxiety.

## HEALTHY STRESS

In one sense, then, stress is good for you – it provides stimulation and the opportunity to achieve. 'Healthy stress' occurs when you are under the amount of pressure that suits you. The signs of healthy stress will differ according to your individual personality, but should generally reflect those listed in Activity 7.1.

If you cannot tick at least half of the items in the checklist, it could mean that you are not responding to your present level of stress very well.

The stress of university life may be making huge demands on your ability to cope. As shown in Figure 7.1, you will have your own natural balance, or 'steady state'. Under optimum conditions, you should exhibit the signs of healthy stress outlined above – subject, of course, to natural differences in underlying temperament and personality.

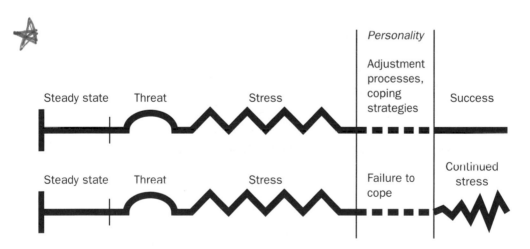

**FIGURE 7.1   Different responses to stress – the Cooper-Cummings framework**

Source: *Stress and Employer Liability*, 1996, Earnshaw, J. and Cooper C. Reproduced with the permission of the publisher, the Institute of Personnel and Development, IPD House, Camp Road, London SW19 4UX

# RECOGNIZING WHEN YOU ARE OVERSTRESSED

When a perceived threat or challenge arises (for example, having to write an essay or give a presentation to your seminar group), the alarm bells ring. Stress can affect your feelings, behaviour and physical wellbeing. Common signs of being over-stressed are listed in Activity 7.2. The signs of being overstressed can be experienced at varying levels of intensity.

The greatest problems are encountered when the challenges or threats of university life habitually exceed your ability to cope and the symptoms continue.

Under such circumstances, the emotional and physical symptoms of stress can contribute to further stress and you enter a vicious, downward cycle.

In order to combat stress, you need to identify your own signs of being overstressed.

---

### ACTIVITY 7.2   Are you overstressed?

Look at the checklist and put a tick by those signs you experience when you are overstressed.

| | |
|---|---|
| ❏ Worry, anxiety | ❏ Lack of appetite. |
| ❏ Feeling fearful. | ❏ Difficulty in making decisions. |
| ❏ Low self-esteem. | ❏ Difficulty concentrating. |
| ❏ Making frequent mistakes. | ❏ Feeling unable to cope. |
| ❏ Tiredness. | ❏ Wanting to cry. |
| ❏ Nausea. | ❏ Emotional outbursts. |
| ❏ Fainting spells. | ❏ Difficulty sleeping. |
| ❏ Headaches. | ❏ Flitting between tasks. |
| ❏ Constipation or diarrhoea. | ❏ Increased drinking, smoking. |
| ❏ Tendency to sweat. | ❏ Greater use of caffeine, drugs. |
| ❏ Frequent indigestion or heartburn. | ❏ Excessive self-criticism. |
| ❏ Food cravings. | ❏ Mood swings. |
| | ❏ Angry outbursts. |

Source: Adapted from *The Stress Work Book*, 1993 by Eve Warren and Caroline Toll, Nicholas Brealey Publishing, London. Used with kind permission

---

If you have ticked more than four of these signs or you have noticed that one or two of them are becoming more intense and difficult to manage, then you may have an underlying emotional or physical problem. You should see your GP for a proper medical assessment. Many GPs now have a counselling service or can refer you to the student counselling services provided locally and they can prove very beneficial.

## RECOGNIZING WHEN YOU ARE UNDERSTRESSED

Lack of interesting work, variety or challenge can lead to boredom, frustration and lethargy. The following are signs of being understressed:

- ▶ low-self esteem;
- ▶ irritability;
- ▶ tiredness;
- ▶ complaining about work;
- ▶ low energy levels;
- ▶ needing extra stimulants;
- ▶ little interest in work;
- ▶ critical of self and others;
- ▶ inertia;
- ▶ unproductive work patterns.

You will notice that some of these indicators are similar to those of being over-stressed. They will not follow a set pattern, nor will they all be experienced by every person. They can serve as a helpful warning sign that you are not receiving sufficient stimulation.

You may notice these responses occurring when you are in a particular environment, especially paid term-time work, which is so often low-skilled and low-paid graft!

# EFFECTIVE STRESS MANAGEMENT

Recognizing what overstresses you is critical to effective stress management.

---

**ACTIVITY 7.3    Recognize your own stressors**

Look at the lists of potential sources of stress associated with university and career choices. Which ones are the most stressful for you? Tick those that apply to you.

**Academic**

- ❑ Writing assignments, essays.
- ☑ Team-based project work.
- ❑ Giving presentations.
- ❑ Examinations.
- ❑ Tutorials.
- ❑ Contributing in seminars.

*continued*

---

- ❏ Skills practice sessions.
- ❏ Using computers, IT.
- ❏ Study v paid work conflicts.
- ❏ Other..........................

**Relationships**

- ❏ Conflict at home, family problems.
- ❏ Bereavement or other significant loss.
- ❏ Rejection by intimate partner.
- ☑ Separation from partner/family.
- ❏ Loneliness.
- ❏ Other..........................

**Personal**

- ❏ Debts.
- ❏ Weight problems.
- ❏ Health problems.
- ❏ Drug/alcohol dependency.
- ❏ Problems at work.
- ❏ Sexual/identity problems.
- ☑ Coping with previous trauma or abuse.
- ❏ Childcare/dependants.
- ❏ Other..........................

**Career**

- ❏ Difficulty in making decisions/no direction.
- ❏ Family pressures.
- ❏ Fear of interviews.
- ❏ Worries about assessment centres.
- ❏ No time to think.
- ☑ Other......Lack of...my skill

You have now identified:

▶ Your own unique stress response pattern;

▶ Your personal stressors.

You need to check out your own level of stress fitness and see if there is room for improvement.

# HOW STRESS FIT ARE YOU?

Effective stress management needs to be tailored to your own unique stress profile and stress response pattern. Your ability to manage stress will be influenced by:

▶ internal factors, such as your self-image and beliefs about your abilities;

▶ external factors, such as circumstances, events and the challenges of university life.

Numerous studies have shown that the way you think, care for yourself, manage your time and studies and keeping to a healthy balanced lifestyle can help combat signs of being overstressed.

You can use the six-step problem-solving model and force field analysis technique outlined in Chapter 6. To reiterate the advice given earlier, if you are suffering from being overstressed, or know you have other personal problems, you may need to see your GP for a referral to suitable help.

Everyone can benefit from an occasional assessment of lifestyle.

Is there anything you can change to improve your ability to cope with the challenges you face? You may be stress fit already. Why not find out by doing the next activity?

---

### ACTIVITY 7.4  Stress fitness test

Use this quick questionnaire to find out how your lifestyle adds up. Circle the answer that most closely describes you.

| Lifestyle activities | Always | Usually | Sometimes | Rarely |
|---|---|---|---|---|
| **Exercise and health** | | | | |
| I exercise for at least 20 minutes twice a week. | 1 | 2 | 3 | 4 |
| I use stairs rather than lifts. | 1 | 2 | 3 | 4 |
| I generally feel well and have plenty of energy. | 1 | 2 | 3 | 4 |
| **Relaxation** | | | | |
| I laugh and have fun. | 1 | 2 | 3 | 4 |
| I know how to unwind. | 1 | 2 | 3 | 4 |
| I sleep well. | 1 | 2 | 3 | 4 |
| **Nourishment** | | | | |
| I eat at least one balanced meal a day. | 1 | 2 | 3 | 4 |
| I limit my intake of alcohol and don't often get totally drunk. | 1 | 2 | 3 | 4 |
| **Emotional support** | | | | |
| I have at least one close friend I can tell anything to. | 1 | 2 | 3 | 4 |
| I can express my thoughts and feelings well. | 1 | 2 | 3 | 4 |
| **Positive thinking** | | | | |
| I am optimistic. | 1 | 2 | 3 | 4 |
| I like myself. | 1 | 2 | 3 | 4 |
| **Study skills** | | | | |
| I feel in control of my studies. | 1 | 2 | 3 | 4 |
| I can concentrate for long periods of time. | 1 | 2 | 3 | 4 |
| I use my time well and effectively. | 1 | 2 | 3 | 4 |
| Totals for each category | | | | |

This activity has identified your areas of strength and weakness when it comes to life-style stress fitness. Take action now in any area you have marked as something you do rarely (4). Improvement in even one of these could make a big difference to your ability to cope with stress, in both the short and long term.

Choose an aspect that you need to improve and take **SMART** action now – **SMART** meaning, you will recall from Chapter 6:

**S** pecific

**M** easurable

**A** chievable

**R** ealistic

**T** ime-limited.

In this way, you will be building up your own ability to cope with the physical and emotional demands of university life. Inevitably, there will be peaks and troughs.

## SUMMARY

When you hit a really demanding episode and you feel overstressed, make sure you follow this six-step stress management plan.

---

**How to manage stress**

---

▶ **Exercise**  Aerobics, team games, swimming, clubbing …

▶ **Relaxation**  A hot bath, listening to your favourite music in candle-light …

▶ **Indulge yourself**  Chocolate, aromatherapy …

▶ **Positive thinking**  Look on the bright side, imagine a positive outcome …

▶ **Get a new perspective**  Read something unusual, go somewhere different, break routines, read a beautiful poem …

---

Developing greater levels of self-awareness and stress fitness isn't just a skill for university. These skills will be invaluable – indeed, essential – in your career. Evidence that you are stress fit will be an added attraction for prospective employers!

## FURTHER INFORMATION

Earnshaw, J. and Cooper, C. (1996) *Stress and Employer Liability*, IPD, London.

Spera, S. and Lanto, S. (1995) *Beat Stress with Strength: Achieving wellness at work and in life*, DBM Publishing, New York.

Warren, E. and Toll, C. (1993) *The Stress Work Book*, Nicholas Brealey, London.

# SOURCES OF HELP

Whatever problems, questions or worries you have, there will always be someone nearby who can advise and support you. Specialist welfare, advice and support agencies will have the necessary skills or professional training that will enable them to help, no matter what your issue is. Whatever your concern, seek advice sooner rather than later. Here are some initial pointers to help you find the right person or organization. (See the Appendix also.)

## NATIONAL ORGANIZATIONS

### BRITISH ASSOCIATION OF COUNSELLING (BAC)

You can contact BAC for a list of trained and accredited counsellors in your area. See the Appendix for contact details for BAC and also try the following:

▶ Gay and lesbian groups
▶ MIND
▶ NUS (your local centre will have a welfare officer)
▶ The Samaritans
▶ Victim Support
▶ Young Minds.

## LOCAL RESOURCES

▶ Your student counselling service.
▶ Nightline telephone counselling and information.
▶ Your student union's advice and information officer.
▶ Your student health centre.
▶ Your GP.
▶ Academic advisory or other learning support services.
▶ Your university chaplain.
▶ Your local church/place of worship.
▶ Local branches of national counselling and advice agencies.

# part II

---

# looking at graduate jobs and employers

# graduate jobs in the twenty-first century – the big picture

## Why do organizations employ graduates?

**In this chapter, you will:**

- [ ] come to understand the changing nature of graduate jobs;

- [ ] improve your business awareness;

- [ ] find out why employers want graduates;

- [ ] understand the links between organizational goals and graduate jobs;

- [ ] discover how to evaluate an organization's business context.

**In the activity:**

**8.1** Linking organizational goals to graduate recruitment

# GRADUATE JOBS IN THE TWENTY-FIRST CENTURY

To be successful in your quest to find a brilliant job, you need to understand that employing you is part of an employer's much wider strategy to be competitive and successful. Job hunting isn't what it used to be.

## THE MILK ROUND – WHAT IS REALLY HAPPENING?

Employers face unprecedented rates of change in the growth of new technology. Markets are expanding and competition ever more challenging as the process of globalization exerts its influence. Organizations are responding to the needs of their customers with increasing speed and sensitivity, so they need to be fitter and more effective than ever before. Some fundamental shifts are taking place in the global economy and these are impacting the opportunities for graduates, traditional milk-round procedures and the jobs on offer are changing.

Many organizations are finding that traditional two- to three-year graduate training programmes are no longer viable. Such traditional practices do still survive, but they are diminishing rapidly – they now co-exist alongside more modern, streamlined and targeted approaches to job design and recruitment. A classification of jobs now available to graduates is included in the next chapter.

The links between graduate jobs and wider changes in the local and global economy are shown in Figure 8.1. Some graduate jobs are designed as part of a strategic approach to managing people – often referred to as human resource management (HRM). The extent to which jobs are strategic and linked will vary, some smaller firms operate on a more *ad hoc* basis, some larger firms are so large and decentralized, it's difficult to see the linkages at all.

What is true for most organizations is that they will have some sort of business strategy that has grown out of its business environment. The firm will have identified a range of critical success factors that it needs to address to ensure that the business strategy is successfully implemented. These could include targets for increasing the share of the market for its products and services, ideas about quality or production targets. In many public-sector organizations, such as local government and education, standards of service delivery are set externally by government or supervisory agencies.

Organizational ability is influenced by the presence of an efficient organizational structure, a good communication network and the right culture. These are supported and maintained by having the best-quality managers working with the right people. Chapter 10 covers these in more detail. The central idea is that the organization's structure, culture and people can together promote superior business performance. This idea is well established in many private, public and not-for-profit organizations.

**FIGURE 8.1  The big picture – graduate jobs in context**

Let us now look at some of the main features of this big picture in more detail.

## BUSINESS STRATEGIES AND GRADUATE JOBS

Employers vary enormously in the level of their sophistication, but most will actually link graduate jobs to their organizational goals and/or to their business strategy – if they have one written down, many do not. They will use job analysis (see Chapter 13) to develop an idea of the specific skills, abilities and attitudes needed to achieve company objectives.

Business strategy is a huge and complicated field. Some of you may have studied this topic as an undergraduate module or even as a substantial part of a first or post-graduate degree. I cannot hope to cover all the complexities and arguments that are waged in academic and practitioner circles here. Rather, I shall draw out the key themes that relate to graduate recruitment. This will enable you to think about the extent to which you actually match the job and organization and will ensure that you target your CV and application towards these things. The essence of this is *matching*. The organization will have done a lot of thinking about its own business strategy, it will have drawn some conclusions about what sorts of graduates it wants to employ and you will need to match the requirements to have a chance of being offered a job.

Business strategy covers the overall scope, structures, financing and investment decisions of an organization. If it is a large organization, it may well be made up of a range of different businesses. In such cases the business strategy will set out how an organization or its constituent business units will compete in their different markets.

---

**What is strategy?**

Strategy involves:

▶ assessing an organization's internal competences and capabilities;

▶ assessing environmental threats and opportunities;

▶ deciding the scope of an organization's activities;

▶ creating and communicating a strategic vision;

---

This tidy, ordered view of strategy is an ideal that organizations hope to achieve, but real life is often untidy and unplanned. Asian markets collapse, hostile takeovers occur, competitors are successful with new products, customers respond unexpectedly to food scares, such as BSE, GM foods, or switch to buying organic products.

Much of organizational life is a constant process of adapting to the external world. Employees are often seen to hold the key to the future success of the organization. Graduates are seen as being talented, flexible and responsive – much-needed qualities in times of uncertainty and change.

## THE BUSINESS ENVIRONMENT – WE LIVE IN TURBULENT TIMES

Globalization means that the world economy is changing in some quite fundamental ways. These developments affect how and where goods and services are produced. Goods, services, money and information flow across international borders. New markets open up, new forms of business allegiance evolve to take advantage of them.

Our economy is now more influenced by global forces than ever before, and these shape the ways in which business and society operates. Tiger economies collapse, new markets open, ideas from around the world influence our thinking. Increased competition, too, affects business life in a number of ways. Organizations are focused on the expectations of shareholders, the need to produce quality goods and services in the most efficient way. Business life is characterized by the constant ebb and flow of merger, de-merger, acquisition and the threat of takeover, often hostile.

The availability of graduate jobs follows patterns in the economy generally, so, at present, this means there is a rise in service-sector jobs such as banking, commerce, management consultancy, leisure and retail. The forever-expanding domain of IT, advent of real-time trading and e-commerce has created new possibilities in every aspect of life – new markets, new products, new ways of communicating and new ways of working, in both public and private sectors.

The last two decades of the twentieth century saw the further decline of traditional manufacturing industries and the rise of the service sector. New domains of work have emerged in commerce, accounting, professional services, retail and leisure.

## PEOPLE AND JOBS – A NEW SETTING FOR GRADUATE JOBS

The notion of building a career within one organization, progressing onwards and upwards over the years, is diminishing rapidly. Employers are sensitive to markets and profitability, they recruit and keep people for hard-nosed business reasons. These pressures also apply throughout the public and not-for-profit sectors.

These and other associated changes in the economy and society generally mean that there have been some quite significant changes in the workplace. These include:

▶ increased business/efficiency focus;

▶ delayering – fewer layers of management, so fewer upward promotion prospects;

▶ outsourcing – using more outside services, such as in IT, training, catering;

▶ constant business restructuring as a result of mergers, acquisitions or reorganization;

▶ new deal/new psychological contracts – no more 'jobs for life';

▶ individualization of jobs;

▶ greater individual responsibility;

▶ changing and complicated career paths – the rise of self-managed careers.

## ORGANIZATIONAL ABILITY

### What senior executives said about graduates

**People are Astra-Zeneca's key intellectual assets … business success depends on transferring and transforming knowledge and ideas into unique, high-value products and services, and this can only be achieved through the intelligence, commitment and energy of our people.** *(Chief Executive)*

**We are successful because of our people, many of whom have risen to senior positions after joining us as graduates.** *(Chairman of Rank Hovis McDougall)*

### The right people in the right jobs

Graduate recruitment and selection are extremely important. Organizations need to select the right people for the right jobs. They then aim to reward, develop, train and motivate individuals to ensure they add value. This is the realm of the human resource management (HRM), or personnel, department of an organization. It contributes to an organization's activities by helping to assess the jobs that need to be done. HRM practitioners also help to identify the right selection criteria – that is, the skills, abilities and experience applicants will need to have to do the job well.

# HOW DOES ALL THIS HELP YOU?

Use the following activity to answer the question 'Why does the organization you are considering employ graduates?'

---

**ACTIVITY 8.1    Linking organizational goals to graduate recruitment**

**1.** Find out if the organization you want to work for has a mission statement, outlining its goals. If not, can you work out what these are, based on what you know from the graduate brochure, job advert and/or financial report?

_____

_____

_____

**2.** Describe the organization's business or operating environment. How is the business doing? Are some businesses/brands/services doing well or badly? What sorts of people does this organization need in order to succeed?

_____

_____

_____

**3.** Who are the organization's main competitors? What are its main commercial and business issues just now?
If it is in the public sector, what are the main issues regarding resources and service delivery?

_____

_____

_____

**4.** Why would this organization want to recruit graduates at all? What sorts of skills, knowledge and attitudes are likely to be important?

▶ **skills** ...........................................................................

▶ **knowledge** ...................................................................

▶ **attitudes** .....................................................................

**5.** Is it possible that this organization may have more than one approach to graduate recruitment – for example, wanting some to go into specialist roles, others for more general training? Where do you fit in?

_____

_____

_____

---

# SUMMARY

▶ The organization you are interested in will have some sort of business strategy – it may not have a formal mission statement, but it will be apparent in any literature.

▶ Think about what the main products or services are that the organization exists to offer.

▶ 'Business strategy' is a nebulous, changing concept as markets can be fickle and fortunes change.

▶ Be aware of the organization's main customers and competitors.

▶ What is happening in these markets or in this area of work at the moment.

▶ Understand the business strategy – think what types of skills or attitudes the organization is looking for.

▶ All organizations will be attracted to someone who is enthusiastic about their products or services.

▶ Many organizations operate a multifaceted approach to graduate recruitment, seeking some graduates for specialist roles, others for more general training.

# SIGNPOSTS TO MORE HELP

The remaining chapters in Part II explore the issues raised here in more depth and provide the further information and contact details that you may need.

In Part III, Chapter 13 provides a more detailed explanation of job selection criteria.

# so, what is a graduate job?

**The traditional graduate job has almost disappeared ... a new set of graduate opportunities has emerged, which graduates need to be aware of and prepared to seize and develop.**

L. HARVEY, *ET AL*. GRADUATES' WORK, 1997

## In this chapter, you will:

- ☐ find a typology of graduate jobs:
  - ☐ high-flyer/fasttrack;
  - ☐ general management;
  - ☐ professional scheme;
  - ☐ technical specialist/ knowledge worker;
  - ☐ 'direct' job entry;
  - ☐ alternative workstyles;
  - ☐ self-employment;
  - ☐ McJobs.

## In the activity:

**9.1** How does your intended job or training scheme measure up?

# THERE ARE MANY WAYS TO ACHIEVE YOUR CAREER OBJECTIVES

You may have already decided on a particular career pathway – you know you want to be in finance, marketing, PR, media or perhaps in management generally. Even if you know the general direction you want your career to take, there will probably be a number of ways of achieving your objective.

You may want to keep your options open, have a 'Plan B' just in case your preferred route doesn't work out. Even if you want a job that will enable you to gain a traditional professional training, there are often several options open to you.

## NEW OPPORTUNITIES FOR GRADUATES

The traditional milk-round-type jobs may sound attractive, but the nature of graduate jobs is changing quickly. The familiar information available in the graduate directories may not be painting a clear enough picture of these present trends. In order to maximize your chances of success and minimize wasted time, you need to know what is *really* happening.

The first few years of the new millennium will be characterized by the emergence of a range of alternative jobs for graduates – the intelligent, flexible and adaptive generation of which you are a part. You need to know about the new wave of graduate opportunities that are emerging in order to make a well-informed choice about your future.

As outlined in the previous chapter, graduate jobs reflect organizations' need to be flexible and responsive to customers. In practice this means there is a confusing array of graduate jobs available.

## SO WHAT EXACTLY IS A GRADUATE JOB?

There follows a typology that you may find useful when thinking about comparing options. I identify seven main types of 'real' graduate job and then McJobs, which are the jobs graduates take because of difficulties finding something more suited to their talents. McJobs are not really true graduate jobs, but I include them because they represent a significant slice of reality for many graduates, at least in the short term.

However, this classification is provided mainly to get you thinking about the real nature of the jobs on offer. Many of the so-called 'fasttrack' and 'general management' schemes run by large organizations may have very similar features to other jobs that sound far less attractive on the surface but are equally, if not more, attractive on closer scrutiny! Don't discount jobs in small and medium-sized enterprises too early.

# TYPES OF GRADUATE JOBS

Any typology brings with it the danger of oversimplification and so it is here – jobs placed in different categories may share some common characteristics. However, you need to start somewhere when evaluating and comparing jobs. Some jobs will, of course, be hybrids and will share features with other types.

When trying to compare one job with another the typology may be of help. It highlights the types of jobs available and points to the differences that exist in the way organizations in the same sector or industry design their jobs. The general types of graduate jobs available are:

► high-flyer/fasttrack;
► general management/graduate traineeship;
► professional scheme;
► technical specialist/knowledge worker;
► 'direct' job entry;
► alternative workstyles;
► self-employment;
► McJobs.

Here are some notes on each of them.

# HIGH-FLYER/FASTTRACK

## FEATURES

Schemes are marketed specifically as for the élite, intended for only high-potential individuals. Usually fiercely competitive and starting pay rates offered are above the average for other types of graduate jobs (with the exception, usually, of specialist IT workers). Challenging, interesting work that may be accompanied by international travel (for example, Civil Service, Fast Stream and police's Accelerated Track). Also features a large amount of training and personal development opportunities.

## BENEFITS

Accelerated start to building a career and gaining responsibility very quickly. Very well paid, Being selected for such posts is often perceived as a great scoop for your CV as it points to both intellectual strength and good interpersonal skills and/or business awareness, according to the organization joined.

## DOWNSIDE

You may waste a lot of time and effort in the process of fighting for these places. The reality of the actual job may not be as exciting or challenging as portrayed. Graduates in other jobs – especially in manufacturing – may quickly catch up to your level of pay. Most organizations recognize talent very quickly. Those that have talent are usually promoted quickly to very demanding and quite senior jobs. Beware that the fasttrack label is sometimes being used to describe what is otherwise an ordinary graduate job opportunity. All that glitters may not be gold.

# GENERAL MANAGEMENT/GRADUATE TRAINEESHIP

## FEATURES

General management jobs often include a brief induction period, followed by a substantial amount of organizational training directed at giving graduates a broad understanding of the business. The traineeship may last two to three years, although the trend is towards shorter timescales. These schemes suggest that you have middle or senior management potential, and this will be a good basis for future career progression.

Some of these jobs offer general management training or have a scheme accredited by an outside body, leading to a Diploma in Management. The main focus is not a specific job, but may involve moving to a different department every three to six months. This is not always the case, however. It is essential that you find out the exact details of the job responsibilities and training scheme.

## BENEFITS

A good broad base of work experience on which to base future career decisions. These schemes usually leave plenty of scope for you to explore different management options and areas. They may give you marketable, transferable skills as well as organization-specific knowledge.

## DOWNSIDE

In reality, you may feel rootless, nomadic and unwanted. Many managers find the bother of delegating a short-term task to a trainee more effort than it's worth. It may be better to look for the sort of job where you are given genuine responsibility at the outset. If you are placed on a set programme of training, you may find this boring and unrelated to the job or role you have. The number of firms offering this generic scheme is shrinking – the trend now is for graduates to go into *real* jobs rather than be seen as trainees. Most employers now want their graduates to hit the ground running and so have training that fits the needs of the actual job.

# PROFESSIONAL SCHEME

## FEATURES

A job that involves responsibilities and activities associated with a particular profession. Examples include teaching, accountancy, legal and actuarial training. The job is usually designed in agreement with a professional body and requires/allows you to receive appropriate training and take specific examinations that will lead to a professional qualification.

## BENEFITS

Clear career focus and direction. On-the-job training, working alongside qualified professionals. A good opportunity to check that this career suits you. You will receive a transferable professional qualification that will enhance your mobility and marketability if you want to move to a different company.

## DOWNSIDE

Very competitive, even cut-throat. Also usually a high-pressure work environment that may involve long hours in the office and years of hard work and study in your own time. Some firms will only continue to employ you if you pass all the exams, so there is little room for failure. You will need to have a back-up plan in case the worst happens. You may also find that your first couple of years involve substantial tedious administrative work on behalf of qualified staff or partners.

# TECHNICAL SPECIALIST/ KNOWLEDGE WORKER

## FEATURES

These jobs require highly specific skills and knowledge, often in a specialist area such as biotechnology, engineering or physics. In particular, information and communications technology is creating a new breed of jobs that involve both technical expertise and interpersonal/teamworking abilities.

These are often highly paid jobs in IT, computing, systems analysis and software/ program design. These jobs include very specialist scientific knowledge in the design or production of high added value products or services. These are often key jobs in an organization, often associated with individuals having a high level of skill on joining. Employees may also have an opportunity to gain a specific professional qualification, but this may not be necessary for career success.

## BENEFITS

High pay and attractive reward packages. Individuals with key skills that are in short supply in the UK are also likely to be given ongoing training and career development support. Really important people are even provided with mentors to encourage them to stay in the organization.

## DOWNSIDE

Some very specialist jobs are fastmoving and mean a lifetime of pressure and constant adaptation. In some areas, such as scientific roles, you may become so specialized that you limit the number of employers who would be interested in your expertise or knowledge.

Levels of pay in specialist markets can be relatively poor, as it often is, for example, in hotels and catering and in areas of media work.

# 'DIRECT' JOB ENTRY

## FEATURES

This category consists of jobs that graduates do but which are not necessarily, restricted to them – they may also be open to people with other qualifications, school leavers or people with different types of work experience. This type encompasses the wide range of occupations in which graduates and non-graduates work alongside one another at the same level doing the same kinds of work. Major examples include supervisory and line management roles, much clerical and administrative work and sales jobs.

The 'direct' entry job emerges from an identified need within the organization for a person to do a 'real job' and not just occupy a training role or apprenticeship. 'Direct' entry jobs would normally be advertised in response to the need to fill a vacancy or create a new role. It would be unusual for such jobs to be closely linked to the milk-round months in advance of the job being advertised.

## BENEFITS

There is no reason, in principle, for such jobs to be anything other than the basis for an enjoyable and rewarding career. A great benefit can be that these jobs offer real responsibility at the outset.

## DOWNSIDE

Pay levels may be relatively low at the beginning. There may be no clear career progression, no well-worn path to promotion. Good people are usually noticed, however.

# ALTERNATIVE WORKSTYLES

This is an umbrella term for a wide range of workstyles that are in the ascendancy at present.

## ALTERNATIVE TYPES OF EMPLOYMENT STATUS

Perhaps it is helpful to distinguish between different types of employment status. There has been an increase in the use by employers of part-time, temporary, casual and seasonal staff to provide them with a flexible workforce. However, even important jobs traditionally done within the organization are now being delivered by outside workers – IT, accounts, catering and training are commonly outsourced activities today.

## 'ALTERNATIVE' EMPLOYERS

### Not-for-profit organizations

A significant proportion of graduates wish to work in the growing not-for-profit and charity sectors. This may involve working for a well-known national charity, in a religious community or for an interest or pressure groups. A number of community group networks and charities enable graduates to work on a year placement scheme.

*Benefits*
Some high-demand outsourced roles can be very well paid. Others are just insecure, uncertain jobs with few prospects – it depends.

The benefits are personal to each individual, but the reward of contributing to a worthwhile cause and following your own values and beliefs can be considerable. Independence and freedom may be more attractive than security. Some people find satisfaction in the risk and entrepreneurship required in some unconventional jobs.

*Downside*

Low pay, uncertainty. Ensure that you have thought about how you might move into a more mainstream work environment if you change your mind.


## SMALL FIRMS

*Features and benefits*

A huge variety of small businesses exists. These can be well-established mature organizations or very recently established. They can offer a traditional structured work environment or progressive, fast-moving methods of organizing and doing work. In many small firms, employees have more access to senior people and can learn a lot about many aspects of the business than in a larger more traditionally structured workplace.

You may have opportunities to get involved in a broad range of activities and can gain insight into many different areas of work.

*Downside*

You are probably more at risk of losing your job in a smaller firm than you are in a big one as they are more vulnerable to failure, especially in their first few years of existence. Personnel and training practices differ enormously – small firms can be good, bad or ugly, so make sure you ask the right questions at interview.

(Read Chapter 11 for some assessment tips.)


# SELF-EMPLOYMENT

Starting a business is an increasingly popular option. In a 1999 survey, 1 in 7 people aged 16 to 25 were considering this as a serious career option with the proportion likely to increase even more in the years ahead. It is not an easy option, though. You will need:

▶ a great business idea;

▶ a business plan;

▶ sufficient finance to begin and maintain the business during the start-up phase;

▶ a demand for your product or services;

▶ the right location, pricing strategy, method of delivery.

You may be able to get help with some or all of these from various agencies and organizations.


## BENEFITS

Being your own boss, being creative, deciding how and when to work, reaping the benefits of your own success.

## DOWNSIDE

You will probably work long hours and will never feel you have left work behind you. You may encounter disappointments, failures and frustrations. You will need the ability to persevere and keep going.

## HELP

If you are aged 16–30, you can get a free *Essential Business* kit from Shell LiveWIRE, which includes a guide to help you develop your ideas, plus a link to a local business adviser. Contact Shell at:

Shell LiveWIRE
Freepost NT805
Newcastle upon Tyne NE1 1BR
*Tel:* 0345 573 252
*Web site:* www.shell-livewire.org

For financial help and advice for 18–30-year-olds, contact:

The Prince's Youth Business Trust
18 Park Square East
Regents Park
London NW1 4LH
*Tel:* 020 7543 1234
*Web site:* www.princes-trust.org.uk

## FURTHER READING

'Alternative Workstyles Including Self-employment', a careers information booklet, is available from most university careers advisory services.

'Starting and Running Your Own Business', Department of Employment booklet.

# MCJOBS

A significant number of graduates end up in low-skilled, low-paid jobs that are unrelated to their long-term career aspirations.

## FEATURES

▶ Low skill level, low pay.

▶ Boring, often repetitive, tasks.

▶ Little or no training – when available, it is usually mechanical.

▶ Limited prospects.

▶ Uncomfortable working conditions – heat, smoke, noise.

▶ Insecure, possibly seasonal or temporary.

## BENEFITS

May provide a short-term source of income/employment after finals. This can help provide the basis for a longer-term job application strategy. This is an increasingly attractive short-term option for many graduates who do not want the pressures of applying for more traditional milk-round-training scheme jobs during their final year. Some low-skilled jobs can be converted to an interesting role if your employer spots your talent and is able to 'grow' the job for you.

## DOWNSIDE

These jobs may be OK in the short term, but they are unlikely to provide an opportunity to develop essential managerial or professional skills in the medium or longer term. However, every type of work experience has the potential to help you learn about yourself and the world of work. Use the activities in Chapter 5 to help you use your McJob experiences to enhance your future employability.

# THINKING ABOUT YOUR INTENDED JOB

Focus on the features, benefits and disadvantages of the jobs you are considering, using the next activity. If you worked through Chapter 3, you may have already completed Activity 3.4 – Design your ideal job. You may find it helpful to refer back to your answers before completing Activity 9.1.

## ACTIVITY 9.1    How does your intended job or training scheme measure up?

Consider the following list of nine job features and find out how good any jobs you are considering actually are. You can use this exercise to compare jobs and find out which one will most suit you.

| Job feature | Questions to ask | Answers |
|---|---|---|
| Comprehensive induction | How long will the induction period last? Will training and courses be with other graduates or with other staff generally? Is there departmental and organizational induction? | |
| On-the-job training | What sort of training and support will I receive? Is there a training or human resource management department? If not, how is this managed in the organization? | |
| Off-the-job training | How many courses (10–25 days per year)? How long and where held – in-house v external training consultant? (Preferably a good mix of both!!) Are courses part of a mandatory/fixed programme or identified to suit my own particular needs according to the job? | |
| Externally recognized qualifications | Is the organization supportive of professional qualifications? Will it pay professional fees, for training and exams and so on? Has anyone here done an MBA recently? | |
| Interesting work | What will I actually be doing – specific tasks, proportion of time doing different duties? How much choice and discretion will I have? Will I have a chance to visit other parts of the business early on? | |
| High degree of responsibility from start | How much responsibility for people, budgets, customers, accounts and so on will I have? Who will manage me? | |
| Rewards | How will my performance be measured? When will my pay and conditions be reviewed – annually, every six months? | |
| Promotion prospects | What career paths are open to me? Can I move sideways to broaden my job experience? Is promotion based on merit? What have others moved on to do after time in this job? | |
| Other features that are important to you | | |

# SUMMARY

▶ There are many ways of achieving your career objectives – make sure you are not narrowing your options down too soon.

▶ There are many different career pathways now open to graduates and they all have advantages as well as a downside. Check out which ones suit you most. This chapter has set out eight main types of graduate jobs.

▶ Alternative workstyles are an increasingly popular option. These include working for not-for-profit organizations or for small firms as well as self-employment or starting your own business.

▶ Many graduates accept short-term jobs that require low levels of skill shortly after leaving university. These can be a stopgap before moving on to a career-related job, but sometimes they can become interesting jobs with prospects.


# SIGNPOSTS TO MORE HELP

Key information sources and Internet addresses are listed earlier.
About occupations – see Chapter 11.


# FURTHER READING

Two readable accounts of the hopes and realities of graduate careers are:

Purcell, K. and Pitcher, J. (1996) *Great Expectations: The new diversity of graduate skills and aspirations*, Institute of Employment Research Department for Education and Employment/CSU.

Purcell, K., Pitcher, J. and Simm, C. (1999) *Working Out?*, Institute of Employment Research Department for Education and Employment/CSU.

# organizational culture and climate

## Culture ... the collective programming of the mind?

**In this chapter, you will:**

☐ understand the concept of organizational culture;

☐ identify the components of corporate culture;

☐ know what influences the development of culture;

☐ find out about the most common types of culture;

☐ come to know how to evaluate your prospective employer;

☐ be introduced to gender cultures;

☐ discover the secrets of organizational climates.

**In the activities:**

**10.1** My prospective employer's values, norms and myths

**10.2** Is it an equal opportunities culture?

**10.3** Characteristics of a healthy organizational climate

# WHAT IS ORGANIZATIONAL CULTURE?

The idea that a company or organization has a distinctive personality is helpful when you consider what it might be like as a future employer. The idea originated in anthropology, but can be applied to the modern world of graduate jobs and the issues you are thinking about.

'Organizational culture' is the pattern of beliefs, attitudes and behaviours that influence how people work together. In many respects, then, culture is one of the most important factors you need to consider when choosing an employer. Culture is a very powerful force at work inside organizations – something deliberately cultivated and passed on to incoming employees. A great deal of the selection process is intended to ensure you will fit in with, and maintain, the existing culture.

In some circumstances, graduates are employed specifically to help change the prevailing culture. Equally, many organizations are in a state of constant change and cultural adaptation. It is still the case, however, that many organizations actively promote the idea of having a strong, distinctive culture. The notion of employer branding is increasingly popular among many leading graduate recruiters and smaller organizations in both private and public sectors are doing it. Your task is to cut through the employer branding rhetoric and the glossy impression management techniques to find out the true nature of the organization you are thinking of joining.

It is worth finding out as much as you can about culture before putting a lot of effort into an application – many graduates do not and end up very disappointed and unhappy in their first jobs! In many cases this is because there is a clear clash between their personal values and approach to work and those of the company they have joined. How can you assess organizational culture? Find out below.

# WHAT CULTURE CONSISTS OF

Organizations don't exist in a vacuum. Figure 10.1 shows the huge variety of external influences on them, embedded as they are in society. Organizational life is affected by the regulations, statutes and norms of society.

Organizational culture, then, is built up, and maintained, by various traditions, values, policies, beliefs and social conventions. These create a dynamic environment that sets the tone for all sorts of conduct, rewards and behaviour. Culture is obviously a complicated notion. There are four basic factors that you need to consider when trying to understand and evaluate culture:

▶ values
▶ norms
▶ artefacts
▶ myths.

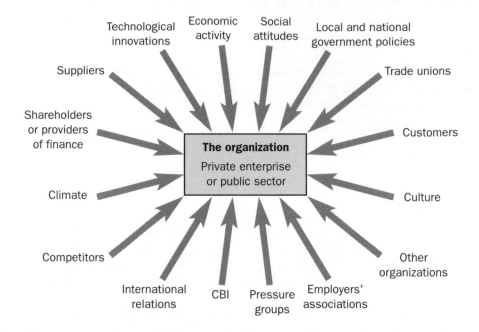

**FIGURE 10.1  External influences on your prospective employer**
Source: L. Mullins, *Management and Organizational Behaviour*, Pitman, 1996

## VALUES

These are the things that an organization believes are important. Many organizations actually produce mission statements. Many include a statement of values in
their promotional material and these are reflected in the nature of the goods or
services produced by the organization. However, these may be part of good PR,
espoused by a few very senior managers but not carried through everywhere in the
organization. The *true* values of an organization can be judged by the emphasis
placed on, for example:

- ► care for customers;
- ► attitudes towards employees;
- ► excellence;
- ► profitability;
- ► competitiveness;
- ► growth;
- ► innovation;
- ► performance/meeting targets;
- ► social responsibility;
- ► equality of opportunity.

## NORMS

These values are converted into organizational culture by means of norms, artefacts and myths. Norms are unwritten codes of conduct and rules that guide employee behaviour. Norms direct what people wear, what they do, what they say, when they say it and to whom. Norms are passed on in numerous ways during selection procedures, the early stages of induction and after entry into an organization. These unwritten rules can exert powerful pressures to conform.

Norms include:

► prevailing management style – open, directive, permissive;

► status – how much importance is attached to position, separate car parking and canteens, titles on doors, first-name terms, permanent staff versus people paid hourly.

► work ethic – what is expected above and beyond what is in the contract, long hours versus flexible working arrangements;

► loyalty – a long service culture versus emphasis on short-term results;

► formality – cool, distant relationships, dress codes, respect for hierarchy;

► power and politics – is the possibility of potential conflict accepted, unions recognized or is a uniformity of interest expected/assumed?

## ARTEFACTS

The artefacts of an organization are its tangible environment. So, the term could include, for example, the number, type, location and design of buildings owned by the organization. The working environment reveals the culture of an organization – the way people speak to each other, the level of aggression and bad language 'allowed' in meetings, the tone of internal communications, such as e-mail. The term artefacts also includes the interface between the company and the outside world – the company's headed notepaper (recycled, environmentally friendly, cheap versus quality), the telephone manner used in handling customer calls (helpful, friendly, curt). These things can all be very revealing about the true character of an organization.

## MYTHS

Myths and stories about leading characters or defining moments in an organization's history are often used to convey and illustrate something about its core values and culture.

## Organizational myths and fairytales

**Risk Ltd**

One very well-known blue chip company with an international reputation for innovation tells all graduates the tale of the young man who joined them and within six weeks was responsible for launching a new product with a budget equivalent to £300,000. The project went badly wrong. The young man was hauled in front of the Marketing Director, apology and resignation speech prepared. Before the Director could begin, he spluttered out his resignation. 'What?', declared the Director, 'leave? No chance! I have just invested £300,000 training you!'

**BBC**

The BBC has the following story to tell on customer care. A young child was queuing with her family to go on one of the big attraction rides at Disneyland. The day was hot, the queue long, so her father slipped off to buy her an ice-cream – little knowing that food and drink were not permitted on the ride. Much to the child's disappointment, Dad had to dispose of it quickly before they were allowed on. The quick-thinking door attendant noticed the problem and organized for a colleague to wait at the ride's exit with a delicious replacement ice-cream.

---

### ACTIVITY 10.1   My prospective employer's values, norms and myths

What values and norms have you noticed your prospective employer/s exhibiting, overtly or covertly?

Have you heard any corporate myths or anecdotes?

# MODELS OF CORPORATE CULTURE

Charles Handy is a well-known business writer. He suggests that there are four main types of culture, the uniting theme being how the organization is structured. His typology addresses the way in which power is distributed, people are coordinated and communication is controlled.

# POWER CULTURE

Usually a company with a power culture is highly centralized, dominated by a key figure or figures in the organization. It is typical in small-scale family businesses. It is also typical of larger-scale organizations dominated by a leading very charismatic figurehead. Such an organization has a structure reminiscent of a spider's web, with power and decision-making located at the centre. Thus it may have only a very limited amount of delegated power. This type of culture can inhibit growth and innovation.

# ROLE CULTURE

In a company with a role culture, power is distributed by virtue of the employees' titles or roles held in the organization. People are coordinated by means of a hierarchical network structure, often by department. Communication is controlled by the formality of the structure, often following the traditional bureaucratic conventions.

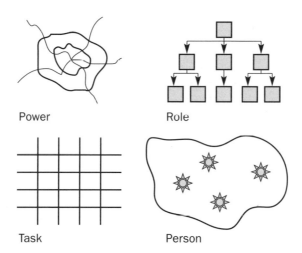

Power       Role

Task       Person

**FIGURE 10.2 Handy's four types of culture**
Source: Adapted from C. Handy, *Understanding Organizations*, (4th edition) Penguin, 1993

# TASK CULTURE

Task cultures focus more on accomplishing tasks and working on projects. Employees may belong to a variety of different teams and answer to different senior managers as required. This is a very flexible and responsive culture, often found in modern private-sector workplaces. A chemist may be part of one team developing a new product and also involved in a marketing team trying to sell an existing product in a new market.

## PERSON CULTURE

Person cultures are characterized by power being distributed among a few key individuals who are specialists or experts in their field. Examples include barristers' chambers, management consultants or doctors' surgeries.

# ORGANIZATIONAL CULTURE AND EQUALITY – IS IT A LEVEL PLAYING FIELD?

**'We are an equal opportunities employer.'**

You will see this and similar statements in most employers' recruitment literature, but what do they really mean? Not all employers are totally committed to equal opportunities. Organizations often mirror the discrimination that is still deeply woven through our society.

Attitudes and behaviour within organizations can amount to discrimination that is the result of unwitting prejudice, ignorance and thoughtless stereotyping with respect to gender, race or disability. Even though you are protected by law against discrimination (see Chapter 12 for more details), both during recruitment and while at work, sexist and racist cultures persist in both the public and private sectors. The findings of the Stephen Lawrence Inquiry and deeply rooted troubles at the Ford Motor Company reflect the pervasive, yet complicated, nature of discrimination.

## WOMEN

Much has been written in recent years about the presence of invisible barriers or 'glass ceilings' that prevent women gaining promotion at work. Organizational traditions and procedures can themselves contribute directly and indirectly to discrimination against women. Those who inhabit the corridors of power maintain a variety of traditions and behaviour patterns that exclude women or are very difficult to penetrate.

In some organizations or professions, women are viewed as being generally less ambitious and less committed than men. This is often linked to an associated belief that women are less mobile, should change of location be necessary. In reality, there are few sex differences regarding motivation and ambition and some studies have found women managers to be more ambitious, in fact, than their male counterparts.

Women may be viewed as less attractive than men because they are more likely to have and care for children. However, studies have found that pregnancy is not a main reason for leaving, and almost 50 per cent of all full-time working women have no dependants. Another pervasive notion is that women have a different and inferior style of management. Men are seen as being more competitive, unemotional and hierarchical, but propose women as collaborative and cooperative leaders, stereotyping them as lacking assertiveness and the capacity to make decisions.

## Gender cultures

There are traditional gender cultures, such as the gentlemen's club, that reinforce stereotypical notions of women as mothers, men as breadwinners. In this cultural environment, men are patronizing, courteous and humane, but women are expected to keep in their place. This culture can arise in organizations where certain tasks and roles are performed only by women, in what has been termed a 'velvet ghetto'. The 'barrack yard' culture is an aggressive environment where women may feel threatened. Managers and even fellow work colleagues may use bullying to get things done. The 'locker room' is an exclusion culture, where men build relationships on the basis of common, but exclusive, interests. Promotion prospects may be enhanced by attendance at male-dominated social events, such as Twickenham, golf or the pub.

Finally, and very common, is the 'long hours/beyond what is specified in your job contract' culture – a high-pressure, performance-oriented culture involving working long hours. This is prevalent in the UK, where the proportion of men and women working long hours (over 45 hours per week) is the highest in Europe. Such organizations show a reluctance to allow flexible working arrangements, such as holding meetings during core times (after 10.00am when children are at school).

## Further obstacles for women

▶ The relative dearth of women in upper management tiers and in some occupations can lead to feelings of isolation and loneliness for those who do make it. In addition, women may be more vulnerable and exposed to sexual harassment. This is a widespread problem for many women in the workplace. These experiences include unwanted sexual teasing, jokes, questions and gestures – all of which can be very stressful.

▶ Studies have shown that having female role models in higher positions can act as a helpful influence and encourage the career aspirations of younger incoming graduates. A good mentor can offer a close, developmental relationship, bring about opportunities for interesting and challenging projects and help mentees to be noticed as potential executive material.

▶ Many organizations are recognizing the reality of these problems and have taken action to reduce discriminatory practices and cultures. Activity 10.2 highlights some features that good employers should adopt. Use it to help you assess the extent to which glass ceilings have been shattered in the organization you are thinking of joining.

*Overcoming the obstacles*

A lot has been, and is being, done on behalf of women. Here are some useful contacts and sources of information.

▶ the Equal Opportunities Commission (EOC) is the lead body in support of equality for women and offers support, information and advice. The EOC (www.eoc.org.uk) gives useful information and contacts, plus advice on how to complain if you feel you have been discriminated against.

▶ Opportunity 2000 is a UK-based initiative that promotes equality for women in employment practices. You can contact Opportunity 2000 to find out if your prospective employer is a member (020 7224 1600).

▶ Know your rights (see also Chapter 12) and be prepared to stand up for yourself during the selection process. Interviews are a very common place for inappropriate questions to be asked. Read Chapter 17. Contact the EOC or your local careers advisory service if you believe you have been discriminated against.

▶ Complete Activity 10.2 to assess whether or not your prospective employer is serious about equal opportunities.

## RACE

Ethnic minority graduates face similar institutionalized problems and prejudices as women. Protection given in the law does not change people's attitudes. There are positive developments and many organizations are attempting to eradicate racism in recruitment, reassessing their working practices and training and promoting equal opportunities policies. These changes are driven by business arguments about the advantages of a diverse workforce and by the penalties of costly race discrimination claims and damage to the company reputation.

Following the findings of the Stephen Lawrence Inquiry and ongoing questions regarding racism at the Ford Motor Company, in the NHS and in many professions, no one can doubt the pervasive nature of institutionalized racism.

## DISABILITY

The same blend of business arguments, legislation and strong pressure group lobbying is leading to improved opportunities for disabled graduates. Some progressive employers want to diversify their workforce to include minority groups, recognizing the business benefits of reflecting their customers and communities. Cando (www.cando.lancs.ac.uk) provides specialist help and advice to disabled graduates in choosing a career and finding a suitable employer.

Further information, contact details and web sites of agencies supporting women, ethnic minorities and individuals with a disability are given in the Appendix.

---

**ACTIVITY 10.2    Is it an equal opportunities culture?**

Organizations that are serious about equal opportunities have the following characteristics. How does your prospective employer rate?

❑ A clearly stated equal opportunities policy.
❑ Job-related selection criteria.
❑ Trained selection interviewers.
❑ Antidiscriminatory policies.

*continued*

---

- ❏ Zero tolerance of all harassment and bullying.
- ❏ Antiharassment training.
- ❏ Senior women role models.
- ❏ Women/ethnic minorities board members.
- ❏ Women and ethnically diverse mentors.
- ❏ Positive images of women, ethnic minorities and disability in corporate brochures.
- ❏ Adhere to all current EU legislation and directives.
- ❏ Family-friendly policies.
- ❏ Monitoring and evaluation.

# THE IMPORTANCE OF SUBCULTURES

Both small and large organizations are complicated structures. Many of their constituent parts have experienced different levels of change and transition through the years. They may have experienced merger or acquisition and so are now a fusion of various organizational cultures and traditions. There may be regional variations caused by local customs and practices or by virtue of a charismatic figure who did things his or her way despite HQ's views. For whatever reason, distinctive subcultures exist in most organizations. The three main ones are listed below. Make sure when you are assessing culture that you take into account the strength of these.

▶ **Site-based subcultures**

Certain sites may have values and a culture that are very different from that of the mainstream organization. This may be due to a long history of, for example, unionization or to local traditions. This often occurs, too, when one site, factory or office is acquired from a competitor where the policies, procedures, values and many original staff are absorbed into the acquiring company.

▶ **Professional cultures**

The rules and practices of a professional body and associated training and codes of conduct may be very powerful. These can dominate an organization or even be contrary to the prevailing culture.

# CHANGING CORPORATE CULTURES

Most organizations are in a process of constantly changing and adapting. They may wish to move from old patterns of thinking and behaviour and adopt new ones. Leadership styles and methods of communication shift, often needing modelling.

It is generally recognized that culture can be changed by:

▶ what leaders pay most attention to, what they measure and control;

▶ leaders' reactions to critical incidents, emergencies and problems;

▶ deliberate role modelling, teaching and coaching by leaders;

- ▶ the criteria for allocating pay, rewards and status;
- ▶ criteria for recruitment, selection and promotion of employees;
- ▶ changing policies and procedures;
- ▶ changing workspaces and working environments;
- ▶ inventing new legends and stories.

Cultures have evolved over time and can be deeply rooted, so they can be difficult to change. Changing behaviour and attitudes takes time, but employing graduates is one way in which organizations can introduce new people who are flexible and willing to do things differently.

# THE ORGANIZATIONAL CLIMATE

Organizational climate is how existing employees feel about the culture that has been created in their department or unit. It has been defined as a relatively persistent set of perceptions held by members of the organization concerning the characteristics and quality of an organizational culture.

Such perceptions can be measured by, for example, opinion surveys. Climate answers the big question 'So what is it really like to work here?'

Some of the most important things you can find out in the process of choosing an employer are the opinions of its employees. The concept of climate invites you to ask questions about the prevailing atmosphere in an organization – the level of morale, strength of feelings, care and goodwill among members. There are eight main variables that influence climate and these are shown in Figure 10.3.

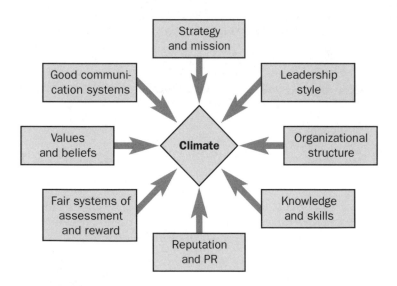

FIGURE 10.3  The factors influencing organizational climate

Activity 10.3 provides you with a checklist of issues to checkout. You can use these as the basis for questions to ask careers advisers and employees during university presentation or at recruitment/selection activities.

---

**ACTIVITY 10.3   Characteristics of a healthy organizational climate**

Check out your prospective employer against this list.

❏ **Equality of opportunity**
Stated equal opportunities policy supported by practices, women, minorities and disabled people in senior positions, board membership.

❏ **Trust**
Good level of morale, staff optimistic, positive, employees trusted by managers.

❏ **Pay and performance**
The pay system and methods of individual assessment are perceived as being fair.

❏ **Shared information and good communications**
Team briefings, company intranet, newsletters, effective works council.

❏ **Open discussions**
Regular team meetings, open management style, questioning and challenging status quo tolerated, canteens shared by all employees.

❏ **Opportunities for development**
Access to training opportunities, career development, coaching, mentoring, possibility of gaining externally recognized qualifications.

❏ **Social responsibility**
Social responsibility statements and policies, community action, open expression of values, aims, mission, published examples of appropriate organizational activities, such as recycling, concern for the environment and so on.

❏ **Respect for all stakeholders**
Seen to value employees, local community (even global community), environment, customers/clients, shareholders.

---

You may choose to work for an organization where staff morale is low or for one where it is very buoyant, but know what to expect.

# SUMMARY

▶ This chapter has reviewed the idea that a company or organization has a distinctive personality. This concept is helpful when you choose a future employer.

▶ Organizations do not exist in a vacuum – certain traditions and values may characterize a career or industry, not just a specific employer.

- ▶ The true values of an organization can be gauged in your experience of the selection process, especially if you have close contact with a range of employees. Various models and types of culture have been described to help you think about your target employer.

- ▶ You may notice considerable differences between various parts of the organization. This can help you find out if particular subcultures have developed and how this may affect you, especially in relation to equality of opportunity.

- ▶ Ask the crunch question – what is it really like to work here? Think in terms of organizational climate. You should think about your intended employer in relation to the characteristics of a healthy organizational climate listed in Activity 10.3.

## FURTHER INFORMATION

Deal, T. and Kennedy, A. (1982) *Corporate Cultures*, Penguin, Middlesex.

Handy, C. (1993) *Understanding Organizations* (fourth edition) BBC Books, London.

Coe, T. (1992) *The Key to the Men's Club: Opening the doors to women in management*, Institute of Management, London.

Davidson, M. J. and Cooper, C. I. (1992) *Shattering the Glass Ceiling: The Woman Manager*, Paul Chapman Publishing, London.

Schein, E. (1988) *Organizational Psychology*, Prentice Hall, New Jersey.

## SIGNPOSTS TO MORE HELP

### Equal opportunities, discrimination and employment rights

See the Appendix for more information and contact details of the agencies that can help and advise you.

You may also find Chapter 17 helpful for knowing how to handle interview questions.

### About employers

See Chapter 11.

# choosing your first employer

## Can you get it right first time?

**In this chapter, you will:**

- [ ] be able to answer the question 'is there a choice?';

- [ ] look at the dilemma of occupation versus ideal employer;

- [ ] discover how to find out about employers;

- [ ] be able to evaluate potential employers;

- [ ] analyse the psychological contract.

**In the activities:**

**11.1** I want to work for a …

**11.2** Prospective first employer checklist

# IS THERE A CHOICE?

I wonder what your first reaction was to the title of this chapter? You may be one of the many students graduating this year who feel that employment prospects are limited. This may be related to your personal circumstances, your expected results or the fact that you don't feel your degree subject is relevant to work. As discussed earlier, lots of students and graduates are now accepting McJob jobs to help start paying off debts rather than picking and choosing.

This chapter shows you that you can choose your first employer with a view to focusing on career development. I understand that, for many, the first job you get after leaving university may not be in that category. However, use this chapter to look forward to the choices that are available to you, whether you are reading this as a student, graduate, are unemployed or stuck in a job that is just paying the rent.

# SIZING UP THE COMPETITION

You are one in a quarter of a million if you graduate in 2000 and beyond ...

Congratulations. Now what?

According to the Higher Education Statistics Agency (HESA), a record number of around 287,000 other students will be joining you in the race for the best graduate jobs. Similarly high, or even higher, figures are expected for the following years, overshadowed a little by the uncertainty of response to the abolition of grants, introduction of fees and student debt generally. You can guarantee that competition for graduate jobs will be as fierce as ever, especially for the best-paid jobs, those offering a fasttrack or high-quality management training (see Chapter 9).

The quality of your final degree result is seen by many students as an important factor in the race for the best jobs. Almost half of all students will get a 2:1 or above. Usually, just a third get a 2:2.

It is also important to note that graduates are a more mixed bunch than ever. In particular, there is a broader age range, with some students working or travelling prior to university, some taking a placement year and others coming to university after several years in a job. Graduates from countries across Europe and elsewhere are seeking jobs in the UK, too, many of them have high-level language skills. This means more diverse characteristics are being taken into account, especially when competing with people who have transferable skills and experiences.

The key points, then, are that:

▶ more numbers are graduating – 287,000 expected in 2000 and beyond;
▶ more diverse characteristics are considered;
▶ more mature students;
▶ more work-experienced students;
▶ almost a third will get a 2:1 or above;
▶ talented Europeans and others are coming this way!

However, keep things in perspective. It is also true that many employers feel that they are competing for you. Many graduates and finalists do have a genuine choice about where to work and who to bestow their talents on.

# OCCUPATION VERSUS IDEAL EMPLOYER?

In today's world of graduate jobs, you may feel that it is not always a 'job' or 'career', but an employing organization that you are choosing. If you are starting out with very little work experience and finding it hard to decide, the traditional graduate training schemes can be very alluring – the offer of paid work now, but little pressure to decide on a final career direction for some time to come.

In fact, most employers are becoming much more discerning these days. When you apply to join even the general schemes, you will find that most of them now ask you to indicate a specific area of work interest. Research suggests that most people will need to choose a particular occupational area as the basis for approaching an employer. There are exceptions (as we shall see in Chapter 14 on jobhunting) when employers come looking for you, but, as yet, this only affects a minority of students.

# THE MOST POPULAR OCCUPATIONAL AREAS

Information about graduates is available from a wide range of sources and each can paint a quite different picture according to which students were asked and how questions about career intentions were posed. There are annual studies by government organizations as well as those undertaken by private consultants, such as Universum (1998), and High Fliers (1999). The private-sector studies mainly concentrate their research at top universities, so please bear this in mind when you look at the information provided in the rest of this chapter.

Two broader studies by Purcell *et al.*, for the DfEE (*Great Expectations*, 1996, and *Working Out?*, 1999) have provided broader study of old, mid-century and new university students, but have not addressed all the issues covered by the private consultants.

Table 11.1 highlights the 20 most popular occupations and work destinations of over 11,000 final-year undergraduates who were interviewed in 1999.

These research findings point to great interest in management consultancy, marketing and media/PR as favoured career paths for the first few years of the next millennium. The figures in Table 11.1 represent the ideal jobs undergraduates would like to get, but not everyone manages to put their Plan A into practice. The entry requirements and selection criteria for some of the very popular occupations can be very high, often based on a combination of A level grades, present university status and anticipated degree result.

**TABLE 11.1  Top 20 graduate occupations**

| Rank | Career sector | % of final-year students |
|:---:|---|:---:|
| 1 | Management consultancy | 14.1 |
| 2 | Marketing | 13.5 |
| 3 | Media | 12.0 |
| 4 | Research & Development | 11.6 |
| 5 | Accountancy | 10.7 |
| 6 | Computing and IT | 10.5 |
| 7 | General management | 10.4 |
| 8 | Engineering | 9.8 |
| 9 | Teaching | 9.7 |
| 10 | Banking or finance | 9.6 |
| 11 | Civil service | 9.2 |
| 12 | Charity/voluntary work | 8.8 |
| 13 | Investment banking | 8.6 |
| 14 | Human resources | 8.0 |
| 15 | Sales | 6.3 |
| 16 | Solicitor or barrister | 6.1 |
| 17 | Retailing | 5.0 |
| 18 | Armed forces | 2.7 |
| 19 | Purchasing | 2.3 |
| 20 | Police | 2.1 |

Source: *The Graduate Careers Survey*, 1999. High Fliers Research Ltd

Don't forget, graduate career paths are becoming more complicated and diverse – there are new options open beyond the traditional patterns. Career aspirations can be fulfilled in a number of ways, so try to adopt a flexible approach and be willing to consider more than one of the options discussed earlier in Chapter 9.

**ACTIVITY 11.1   I want to work for a …**

How would you finish this sentence? Multinational, charity, small firm?

_____

_____

Once you have decided on a general area in terms of occupation or career, you will need to think about the type of organization you want to join. Of course, it may not be a matter of joining an organization – you may wish to work for yourself. However, most graduates do end up working for someone else, at least at first. Activity 11.2 at the end of this chapter gives you an opportunity to evaluate prospective employers using a checklist of qualities.

# FINDING OUT ABOUT EMPLOYERS

How many employers can you name that offer jobs in your chosen field?

Finding out about different employers is an important part of jobhunting. You need to find out what information is available and then find some criteria as a basis for comparing them.

## SOURCES OF INFORMATION

Some of the most commonly used sources of information about employers are listed below. Much of the hard information is available from your local university careers advisory service.

- ▶ company directories;
- ▶ career publications;
- ▶ company presentations;
- ▶ promotional materials;
- ▶ the Internet (see below and Chapter 14, Jobhunting);
- ▶ videos, at presentations and many held in careers advisory service libraries;
- ▶ recruitment fairs;
- ▶ university networks;
- ▶ direct work experience or contacts who work there;
- ▶ articles in the media;
- ▶ reference books;
- ▶ libraries.

### Traditional graduate directories and careers advisory service information

Unsurprisingly, the most frequently used directories are those published in the UK especially for final-year students and graduates. These include very brief descriptions of the organizations, the sorts of jobs available and the types of people the organizations are seeking. The most popular directories of this sort include *GET*, *Prospects*, and the GTI series. *The Times Top 100 Graduate Employers* is a new directory launched in 1999, and gives basic information and the web site addresses of leading UK graduate recruiters. These are all available from your local careers advisory service.

In addition, most of the information is available on-line – try:

- ▶ www.get.hobsons.com
- ▶ www.prospects.csu.ac.uk

Many careers advisory services have well-stocked employer files that are often a source of rich additional material – some have recent clippings and newspaper articles.

The standard sources of information can provide a quick and easy starting point, but don't rely solely on these. When you have produced an initial short list of possible employers, you need to do some more resourceful researching, as suggested below.

## Libraries and the Internet

Your university library or local public library can provide a comprehensive collection of sources, such as:

▶ UK and foreign trade directories;

▶ company reports;

▶ company and financial information services;

▶ market research reports;

▶ CD-ROM sources, including UK and European employer databases;

▶ local company databases and reference books;

▶ information about working in Europe and contact details for European employers.

If you have a particular interest in working in Europe, the *Prospects* directory has details of many European and multinational companies that recruit UK graduates. There are various European graduate employer directories similar to *GET* and *Prospects*. Many local careers services will have a reference copy or you can visit their web sites (given above).

## Important directories

These include the following:

▶ *Key British Enterprises: Top 50,000 UK businesses* free to inspect hardcopy directory, usually available at public libraries, but a fee is usually payable for further details and analysis;

▶ *Kelly's Industrial Directory* www.kellys.co.uk

▶ *Kompass Register of British Industries and Commerce* similar to *Key British Enterprises*, revised annually.

Company reports of large UK companies are available on-line at: www.carol.co.uk/index.html

As you can see, some of these information sources are also available on-line to students and recent graduates. Ask at your university or local library for help as some services are only available subject to access status. Many university libraries are now forming information consortia, so find out what is available near you.

If you are wanting to find organizations that specialize in a particular product or service, you can search using an on-line directory service based on the *Thompson Local Directory*: www.infospace.com/uk/thomw

### Do they tell it how it really is?

There can be several problems with some organizational promotional material. Organizations do not necessarily intend to present a false picture, but the high rates of staff turnover and disillusionment of many graduate entrants is sufficient to be wary. The problem of graduate staff feeling disenchanted with false images of their organizations have been reported frequently in both professional and academic human resource management journals.

In assessing promotional material, apply the following four tests.

▶ **Origin of material/authorship**

Ask who wrote the material and why. The majority of graduate recruitment literature is written to attract you. View this as the organizational equivalent of a CV. The same rule applies when you read material in professional journals and in some newspapers. How objective is the information you are reading?

▶ **Accuracy**

Some promotional material can quickly be out of date – circumstances can change inside organizations following takeovers and mergers that radically change prospects. Some organizations are so large and complicated that general descriptions cannot do justice to enormous differences between one part and another.

▶ **Depth**

How much detail are you being given? Does the brochure talk generally of training or does it set out exactly what is on offer?

▶ **Omissions**

There is probably a lot going on inside organizations that you are not told. There may be worries or concerns about commercial success, restructuring or ongoing problems of morale or high staff turnover. This happened to a number of graduates in 1999 when Marks & Spencer withdrew offers of graduate training scheme places because of commercial problems.

# HOW TO OVERCOME ORGANIZATIONAL IMAGE MANAGEMENT

▶ **Recognize that it happens**

Graduate recruitment brochures and adverts are often part of a wider PR campaign to raise the company profile among investors, customers and competitors. Many organizations are now recognizing that the practice of inflating graduate expectations can create problems for both the individual and the organization. Thus, many organizations are now trying hard to tell it like it is, and avoid giving too rosy a picture, but it is very hard to know what is rhetoric and what is reality.

► **Get off the beaten track**

Don't just rely on the traditional graduate sources of information. Think of some alternative ones. Use the Internet and your university library to find out as much as you can about companies. Good sources include *Financial Times* and other broadsheets, professional journals and trade magazines.

► **Get an inside picture**

The best way to find out about a company is to have worked there yourself. If you are still an undergraduate, you could target a particular organization for your dissertation, project or a vacation job. Next best is to find someone who works there. You can try your careers advisory service – some keep contact with recent graduates for this very reason. Your university lecturers may have contacts with recent graduates or with staff unconnected with the recruitment process.

► **Resourceful researching**

Go to company presentations and recruitment fairs armed with probing questions. In particular, ask recent graduates specific questions about the organization and how it has met their expectations. If you get through to an assessment centre, you will probably have an opportunity to do this at some length.

Other published sources of details about employers include books such as *The 100 Best Companies to Work for in the UK* (Nightingale Multimedia, Millennium Edition). This book measures organizations in terms of pay, benefits, communication, training, career development and morale. It also gives figures for the number of graduates employed each year and other facts, such as the annual staff turnover rate.

# WHICH ARE SEEN AS THE TOP GRADUATE EMPLOYERS?

Over 11,000 final-year students were asked 'Which employer do you think offers the best opportunities for graduates?' Respondents mentioned over 800 different organizations, including a range from small local employers to well-known multinationals. The companies students mentioned most often are shown in Table 11.2.

Of course, students and graduates differ enormously in terms of their reasons for choosing a particular employer. Reputation, image and financial success may be important. Views can be influenced when employers are active in a particular university, if they are featured in traditional graduate directories or have an impressive advertising campaign.

In today's turbulent world, success and popularity can be a roller-coaster, and league table positions can change very quickly.

The problem with considering the 'top 100' companies is that competition for jobs is fierce. You may well decide that, in spite of their 'ideal' status, the time and effort it takes to complete application forms and attend interviews may be better invested where the chance of success is much higher.

**TABLE 11.2** The top graduate employers in 1999

| Rank | Company | Rank | Company |
|------|---------|------|---------|
| 1 | Anderson Consulting | 51 | Linklaters |
| 2 | Arthur Andersen | 52 | Data Connection |
| 3 | Price Waterhouse Coopers | 53 | Allen & Overy |
| 4 | Proctor & Gamble | 54 | J. Sainsbury |
| 5 | Civil service | 55 | Foreign Office |
| 6 | British Airways | 56 | Royal Navy |
| 7 | Marks & Spencer | 57 | Police |
| 8 | KPMG | 58 | Microsoft |
| 9 | Unilever | 59 | McDonalds |
| 10 | Boots | 60 | Citibank |
| 11 | Ford | 61 | Standard Life |
| 12 | Glaxo Wellcome | 62 | Eversheds |
| 13 | Ernst & Young | 63 | Rolls-Royce |
| 14 | BBC | 64 | Bank of England |
| 15 | Army | 65 | NatWest Bank |
| 16 | Deloitte & Touche | 66 | Virgin |
| 17 | IBM | 67 | Saatchi & Saatchi |
| 18 | Mars | 68 | Peugeot |
| 19 | Esso | 69 | Hewlett-Packard |
| 20 | BP | 70 | British Steel |
| 21 | Shell | 71 | Mott Macdonald |
| 22 | McKinsey & Co. | 72 | Marakon Associates |
| 23 | British Aerospace | 73 | Cable & Wireless |
| 24 | Kingfisher | 74 | Abbey National |
| 25 | Goldman Sachs | 75 | United Biscuits |
| 26 | Astra-Zeneca | 76 | Sony |
| 27 | NHS | 77 | Salomon Smith Barney |
| 28 | J.P. Morgan | 78 | Oliver, Wyman and Co. |
| 29 | HSBC | 79 | Norton Rose |
| 30 | BT | 80 | European Union |
| 31 | Pfizer | 81 | Deutsche Bank |
| 32 | Warburg Dillon Read | 82 | Walkers Snack Foods |
| 33 | Clifford Chance | 83 | SmithKline Beecham |
| 34 | Barclays Bank | 84 | Royal Bank of Scotland |
| 35 | Schroders | 85 | PA Consulting |
| 36 | Schlumberger | 86 | Nortel |
| 37 | Reuters | 87 | Mitchell Madison |
| 38 | Ove Arup | 88 | EDS |
| 39 | Logica | 89 | Druid |
| 40 | GKN | 90 | Boston Consulting Group |
| 41 | Bass | 91 | BNFL |
| 42 | Chase | 92 | Slaughter & May |
| 43 | L'Oréal | 93 | Philips |
| 44 | DERA | 94 | P&O |
| 45 | RAF | 95 | DESG |
| 46 | Nestlé | 96 | Credit Suisse |
| 47 | Lloyds TSB | 97 | Capital One |
| 48 | Merrill Lynch | 98 | British Sugar |
| 49 | John Lewis | 99 | Bank of Scotland |
| 50 | ICI | 100 | Tesco |

Source: *The Graduate Careers Survey*, 1999. High Fliers Research Ltd

In any case, judging the merits of a potential employer is essentially a personal matter, dependent on your own values and aspirations. The final section in this chapter gives you an opportunity to evaluate any of the organizations you shortlist.

# EVALUATING POTENTIAL EMPLOYERS

When you have decided the general area or occupation you're interested in, the next big job is to decide which employer. There are so many to choose from and organizations vary in many ways, such as culture, size, location. This section provides you with a framework for evaluating potential employers.

You can identify positive characteristics you would wish to find in an ideal employer and use this as a checklist when comparing different organizations. An example of the sorts of issues you may like to consider in your evaluation is given in Activity 11.2.

Why not photocopy Activity 11.2 and use it to compare different employers – especially handy if you are fortunate enough to have more than one job offer!

You may feel that one of the features listed above has overriding importance for you. For example, it could be important that your employer is within easy commuting distance of your present address. You can personalize this exercise even more by weighting or ranking the various features I have suggested or adding your own in the blank space provided.

You can use your answers to the checklist again when your prepare your application and for interviews or assessment centres.

# SUMMARY

▶ This chapter started by considering the fierce competition for many graduate jobs.

▶ Many graduates prefer to opt for a big employer and join a general training scheme as this allows flexibility before they commit themselves to a professional career path.

▶ The most popular occupational areas for 2000 and beyond are likely to be management consultancy, marketing, media, research and accountancy. Competition for these jobs is fierce.

▶ We have looked at the various types of employer by sector (private, public or not-for-profit) as well as organization size (large versus small) and extent (local versus global).

| Qualities | Important to you? | Your rating | | | | |
|---|---|---|---|---|---|---|
| | | Excellent | Good | Average | Below average | Poor |
| Successful organization/market leader | Y N | 1 | 2 | 3 | 4 | 5 |
| Blue chip reputation | Y N | 1 | 2 | 3 | 4 | 5 |
| Attractive work locations | Y N | 1 | 2 | 3 | 4 | 5 |
| Good on my CV for my future career | Y N | 1 | 2 | 3 | 4 | 5 |
| International career opportunities | Y N | 1 | 2 | 3 | 4 | 5 |
| Work benefiting people or society | Y N | 1 | 2 | 3 | 4 | 5 |
| Opportunities to reach management level | Y N | 1 | 2 | 3 | 4 | 5 |
| Employs many other graduates annually | Y N | 1 | 2 | 3 | 4 | 5 |
| Variety of assignments and tasks | Y N | 1 | 2 | 3 | 4 | 5 |
| Opportunity to become a specialist | Y N | 1 | 2 | 3 | 4 | 5 |
| Graduate training programme | Y N | 1 | 2 | 3 | 4 | 5 |
| Concern for the environment | Y N | 1 | 2 | 3 | 4 | 5 |
| Dynamic/progressive approach | Y N | 1 | 2 | 3 | 4 | 5 |
| Supports professional development | Y N | 1 | 2 | 3 | 4 | 5 |
| Allows a "work–life" balance | Y N | 1 | 2 | 3 | 4 | 5 |
| Exciting, attractive products or services | Y N | 1 | 2 | 3 | 4 | 5 |
| High ethics and morals | Y N | 1 | 2 | 3 | 4 | 5 |
| Other | Y N | 1 | 2 | 3 | 4 | 5 |

# your employment rights at work

**Working during term-time? Graduate career? Everyone has basic rights – make sure you know yours!**

**In this chapter, you will:**

- ☐ find out if you want to be an employee or not;

- ☐ see what the implications are of being an employee;

- ☐ learn about your contract of employment;

- ☐ find out about statutory provisions;

- ☐ look at pay and the minimum wage;

- ☐ see what hours of work are expected;

- ☐ think about health and safety issues;

- ☐ discuss discrimination;

- ☐ consider what is and isn't fair dismissal.

# INTRODUCTION

Everyone has basic rights at work. This chapter focuses mainly on individuals who have employee status, although some employment rights are common whatever your status at work. Rights such as protection from unlawful discrimination, for example, extend far beyond the realm of work.

The information provided here is intended to offer general guidance. However, employment law is very complicated and may require legal expertise to interpret the facts of each unique case. The information is correct at the time of writing, but new laws are introduced regularly, so seek advice.

Contact details of local agencies that can help you are given, along with web site addresses, so you can quickly find the most up-to-date information and guidance you need.

# WILL YOU BE AN EMPLOYEE?

The nature of work is changing rapidly, there are many new forms of employment relationship. An increasing number of graduates are leaving university to become self-employed or offer services on a freelance basis under a 'contract for services', not a 'contract of employment'. It is important that you are clear about your employment status when you accept work following graduation.

Knowing your status is also important to undergraduates who are working part time while at university. Part-time workers have traditionally been in a much weaker position than full timers regarding statutory employment rights. However, the more recent legislation has helped to improve the situation. There can be problems in establishing that you do have employee status if the work is casual with no 'mutuality of obligation'. You would be unlikely to have employee status if, for example, you are just 'on the books' of a local employment agency with freedom to accept or turn down work when it is offered. Ask your employer or agency to confirm your status as an employee. If in doubt, seek advice.

## THE IMPLICATIONS OF BEING AN EMPLOYEE

► Some statutory employment rights (such as unfair dismissal provisions) are only available to employees.
► Tax and National Insurance deductions can be made from your pay by your employer;
► Many social security benefits are reserved for employees.
► An employer has a greater duty of care towards employees than to self-employed workers.

# YOUR CONTRACT OF EMPLOYMENT

First, it is important to distinguish between your 'contract of employment' and the 'written statement of terms and conditions'. The contract may or may not be written. Employers are required to provide a statement of the main terms and conditions, but a contract is still formed even if no written material or other correspondence changes hands. Your contract of employment is comprised of 'express' and 'implied' terms as follows:

## EXPRESS TERMS AND CONDITIONS

These terms include those appearing in a job advert, oral terms discussed at interview and the written contract provided after interview/selection or after you have started work.

Express terms in your contract of employment may come from existing collective agreements, especially in public sectors where trade union membership is still quite high. For example, pay increases and changes in conditions of service (holidays) may be routinely included. You may be asked to sign an acknowledgement that specific works rules form part of your contract of employment.

## IMPLIED TERMS

These are derived from the courts as part of all contracts of employment. The employer has a duty to pay you, take reasonable care of your health and safety and treat you respectfully. The employee has corresponding duties, such as obedience, honesty and loyalty.

# WRITTEN STATEMENTS OF TERMS AND CONDITIONS

The terms and conditions of your employment are probably the focus of keenest interest. You have a legal right to a written statement, but, unfortunately, your employer does not need to issue this for up to two months *after* you start work at the company.

The terms and conditions should include:

▶ the names of the employer and employee;

▶ the date when the employment began;

▶ the date on which the employee's period of continuous employment began (usually the same as the starting date, but work with another employer might be included);

▶ the scale, rate and method of calculating remuneration;

- the pay intervals (for example, monthly);
- terms and conditions of hours of work;
- holiday entitlement;
- sickness and incapacity details and entitlements;
- pension scheme details, if applicable;
- notice entitlement;
- job title or brief description of the work;
- if the job is not permanent, the period for which it is meant to last, including any fixed term;
- the expected place of work and address of the employer;
- any collective agreements affecting the employment, including things such as national agreements;
- details of any work abroad lasting more than one month;
- a note specifying any grievance and disciplinary rules applicable to the employee (though where there are fewer than 20 employees at the date employment began, the details need only relate to the person from whom the employee can seek redress).

# EMPLOYMENT LEGISLATION

Employment legislation is best viewed as a foundation on which your contract of employment rests. Employment law is an enormous, complicated and ever-changing field. In summary, here are some of your key rights:

- not to be unlawfully discriminated against in terms of sex, race and disability (but not age in the UK);
- not to be unfairly dismissed;
- not being paid below the minimum wage;
- not to work excessive hours (Working Time Directive);
- to receive a written statement of the main terms of your employment;
- an itemized payslip;
- maternity pay, time off and return to work;
- not to be dismissed for trade union membership and participation in its activities;
- minimum periods of notice;
- time off without pay for certain public duties;
- redundancy pay for those with two years' service;
- time off with pay for trade union duties and training;
- time off without pay for trade union activities;
- time off with pay for safety representative and safety training.

# PAY AND THE MINIMUM WAGE

The minimum wage started on 1 April 1999. If you are 22 or over, you should be paid at least £3.60 per hour. Some employers offer recognized training and pay at a lower rate of £3.20 for up to six months. The minimum for those between 18 and 21 is £3.00. (Rates are revised regularly. Check the current situation at www.tuc.org.uk.)

It is also worth noting that the minimum wage does *not* apply to:

▶ undergraduates on sandwich courses while they are placed with an employer for up to one year;

▶ trainee teachers placed with schools or colleges as part of their course;

▶ au pairs, nannies or other childcare helpers who live in, are treated as part of the family and join in with family activities, such as household chores and leisure activities.

## YOUR PAYSLIP

**'My employer pays me once a week, but I never know how he works out what I'm paid or what the deductions are for'.**

You have a right to a payslip that shows your gross pay, deductions and net pay. You should receive a payslip regularly, regardless of the number of hours you have worked. Your employer has the right to deduct tax and National Insurance. If you don't think you will earn above the tax allowance (£4195 in 1999/2000), you can fill out a P38, which you can obtain from any Jobcentre or at most NUS offices. You can also contact your local branch of the Inland Revenue for further help and information.

**'My boss doesn't want to put my wages through the books – she doesn't bother with payslips.'**

Many students are asked to work on an informal 'cash in hand' basis. Avoid this because you may find it hard to prove your employee status and put yourself at risk of losing your employment rights. The courts view these arrangements as 'tainted with illegality'.

## TIPS AND GRATUITIES

Many students find part-time jobs in the service sector, especially hotels, catering, bar work and restaurants. If you are working in a bar, café or club, you may find there is a set system for handling tips. Tips are usually put into a pot and divided up, with each employee receiving a percentage relating to the job they do.

**'My employer collects my tips and I never see them.'**

Some employers – especially those who paid below the minimum wage prior to 1 April 1999 – tried this approach to avoid paying out any more, but still appear to be raising the hourly rate to the required level. This is not acceptable and is really an unlawful deduction from pay. It may be very difficult to stand up to an employer on your own, so seek help and support form your NUS office, Citizens Advice Bureau (CAB) or from a union. Your NUS or CAB can advise you which are the most appropriate unions for your sector of work.

# HOURS OF WORK

The Working Time Directive came into force on 1 October 1998. The rights are very complicated and cover a wide range of workers, so it is not possible to set out all the provisions in detail here. If you are interested in finding out more, you can visit the government web site:

www.hmso.gov.uk/si/si1998/81833–b.htm

The following rights are those of *all* workers, not just employees:

► a ceiling of a 48-hour maximum average working week, including overtime;

► a paid, 20-minute break when the working day is more than 6 hours long;

► a rest period of 11 hours every working day;

► a minimum of 4 weeks' paid holiday every year after being in a job for 13 weeks.

**'My employer has asked me to *opt out* of my rights. Can I say no?'**

Yes, you can say no! Under the present regulations, your employer can *ask* you to agree to waive your right not to work above the 48-hour maximum average working week (often known as 'opting out'). Your employer may ask you to opt out indefinitely or for a specific period. However, you have the right to refuse to opt out. You also have the right to change your mind by giving written notice to your employer. The law states that the notice period for 'opting back in' is no more than three months.

If you are dismissed for refusing to opt out, the one-year qualifying period does not apply and you can appeal to an employment tribunal.


# HEALTH AND SAFETY

Your employer has a duty of care towards you. This means your employer must ensure that:

► your fellow employees are competent;

► you work in safe surroundings and with safe equipment;

► there is a safe system of work – for example, tools, machinery and equipment should be properly maintained, health and safety procedures set out and followed and training given to all employees.

This means your employer needs to protect you from, for example:

► tripping or slipping at work;

► hazardous substances;

► lifting injuries by ensuring that you are trained in the correct procedures;

► excessive noise and vibration;

► vehicles in the workplace, such as cars, vans and fork-lift trucks.

'One of my work colleagues got badly scalded in an accident at work last week. One of the waiters always uses the "out" door as a short cut to get back into the kitchen.'

You are entitled to complain if anyone you work with behaves in a way that puts you at risk. You should approach your supervisor first or, if that is the person you are having problems with, their superior.

This is always hard on your own, so get advice from your Health and Safety Executive (HSE) branch office (which helps workers in construction, engineering, textiles and utilities) or local Environmental Health Department (which advises workers in retail, catering and leisure industry jobs), NUS or CAB first.

'I spend most of my time at work in front of a VDU. I think I need glasses for the first time in my life.'

If your employment involves regular use of a VDU, your employer must pay for an eye test and, if necessary, for a pair of glasses. If you fancy a pair of designer frames, though, you can dig into your own pocket – your employer is only obliged to shell out for a *basic* pair of specs. If your work is wholly in front of a VDU, you are entitled to take a 15-minute break every 50 to 60 minutes.

# DISCRIMINATION

You have a right not to be unfairly discriminated against on the basis of your sex, race, marital status or disability during recruitment for work or at work. You also have protection against being victimized for bringing a claim after you have finished working for an organization – for example, being refused references for a new job on the grounds that you took your last employer to a tribunal.

'Direct' discrimination occurs when an employer treats you less favourably than another based on one of the above prohibited grounds.

'One of the other bar staff always touches me up when he walks past. I've asked him not to do it. All he does is say I should regard it as a compliment. I need this job but I can't cope for much longer. What should I do?'

It sounds as though you are being sexually harassed, which is a form of direct discrimination. You should tell your employer about this unwanted sexual attention and they should take action to stop it. If the person doing this is your boss, you should contact their immediate superior. Your employer should take your complaint very seriously as they may be liable for uninvited sexual behaviour. Your colleague will probably be disciplined under your employing organization's formal procedures. You are entitled to see these procedures and should have been told about them when you were employed.

If it is a small organization and the harasser is your employer, you should seek advice from the Equal Opportunities Commission (contact details are provided at the end of this chapter) or from a union representative.

'I am the only Asian worker in the shop. I applied for an internal promotion, but didn't even get an interview, even though I have more experience and the same qualifications as the bloke who got the job.'

It sounds as though you have received less favourable treatment on the grounds of your race, which is unlawful. You need to seek legal or professional advice from your local CAB or the Commission for Racial Equality before approaching your employer as each situation has to be handled in different ways depending on the unique facts of the case.

**'Indirect' discrimination** is when an employer applies some requirement or condition to an employee or job applicant that is harder for a minority group (such as women) to meet than another group (such as men). The condition is not justified by the requirements of the job and being unable to comply is to the detriment of the minority group.

**'I regularly work 20 hours a week and have been with this firm for seven months now. They have just told me that part-timers are not entitled to pensions or paid holidays.'**

If you are a full time undergraduate, working 20 hours a week is too much anyway! This can really wreck your studies and degree result! If you are working such long hours because of financial worries, seek some help and advice, and try to keep your hours down to below a total of 15.

You *may* have a strong case for indirect discrimination. Any restriction of benefits to full-time employees is likely to treat men better than women. Your employer may not intend to discriminate, but that is the effect this policy has on women. You also have a right not to be victimized because you have made a complaint about discrimination.

*All* workers are entitled to four weeks' paid holiday after 13 weeks' employment.

# MATERNITY RIGHTS

Women have specific statutory rights in relation to pregnancy and childbirth. The law relating to employment rights of pregnant workers is very complicated and changes are made regularly to bring the UK into line with European law. If you are pregnant, you should consult a NUS adviser or your local union branch for advice, but you should have the following rights to:

▶ time off with pay for antenatal care, for a reasonable number of visits to the clinic and parentcraft classes if they occur when you normally work;

▶ protection against dismissal because of pregnancy;

▶ maternity pay – for women who have worked for 26 weeks by the end of the 15th week before the baby is due and earn at least £66 per week (this figure changes annually so check);

▶ 18 weeks' ordinary maternity leave, but you must give your employer 21 days' notice before you intend to take your maternity leave;

▶ additional leave (up to 29 weeks) after the birth if you have worked for your employer for a year or more.

The detailed provisions and methods of working out entitlement can be found at any Jobcentre, from the Equal Opportunities Commission and your local NUS Welfare Office.

# DISMISSAL

You have the right not to be unfairly dismissed. However, in order to qualify to make a claim against any of the following four 'potentially fair' reasons for dismissal, you must be an employee with at least one year's continuous employment. You must also claim within a certain time period (which is three months for unfair dismissal). There are some further limitations regarding qualification to claim. For example, employees who work past retiring age and those who usually work outside the UK are excluded. If in doubt, seek help from a trade union or get legal advice.

If you are sacked, it can be viewed as either 'potentially fair' or 'automatically unfair'.

## POTENTIALLY FAIR REASONS FOR DISMISSAL

The potentially fair reasons for dismissal are:

▶ concerning your ability to do the job – for example, that you constantly make serious errors or are not as competent as you claimed to be;

▶ your conduct – for example, breaking organizational rules, such as drinking at work, theft, assaulting a colleague;

▶ redundancy – where the business closes down or fewer workers are needed;

▶ statutory illegality – for example, on the expiry of a work permit, if you are employed as a driver but lose your driving licence.

In addition to having a potentially fair reason for dismissing you, an employer must act reasonably. For example, they should follow a fair procedure in the manner of your dismissal. Good employers will have a written disciplinary procedure that you should be familiar with as part of your induction. You should be given a chance to explain events and defend yourself. In most cases, you should be allowed to bring witnesses, be supported by a colleague and appeal against the initial decision. Most companies will allow an appeal that should be heard by a different manager from the one originally involved.

**'I lost my job for smoking in the kitchen. It was raining outside and I was desperate for a fag.'**

You should have been told about the no smoking rule when you joined. In addition, you should have been given a chance to explain yourself as part of a properly conducted disciplinary hearing. This offence is usually referred to as gross misconduct and has instant dismissal as a penalty. You have probably been fairly dismissed, but do check with an adviser that your employer followed the correct disciplinary procedure and gave you a fair hearing. Even a potentially fair dismissal can be unfair if it has been handled badly.

## AUTOMATICALLY UNFAIR REASONS FOR DISMISSAL

These claims do not depend on length of service.

The following are automatically unfair reasons for dismissal:

▶ pregnancy or maternity;

▶ shop and betting workers who refuse to work on a Sunday;

▶ trade union membership;

▶ health and safety reasons;

▶ being on strike during the first eight weeks of a lawful dispute;

▶ refusing to opt out of your rights under the Working Time Directive.

If you are dismissed for any of these reasons you can take your case to an employment tribunal, however long you have worked for your current employer. The ceiling for compensation for unfair dismissal has gone up to £50,000.

# WHERE TO GO FOR HELP AND ADVICE

If you need advice on your own specific case, you can contact your local NUS office or CAB. Alternatively, contact your local professional association, institute or an appropriate trade union once in work. Some students join trade unions even as part-time workers.

The Advisory, Conciliation and Arbitration Service (ACAS) provides free help and advice on issues such as unfair dismissal and can help settle disputes and overcome problems at work.

The TUC has an excellent web site, full of current information and advice about employment rights:

www.tuc.org.uk

The Equal Opportunities Commission and the Commission for Racial Equality can provide help and advice on sex and race discrimination and harassment.

### ACAS (Advisory, Conciliation and Arbitration Service)

National headquarters
*Tel:* 020 7210 3642

Regional offices include:

Birmingham
*Tel:* 0121 456 5856

Cardiff
*Tel:* 029 2076 1126

London
*Tel:* 020 7396 5100

Glasgow
*Tel:* 0141 204 2677

Manchester
*Tel:* 0161 833 8585

Free leaflets available from ACAS Reader Ltd
*Tel:* 01455 852225

Further details from its web site at:
www.acas.org.uk

## CAB (Citizens Advice Bureau)

Refer to your local telephone directory for your nearest one.

## CRE (Commission for Racial Equality)

Elliot House
10–12 Allington Street
London SW1E 5EH

*Tel:* 020 7828 7022
Web site: www.cre.gov.uk

## DTI (Department of Trade and Industry)

Free national helpline:
*Tel:* 0500 848489

## EOC (Equal Opportunities Commission)

Overseas House
Quay Street
Manchester M3 3HN

*Tel:* 0161 833 9244
Web site: www.eoc.org.uk

## HSE (Health and Safety Executive)

Refer to your local telephone directory for your nearest office.

Helpful HSE advice booklets are available free of charge. They can also be obtained from your local government environmental health office.

**NUS (National Union of Students)**

Nelson Mandela House
461 Holloway Road
London N7 6LJ

*Tel:* 020 7272 8900
Web site: www.nus.org.uk

**TUC (Trades Union Congress)**

Congress House
Great Russell Street
London WC1B 3LS

*Tel:* 020 7636 4030
Web site: www.tuc.org.uk

# part III

## key steps towards getting the job you want

# secrets of graduate recruitment and selection – the inside information

## Your future employer's strategy revealed!

**In this chapter, you will:**

- [ ] have an overview of the graduate job selection process;

- [ ] learn of the key stages employers follow in recruitment and graduate selection;

- [ ] find an explanation of what employers are doing and why;

- [ ] find advice on what you can and should know about the process;

- [ ] discover job selection criteria can be made simple;

- [ ] discover details of the competences most employers look for.

**In the activity:**

**13.1** How to identify the selection criteria for your intended job

# THE RECRUITMENT AND SELECTION PROCESS – AN OVERVIEW

Graduate recruiters employ a wide range of methods to attract, find and then select from the right graduates. This section tells you everything you need to know to plan your strategy to ensure they pick you. Look inside the mind of a graduate recruiter and find out what tactics are used on the other side of the desk!

I am not suggesting that graduate recruitment and selection is an exact science. Far from it – in fact, employers vary enormously in the approaches they take. The big blue chip organizations and familiar milk round names will probably follow the steps I describe below. However, there is often a divergence between theory and practice. Not all employers follow best practice and many have not developed such a wholly systematic and integrated approach as that described below.

Knowing the steps being followed by the other side will help you feel more confident in your own jobhunting activities. You will come across as knowledgeable and have better understanding of what recruiters are doing.

Employers often distinguish between 'recruitment' (attracting you) and 'selection' (screening and weeding). I don't want to claim that all recruiters keep strictly to this path. You may well encounter examples of poor practice on a number of counts. If you know about the stages outlined below, though, you will be well on the way to developing an intimate knowledge of the way your future employer thinks.

| Candidate's perspective | Stage in the process | Employer's perspective |
|---|---|---|
| Decide your general career direction | 1 | Define the job |
| Self-assessment, career SHAPE | 2 | Develop selection criteria, list of competences |
| Define career aspirations, type of employer | 3 | Identify the labour market |
| Start serious jobhunting | 4 | Attract the students/graduates |
| Make applications | 5 | Screen applications |
| Fight for a job! | 6 | Assess candidates – by means of interviews, tests and so on |
| Success (or failure and review) | 7 | Decision |
| Accept the job, start work | 8 | Induction |

FIGURE 13.1  Parallel perspectives on graduate jobhunting

You will see from Figure 13.1 that your own jobhunting activities closely mirror those of the employer. You have a great deal in common. Understanding the employer's strategy can help you plan your own approach and give you a tactical advantage over the other, uninformed, applicants.

Of course, real life is not always quite this simple. There are a number of obstacles embedded in the selection process itself, and I shall outline these below. Most jobhunting guides avoid this topic, so, if you are reading selectively, make sure you read the next bit.

# PROBLEMS WITH THE SELECTION PROCESS

The selection process aims to be effective in matching people (you) to jobs. However, there is plenty of room for miscommunication in the form of error and impression management. Figure 13.2 shows the extent of the information that passes between you and your prospective employer during recruitment. You will see that there is plenty of scope for problems to arise.

| Candidate | | Selector |
|---|---|---|
| Image | CV | Nature of job |
| Personality | Application form | Promotion prospects |
| Specific qualities, e.g. leadership | Interview | Training opportunities |
| | Selection methods | |
| Knowledge | Via third party, e.g. agency, headhunter, referee | Conditions of work |
| Skills | | Salary – increments, components (basic, bonuses) |
| Previous employment history | | |
| Previous salary | | Future of company |
| Previous experience | | Selection procedures |
| Commitment | Advertisement | |
| Motivation | Agency | Career advancement |
| | Company brochure | |
| Ambition | Tour round site | Company culture |
| Health | Interview | |
| | Verbal and written communication | Company policies, e.g. |
| Biographical information | | equal opportunities |

FIGURE 13.2   Information exchanged in jobhunting

Source: *Deception in Selection*, Whalley L. and Smith M., 1998. Reproduced by kind permission of John Wiley and Sons Ltd

Organizations can make mistakes in the way they advertise and promote themselves and their jobs. Their screening and selection procedures may be imperfect due to poor administration, image management and plain human error. Candidates can also contribute to problems by exaggerating skills and experiences or by omitting important facts. This is a minefield, but you need to work your way safely through it to make sure you get the job you want – and want the job you get!

# THE KEY STAGES IN THE RECRUITMENT AND SELECTION PROCESS

The recruitment and selection process has seven main stages (as shown in Figure 13.1). This chapter provides a brief overview of them, while the following chapters cover these steps in more detail, with advice and help to ensure you succeed.

As mentioned before, employers will vary in the amount of time and effort they put into each stage. Some employers may not adhere to best practice or else attach greater importance to particular steps and not to others. Time spent thinking about the employer's perspective will not be wasted – it is the one thing that all employers regularly say job applicants lack, so read this and you will stand out from the crowd!

## DEFINE THE JOB

The link between organization strategy and graduate jobs generally has already been explained in Chapter 8. The first practical step employers should take is to analyze the job about to be advertised.

In many firms, recruitment takes place frequently, but there will usually be at least an annual review of the job. There are increasing pressures on all employers to re-design and restructure work, so working practices and the skills required change quickly. It is also an indication of a genuine equal opportunities employer that jobs have been properly assessed. 'Job analysis' is the process of collecting information about the tasks and responsibilities involved in a job or role. This information can be used to produce a 'job description'. Job descriptions usually include:

- ▶ job title;
- ▶ location;
- ▶ who you are responsible to;
- ▶ who you are responsible for (that is, other staff);
- ▶ main purpose of the job;
- ▶ main duties;
- ▶ working conditions.

Job descriptions may exist in your prospective organization, but not all employers are keen to let you see them. I therefore provide an example in Figure 13.3.

# Post **MOTOROLA**

---

## GRADUATE SYSTEMS ENGINEER

**Location: Swindon**          **Grade:**          **Department:**

### Purpose of the job

The cellular world is moving into IP and packet switching. In GSM, the world's most successful digital cellular standard, packet-based data transmission is to be introduced to enable high-speed and efficient data transfer which will result in a whole new range of cost-effective value-added services. This new offering is known as General Packet Radio Service (GPRS) and it provides the evolutionary step into the 3rd generation Universal Mobile Telecommunications System (UMTS). Motorola is playing a leading part in this revolution, creating many exciting opportunities to work with a world leader.

You could play an exciting role in this high-growth technology by joining the Advanced Network Development Centre at our Swindon facility. In doing so you will have the opportunity to use your technical skills to be creative, effective and valuable in the support of the Internet Protocol (IP) component of GPRS systems across our customer base.

### Key responsibilities

The incumbent will be required to develop detailed understanding of the philosophy and operation of telecoms and data coms equipment and use that knowledge to contribute to the design of optimal system architectures for commercial cellular systems. The types of networks covered will range from point-to-point transmission links to whole system architectures for supporting value-added services such as e-commerce, mission critical data transfer, telemetry, 'infotainment', etc. Special attention to IP-based data and voice transport will be a significant part of the job. Responsibilities will include a major subset of the following:

- integration of IP-based networks with Motorola and third-party equipment;
- analysis of system architecture strategies;
- development of analytical tools and utilities;
- application engineering using third-party software tools;
- engineering support to the customer base on a consultancy basis.

### Skills and experience

You should expect to graduate with at least a 2:1 degree or to complete a Masters degree in electronics or communications or computing engineering.
Essential: Knowledge of at least one programming language and an interest in software, should be accustomed to PC technology (upgrades, configurations), good communication skills, should be self-motivated and able to operate independently when away from the office, willingness to undertake significant international travel.
Desirable: Knowledge of HTML and/or Java, basic knowledge of a major foreign language, prior work experience in an engineering environment.

### Further information:

All vacancies include a full relocation package and a competitive salary.

---

**FIGURE 13.3  Job description of a job at Motorola**
Source: Used with kind permission of Motorola.

## SELECTION CRITERIA AND PERSON SPECIFICATIONS

Job descriptions can be limited to outlines of the work-related tasks rather than the personal qualities needed to be successful in doing the job. Many employers now recognize the need to specify the qualities the job holder will need to have to fit in with the company culture and the requirements of the particular job. These are usually referred to as 'person specifications'. They may distinguish between the qualities/skills/experience that are *essential* for the job and those that are *desirable*. A person specification will usually include:

▶ attainments, qualifications;

▶ general intelligence;

▶ special aptitudes – for example, using IT, foreign language;

▶ interests – demonstrate interest in the job/career;

▶ disposition – such as team player, cooperative;

▶ circumstances – for example, willingness to be mobile.

You may notice that there is a similarity between the person specification and the information required on a standard application form and many employers' application forms. This is no coincidence! A person specification, or its informal equivalent, are used to generate the selection criteria. These are the benchmark for assessing your suitability for the job. An example is given in Figure 13.4.

### Competences

It is increasingly common for employers to use competences as a basis for job selection. A competency is 'an underlying characteristic of a person that results in effective and/or superior performance in a job'. They are sometimes also referred to as 'personal attributes' or 'dimensions'.

Organizations that adopt a competency-type of approach believe that managerial and professional jobs can be broken down into their essential elements and then described in performance terms. If you have looked at any typical graduate jobs advertised in the *Prospects* or *Get* directories, you will have encountered competences. Most competency listings will include general attributes, such as teamworking, motivation, communication and problem solving. However, the actual blend required in any one case may differ quite considerably from that required for another, depending on both the type of organization and the type of role.

Many employers have a set of core competences that all successful candidates must have, but produce other lists of competences that are job-specific. An example of the way core and job-related competences are used at BT is shown in Table 13.1.

In addition to the BT specified competences, it is also very common to find selection criteria such as self-confidence, tenacity, sensitivity to others, imagination and drive.

## GENERIC MULTIMEDIA JOB SPECIFICATION

> **Job designation:** Broadcast journalist
>
> **Job purpose**
> To initiate and produce, as part of a team, a wide variety of news and current affairs material for radio and/or television.

**Key behaviours**

1  To carry out in-depth research to a broad brief, with minimal supervision across the whole range of regional broadcasting news and current affairs output.
2  To write material for programme scripts, bulletins and links, exercising editorial judgement, maintaining professional journalistic standards and adhering to BBC policy and legal and contractual guidelines.
3  To undertake interviewing and reporting duties, under broad direction in both recorded and live situations, in studio or on location, for both radio and television.
4  To prepare and present bulletins, including assessing incoming copy, subediting news copy and deploying the necessary resources.
5  To produce live and pre-recorded radio news and current affairs programmes and to prepare radio and TV packages under supervision.
6  To originate and develop programme ideas; to assist in forward planning of material for future programmes.
7  To provide briefings for reporters, camera crews and other resources staff and contributors.
8  To operate broadcast equipment: in radio, portable recording equipment, self-operating outside broadcasting vehicles and studio equipment; in television, to direct camera crews on pre-recorded and live coverage, to oversee editing and operate gallery equipment.
9  To liase with, and service the requirements of, the network newsrooms.
10  On occasions, to administer programmes budgets, ensuring effective use of money and resources, and to supervise the work of broadcast assistants.
11  To develop and maintain local contacts and fulfil a public relations role, e.g. responding to enquiries from the public.
12  At all times, to carry out duties in accordance with regional broadcasting health and safety guidelines policy.

**Skills, knowledge and experience**

This is the core professional level in journalism within regional broadcasting. Journalists are employed across a range of functions and with different skills, knowledge and experience. There is staged progression through the level which is related to review of performance and the achievement of specific objectives at every stage.

1  On initial recruitment, either a recognized journalistic qualification or substantial practical experience in journalism (likely to be around three years).
2  People with similar amount of experience in broadcast journalism may be appointed at a higher level within the salary range.
3  First-class news judgement.
4  Good broadcasting and on-air skills where appropriate.
5  Good writing skills.
6  Ability to originate and develop programme stories.
7  Ability to work cooperatively as part of a small team.
8  Knowledge of production techniques and facilities in both radio and television and the ability to develop multimedia production skills.
9  An understanding of the BBC's producer guidelines and awareness of legal considerations applying to all types of output.

**FIGURE 13.4  Person specification for a job at the BBC**
Source: Used with kind permission of the BBC

## TABLE 13.1  BT's competences

| Core competences | Job-related competences |
|---|---|
| **Commercial and business awareness**<br>Understand the organization's mission, strategy and goals and the contribution you make as an individual and work to increase profitability. | **Financial awareness**<br>Demonstrate an understanding of financial terms and concepts appropriate to the needs of the role. |
| **Customer focus**<br>The ability to see BT through the eyes of the customer and work individually and lead others to improve customer service and satisfaction. | **Global awareness**<br>Demonstrate an understanding of different international cultures and the implications of these for the organization's international interests and operations |
| **Performance and results**<br>Set clear performance standards and objectives for self and others, monitor progress and take appropriate action to achieve delivery of results. | **Strategic vision and direction setting**<br>Demonstrate an understanding of strategic issues, taking into account customer and business needs and new technology. |
| **Teamwork**<br>Contribute fully as a team member, resolving conflicts, building appropriate alliances and networks and helping others to do the same. | **Creative thinking and innovation**<br>Identify new opportunities, generate new ideas and produce innovative proposals.<br><br>**Planning, organizing and project management**<br>Produce workable plans, define priorities and set realistic milestones and deadlines. |
| **Effective communication and impact**<br>Communicate clearly, listen, demonstrate good interpersonal skills, influence others sensitively and encourage two-way communication. | **Problem solving and decision making**<br>Use established techniques effectively to assess and analyze risks, and make timely and workable decisions. |
| **Continuous improvement and managing change**<br>React positively to and lead change, improve performance by challenging established methods. | **Self-management and personal development**<br>Demonstrate flexibility, adaptability and persistence in the achievement of goals and tasks in dealing with changing business priorities.<br><br>BT also lists a number of further professional or technical competences – see more at www.bt.com/careers |

Source: Reproduced with the kind permission of BT

The organization you are applying to may be very different to BT, so do not expect these competences to be universal. However, the BT framework does contain many of the elements that all employers are looking for. Many employers do not state their selection criteria as openly as BT. Use the information provided in the job descriptions for Motorola, the BBC and BT's competences as a starting point for working out what your intended employer's selection criteria might be.

The following activity gives you a framework for your assessment. These insights into employers' selection criteria should be of assistance in making job applications and preparing for interviews and assessment centres.

---

**ACTIVITY 13.1    How to identify the selection criteria for your intended job**

Use the contents of typical person specifications and competences to write a job description for the next job you apply for. Even if your intended employer does not use a competency framework, most will identify attributes such as teamworking, adaptability and motivation in the recruitment advert or literature.

After you have done this, compare your own qualifications, skills and personal attributes to it. How do you compare? Use this to check whether or not you have a strong chance of success and as a basis for completing the application form or framing your CV. This 'matching' principle is the foundation for successful jobhunting.

For more details and ideas, see Activity 15.2 in Chapter 15.

---

## IDENTIFY THE LABOUR MARKET

Employers are aware of the cost of recruiting and selection. There is an increasing tendency for employers to identify particular students by the university they attend or the subjects they study. You can read more about these practices in the first half of the next chapter.

## ATTRACT STUDENTS/GRADUATES

In books about jobhunting, it has become commonplace to find the authors advising that you are marketing yourself, your CV is your personal promotional material. I don't dispute that these are helpful ways of seeing things, but the irony is that employers are at the same game!

Many graduate recruiters produce brochures that can be compared to product brochures, describing features and benefits of their particular jobs. In many cases, employers are fighting each other for graduates. It might not feel like it, but many employers still report difficulty in finding the right people. Chapter 14 highlights some of the issues regarding job adverts and gives practical ideas about where to find jobs.

## SCREEN APPLICATIONS

Many jobs attract hundreds of applications, even for jobs in local, small and medium-sized firms. Organizations operate within recruitment budgets and use a number of techniques to weed out unsuitable applicants.

Employers may adopt a number of screening techniques, including telephone interviews, electronic scanning, and have various ways of checking CVs and application forms. Some even use handwriting analysis or 'scientific' approaches, such as biodata (a way of assessing you based on biographical information) to screen you in or weed you out. Find out more about these techniques and how to handle them in Chapters 15 and 16. In addition, there is specific advice and skills practice provided in Chapter 17 for anyone who wants to know about telephone interviewing.

## ASSESS CANDIDATES

Organizations vary enormously in the number and type of selection techniques they adopt to find the right candidate or candidates for jobs. The most common technique is the interview, which is still used by almost all UK recruiters. Many firms also offer a second interview or an assessment centre and an increasing number use aptitude or ability and personality testing. You can find out more about these in Chapters 17, 18 and 19.

## DECISION

When you are offered a job, it may be subject to various conditions, such as degree results, health checks and references. It may be possible to negotiate attractive terms and conditions. This final stage defines your future employment relationship, so I have devoted a whole chapter to the topic – Chapter 20.

## INDUCTION AND STARTING WORK

The longed-for moment arrives! However, you need to know what to expect and be well prepared. Chapter 21 tells you how.

# SUMMARY

- ▶ This chapter has provided an overview of the selection process, highlighting the parallels between the activities of job applicants and employers.
- ▶ The main methods of assessing jobs and determining selection criteria have been described.
- ▶ A number of very common personal attributes that graduate employers are seeking have been outlined.

# SIGNPOSTS TO MORE HELP

**About human resource management generally, with good sections on recruitment and selection:**

Marchington, M. and Wilkinson, A. (1996) *Core Personnel and Development*, IPD, London.

Armstrong, M. (1996) *A Handbook of Personnel Management Practice*, Kogan Page, London.

**About impression management:**

Whalley, L. and Smith, M. (1998) *Deception in Selection*, John Wiley, Chichester.

# jobhunting – how and where to look

'He who would search for pearls must dive below ...'

ALL FOR LOVE, PROLOGUE, JOHN DRYDEN

**In this chapter, you will:**

- ☐ develop a jobhunting strategy;
- ☐ find out when to start looking;
- ☐ identify job vacancies;
- ☐ learn about recruitment agencies;
- ☐ look at jobhunting on the Internet;
- ☐ set about a creative job search;
- ☐ discover direct approaches;
- ☐ learn about networking;
- ☐ look at headhunting – when jobs come looking for you!

**In the activity:**

**14.1** Identify your network

# YOUR JOBHUNTING STRATEGY

If you have got to this stage you probably know what you want to do or have identified the sort of employer you are looking for. Of course, it may be several months since you graduated and your parents/partner/bank manager are telling you to get going.

In designing your strategy, take account of:

▶ your personal goals and objectives;

▶ your own marketability in the field you have chosen;

▶ the time you want to allocate to the task.

Prior to the application stage (discussed in Chapter 15), it is helpful to think about your overall approach. Are you aiming at a particular market or specialist area or is a more broad-brush approach attractive?

This is important as it will influence how and where you look for jobs, as well as how to actually craft your applications and design your CV. You may decide to proceed on both fronts simultaneously – targeting the really hoped for jobs and going for a high-volume CV splatter as a back-up strategy (on the advice of your bank manager).

# WHEN TO START LOOKING FOR JOBS

The traditional careers service recommendation is to start thinking about jobs in your penultimate year. This is good advice for those who can cope with pressures of academic assignments and term-time jobs. For many of you, though, this is an unachievable objective. The third or final year is even more demanding than the previous ones and many are now deciding that 100 per cent effort is going to be devoted to getting the best degree result possible.

As you might expect, those undergraduates and postgraduates who are studying vocational-type courses, such as business, IT and engineering, do get started sooner than others.

A High Fliers survey (1999) showed that, on average, students made six or seven visits each to their local careers service during their final year. Don't be too alarmed, though – around one in five students didn't manage to get there at all! The first group includes very focused people – perhaps not an accurate reflection of average student jobhunting activity. Perhaps the key question is when serious jobhunting actually begins. A comprehensive study (Purcell *et al.*, 1996) asked students at red brick, traditional and 'new' universities if they had started searching for employment, in May just prior to finals. The results (see Figure 14.1) show that many undergraduates hadn't started at all, and note the big differences between disciplines.

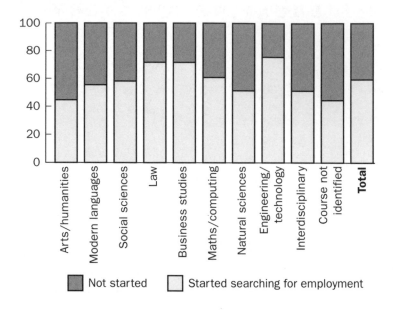

**FIGURE 14.1  Undergraduate jobhunting before finals**
Source: Purcell *et al.*, *Great Expectations*, 1996

Don't forget, though:

▶ you will need to demonstrate some evidence of career-directed thinking at application stage;

▶ to get at least some work experience;

▶ job/career decisions are not for life – everything is reversible;

▶ access to careers services and closeness to friends going through the process are a big help;

▶ don't panic – help is still available after you have graduated.

## THE CLOSING DATE FOR APPLICATIONS IS ...

When it boils down to basics, you will either be recruited several months in advance or get an immediate start job. The advance recruitment type is the domain of the traditional milk round. Many employers still operate a traditional milk round annual recruitment cycle: campus presentations, late in the autumn term or January, and interviews and second interviews at assessment centres in February/March. When you apply is clearly crucial for these jobs, so make sure you are clear about closing dates for applications.

It has to be said that many recruiters are aware of the trend for you to defer applications. This means they may run two or more intakes a year – one in the autumn and another during June/July after graduation. Others recognize that many degree courses (part time, postgraduate and so on) don't end in May/June. Many firms (for example Citibank, Price Waterhouse Coopers, SmithKline Beecham) now offer 'continuous recruitment'. In some jobs, such as law, you usually apply at least two years in advance.

## DIRECT ENTRY AND 'JUST-IN-TIME' JOBS

Big blue chip companies and smaller firms offer graduates direct entry jobs. Job adverts for these appear when the vacancy arises (hence the term 'just-in-time'). As described in Chapter 9, these jobs can be as challenging and interesting as the traditional milk round versions – some more so. These jobs may suit you if you intend to wait until after finals to sort out the next step.

# IDENTIFYING VACANCIES

Recruitment and selection practices are changing dramatically in response to the advances in IT and changing trends and expectations of students and recent graduates about when you want to start work.

## ADVANCE RECRUITMENT – THE MILK ROUND

The two major hard sources of information on advance recruitment jobs in the private sector are the *Prospects* and *Get* directories. Updated annually, these provide A–Z listings of many leading, well-known employers across diverse industries offering careers from accountancy to zookeeping (well, almost).

They are a popular source of information, giving very brief potted accounts of employers, jobs available and closing dates. You may have already used these materials to choose the sort of career and employer you are looking for. The problem is that, because they are so easily accessible, large numbers of undergraduates and recent graduates apply for these jobs. Some information in the directories is also held on-line at the directory web site or at the company's own web site.

The usual milk round includes a visit to a careers fair or to give individual company presentations. These are good sources of information about companies. Given the long lead times necessary to produce company directories, these events can also be a good opportunity to find out about any other vacancies coming on stream.

Research by IES/AGR (1999) shows that as many as 65 per cent of the traditional milk round-type employers are now targeting specific universities with their recruitment drives (see Pearson *et al.*, 1999). If you are not at one of the 'premier division' establishments, you can often find out where employers are going. Try visiting their web site. Some companies publish their milk round schedule. Alternatively, visit the web site of a large, well-known university close to you, find out which recruitment fairs your preferred employer will be attending and go!

## RECRUITMENT FAIRS

Recruitment fairs, are essentially, opportunities for jobhunters to meet prospective employers face to face. Companies and public-sector organizations set up stands and offer you an opportunity to find out about their organization and vacancies. Watch out, though, these can be high-octane meetings – the informal chat can translate into a formal interview there and then. Some offer you an interview after the fair at the careers service or their offices.

Companies at such fairs vary from large multinationals to small local firms and so they are well worth a visit. You can usually find details of which companies will be attending on the local careers service web sites or at the main *Prospects* directory site at www.prospects.csu.ac.uk. There are usually two late autumn tours – one in London, one in Glasgow – and more summer fairs spread out nationally. In 1999, the summer fairs took place at 17 venues in the north of Scotland, Northern Ireland, North East, North West, Midlands, Wales and throughout the south of the UK. You may also notice recruitment fairs advertised in the national newspapers.

---

**Recruitment fair tips**

Recruitment fairs have the potential to really accelerate the jobhunting process – make sure you're ready!'

- ▶ Dress smartly – don the interview suit.
- ▶ Take plenty of copies of your CV.
- ▶ Check out the employers you really want to target – do your homework beforehand.
- ▶ Assume the immediate interview scenario and go prepared – read Chapter 17, Interview success.

---

Recruitment fairs also run in late autumn and early spring and coincide with their presence on campus for first interviews. Specialist fairs, such as those for postgraduates, engineers, IT, alternative occupations and finance, also run at various times during the year. Find out the details from your own careers advisory service.

If you have already graduated and moved away from university or back home, you are probably entitled to help at a careers advisory service near to you under a national mutual aid scheme. Contact your nearest office to find out more details.

# JOB VACANCIES ON THE INTERNET – WHAT IT CAN DO AND WHAT IT CAN'T

The Internet offers you access to information about employers and job vacancies as well as the chance to send CVs or fill in application forms on-line. You can:

- ▶ search for job vacancies;
- ▶ find out about prospective employers;

- ▶ register to receive news of suitable vacancies;
- ▶ post your CV for employers and agencies to read;
- ▶ receive incoming e-mails about jobs;
- ▶ join newsgroups and interactive job sites;
- ▶ search for information worldwide, using a search engine such as AltaVista, Yahoo! or your own favourite.

However useful, the Internet also has its shortcomings. In most fields, only a minority of jobs are advertised in this way at present. You are best advised to use it as a supplement to your other jobhunting activities – do not rely on the Net as your sole job search technique.

A disadvantage is that any of the text-based techniques used to process CVs and select jobs are not highly advanced. Improvements are being made, but the top-quality systems, using artificial intelligence technology, are very expensive to run.

You may also need to e-mail prospective employers or their agencies to find out more details about a job. One problem with very brief job profiles is that they can distort the full picture because of their brevity and what they omit to mention. So, make sure you get the full picture!

## INTERNET JOB BOARDS

Most job board sites are interactive. You can read details of jobs and apply on-line. The approaches vary. With some, you can post your CV and details and the system will continually scan for matches and then send them to you. Even the largest site – such as Monsterboard, which advertises around 2500 jobs – is still very small compared to jobs advertised through traditional means. Many jobs posted on the Net appear in the traditional media as well.

In brief, using the Internet can add value to your jobhunting strategy, but be realistic about what it can do and about the limitations.

## SENDING YOUR PERSONAL DETAILS OVER THE WWW

- ▶ Access is often unrestricted – be cautious about where you post personal information.
- ▶ Many text-based systems look for key words, so find out as much as you can and use words that are sure to touch the spot. Always, always include 'IT' somewhere in your CV.
- ▶ Check the specific guidelines – many job boards or newsgroup sites have different rules and procedures.

# COMPANY BROCHURES AND RECRUITMENT LITERATURE

Companies large and small view their company brochures as being part of their broader public relations campaign. They are intended to make you want to join. They do provide company information and job details, but with a slant. Good job advertising is big business, and even attracts annual awards. Many students are aware of the PR spin and the specially selected nature of graduates' comments quoted in case studies.

These brochures can, nevertheless, be a source of really useful information, especially about what the company is looking for. Don't be fooled, though – recognize impression management for what it is.

The adverts in Figure 14.2 are examples of the impact good advertising can have. These won Advertising Industry Awards in 1999. Enjoy the quality, but follow up with some searching questions when you get the chance.

# CAREERS SERVICES' VACANCY BULLETINS

Many careers services produce their own in-house job vacancy publications. They are notified about a wide range of national and local jobs via a well-established network. In some, they have staff dedicated to searching the newspapers on your behalf. You can collect the bulletins weekly or, after graduation, ask for them to be posted to you.

# NATIONAL, REGIONAL AND LOCAL NEWSPAPERS

Not all the big multinationals and 'brand names' use the *Prospects* or *Get* directories, so don't limit yourself to one resource. Some national newspapers regularly advertise jobs in a specific area or industry on a particular day, as shown in Table 14.1. In addition to the papers shown in Table 14.1, *The Daily Telegraph* has a jobs supplement that covers everything on a Thursday and *The Independent on Sunday* has a repeat of the jobs advertised in the previous week. *The Daily Telegraph* also has a good searchable vacancy database at www.appointments-plus.co.uk.

Many regional and local newspapers also have adverts on a certain day of the week. You may also find that some newspapers produce a job vacancy summary as an independent publication or on a set day of the week. For example, the London *Evening Standard* produces 'Just the Job' on Mondays. In the Manchester area, job vacancies are summarized in the publication *Jobs North West*. Jobs are also advertised on-line at www.manchesteronline.co.uk/fish4jobs.

In addition, there are several sites that link to most UK national and local classified job adverts at http://www.jobhunter.co.uk. You can also visit European and international newspapers on the Web at www.papers.com and www.worldnews.com. More web site addresses are given in Table 14.2 and in the Appendix.

**TABLE 14.1** Newspapers advertising jobs in particular sectors on particular days

| | The Guardian www.Jobs unlimited.co | The Independent www.Independ ent.co.uk | The Times www..the-times.co.uk | London Evening Standard | Manchester Evening News |
|---|---|---|---|---|---|
| Mon | Media, marketing, sales, PR, secretarial | Marketing, sales, PR, media, IT | Graduates | 'Just the Job' vacancies supplement | General |
| Tues | Education and higher education courses | Media | Legal, business | Financial, general, sales and office | Finance, management IT, sales and marketing |
| Weds | Environment, finance, agencies, social services, public sector | City, banking, insurance | IT, secretarial | IT and media, creative, marketing | Engineering, building, education |
| Thurs | On-line IT, graduates | Education, university courses | General, public sector, senior management | Retail, sales and security | Public sector, creative,media, finance, retail, miscellaneous |
| Fri | | | Education, media, marketing | | General secretarial, and *Jobs North West* |
| Sat | Graduate jobs supplement, 'Rise' | | | | |

*Note*: Newspapers vary their schedules for job adverts from time to time, so check out the up-to-date patterns at your local university or public library or go on-line.

Source: Adapted from the University of Manchester and UMIST Careers Service Guide 1999

# PROFESSIONAL AND TRADE JOURNALS

Many disciplines and job areas have a journal, often produced by their own professional body or association. Recruiters want to find discerning, well-informed students and so place adverts into these publications with the advantage of only attracting the well-informed, keen and intelligent among you.

Competition judge comments about these ads:

"Powerful photography married to excellent copy. This no nonsense advertisement is frank and honest, and clearly sets out the challenge of what the job entails."

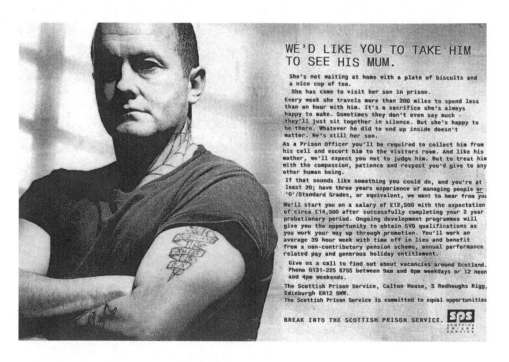

**FIGURE 14.2   Examples of good job adverts: award winners 1999**
Source: Used with the kind permission of Druid/Barkers and Scottish Prison Service/Riley

Comments made about the Druid brochure:

"A simple and well worked theme, you get a really good idea of the personality of the company. Excellent use of copy that was very easy to read, informative, relevant, with good attention to detail. An unusual format that's a bit different and adventurous. Just right for its target audience."

Courtesy of Carlton International Media Limited
© ITC Entertainment Group Limited

## TABLE 14.2  Useful publications

| Title | Type of information | Published |
|---|---|---|
| *The Actuary* | Actuarial work | Monthly<br>www.actuaries.org.uk |
| *Biomedical Scientist* | Biomedical jobs | Monthly<br>Jobs and advice at www.acb.org.uk |
| *The Bookseller* | Publishing, book trade | Friday<br>www.thebookseller.com |
| *Broadcast* | TV and radio jobs | Weekly |
| *Campaign* | Advertising, marketing, market research, PR | Friday |
| *Community Care* | Social work, community work | Thursday<br>www.community-care.co.uk |
| *Computer Weekly and Computing* | IT jobs | Thursday<br>www.computerweekly.co.uk<br>www.thebusiness.vnunet.com |
| *The Economist* | Finance, economic research | Friday<br>www.economist.com |
| *The Grocer* | Retailing, food | Weekly<br>www.grocerjobs.co.uk |
| *Health Service Journal* | NHS administration, personnel | Thursday<br>www.hsj.co.uk |
| *ILAM* | Sports/leisure management | Weekly<br>www.ilam.co.uk |
| *Information Week* | Business and technology managers | Weekly<br>www.informationweek.co.uk |
| *Inside Housing* | Housing | Friday |
| *Jobs Update* | Local government jobs (each authority publishes its own edition) | Monday |
| *Law Society Gazette* | Solicitors, paralegal and legal assistant jobs | Weekly<br>www.lawgazette.co.uk |
| *Management Today* | Company profiles, some jobs | Monthly<br>www.bestpractice.haynet.com |
| *Marketing Week* | Marketing, advertising, sales, PR | Friday<br>www.marketing-week.co.uk |
| *Museums Journal* | Museum work, art galleries | Monthly |
| *New Scientist* | Science/engineering, research associations, Scientific Civil Service, R&D graduate vacancies | Thursday<br>www.newscientistjobs.com/graduates |
| *New Statesman* | Charities, political research, pressure groups | Friday |
| *Opportunities* | Public services, local authorities | Thursday<br>www.opportunities.co.uk |
| *Personnel Today* | Personnel/human resource management | Fortnightly |
| *Planning Week* | Planning jobs | Weekly<br>www.planning.haynet.com |
| *Public Finance Weekly* | Finance and accountancy | Weekly<br>www.publicfinance.co.uk |
| *The Spectator* | Charities, political research, pressure groups | Friday |
| *The Times Educational Supplement* | School teaching, FE college lecturing, education administration | Friday |
| *Times Higher Education Supplement* | University/college lectureships, research assistantships and awards, HE administration | Friday |

Source: Adapted from University of Manchester and UMIST Careers Service Guide 1999.

Many of these publications are available at your local careers advice service and/or at a main public library. As indicated, some can be visited on-line.

# JOBHUNTING AGENCIES

There is an almost bewildering array of agencies available to help you find a job, ranging from the not-for-profit Jobcentre at one end to the competitive private recruitment agencies at the other.

The agencies offer a whole range of different services, some serving primarily your interests, others serving specific employers.

## JOBCENTRES

A source of information, often about mainly local jobs. They do offer vacancies suitable for graduates. Watch out for plans for job vacancies to go on-line by early 2000 (www.employmentservice.gov.uk). A must if you register unemployed after finals and a very good source of information about immediate access jobs while you are planning your longer-term future. Like other State-sponsored agencies, one of the main advantages is the service is free.

## RECRUITMENT CONSULTANTS

Recruitment consultants often take over a large part of the process on behalf of employers. They are used by around 15 per cent of the major companies to, for example, handle advertising and sift applications. Therefore, our first contact with the organization itself may only occur at first interview stage. The employer is probably being charged between 10 and 25 per cent of your first year's salary.

Don't confuse these with advertising consultants who produce the glossy graduate recruitment brochures and showy adverts. They are paid for filling the vacancy and so may not have your career plans at heart. On the other hand, they aim for repeat business and may genuinely aim to make a good match. Any human resources practitioner can tell you they cover a range, including the good, the bad and the ugly!

## EMPLOYMENT AGENTS

This group of agencies are the commercial agents that offer to help you find a job. You can register with them, leaving your details, and they will search their client base and scan job vacancy publications on your behalf, often for a fee. The better-quality agencies will provide a comprehensive service of career choice, CV production and help with applications. They may also brief you on interview tactics.

If you do decide to use an agency, check:

▶ what the costs and charges are and whether it is you or the employer who pays;

▶ how they match your job requirements to the vacancies they have;

- ▶ where the vacancies come from;
- ▶ how much help they will give you with CV preparation and application form filling;
- ▶ the timescale – do you have a fixed period to find a job?;
- ▶ are there any extra costs if you are offered a job but turn it down?

In many cases, commission makes up a significant proportion of staff salaries, so there may be a conflict of interests in getting you placed quickly rather than necessarily appropriately.

## DEDICATED GRADUATE SEARCH AGENCIES

Some universities are now providing specialist graduate agencies and have dedicated graduate recruitment services. In most cases, the service is free to graduates. You are given access to an extensive database of companies with graduate opportunities.

# HEADHUNTERS LOOKING FOR BRIGHT YOUNG THINGS

The domain of headhunting has been most widely used to fill top management posts. The agencies prefer to be called 'Executive search' agents. Headhunters are often part of a recruitment consultancy and, traditionally, they approach individuals already in employment.

From an employer's point of view, that there are increasing numbers of undergraduates, mystifying degree subjects and modules and 200 universities is making it hard to find the right people. Indeed as one survey put it, 'like finding a needle in a haystack'. Some employers therefore decide to approach students who are studying subjects they view as relevant at universities they know and respect. Adam's story was recorded in *People Management* journal in 1999.

---

**CASE STUDY**  **Adam Williams, at Durham, on headhunting**

---

Adam Williams was flattered, not to say amazed, when headhunters acting for a management consultancy approached him during his final year at the University of Durham. He and around 12 other undergraduates had been recommended by tutors at Durham to the headhunters Moloney Search.

Adam had an initial screening interview before receiving job offers from the company's client.

Two years on, Adam is with the same employer and is set to make management consultancy his career. Adam doubts that he would have applied to the firm if he hadn't been approached:

'Having somebody come to you and say, "Have you considered this, because you seem to fit our profile?" helped me move to where I am now.'

---

There are many other agencies engaged in headhunting for dozens of employers who approach hundreds, if not by now, thousands of graduates. Of course, head-hunting is generally a method adopted by organizations in sectors where there is intense competition between employers for students. Few of us are in that enviable position.

# OTHER APPROACHES BY EMPLOYERS

Another growing trend is for an employer to target students in a particular department or on a certain course. This was an approach favoured by 45 per cent of graduate recruiters surveyed in 1998 (1998 survey by the Association of Graduate Recruiters), so keep your eyes open – it could be happening in a corridor near you!

If employers can target specific universities and departments, then why shouldn't you target *them*. Read on for proactive jobhunting techniques.

# THE CREATIVE JOB SEARCH

Most of the discussion so far has focused on responding to advertised job vacancies. Many pre- and postgraduate students successfully find jobs using more creative approaches. These can range from the complete 'cold call' to diplomatic massaging of existing social, family, work experience or academic networks.

Many jobs are not formally advertised because:

▶ the employer receives enough approaches from people like you to save a fortune in recruitment costs;

▶ they already have strong links with university departments and tutors – via work placements and so on, so, for example, an organization may be impressed by your work during a summer placement, project or assignment;

▶ the job doesn't exist yet, but you can convince them they need you;

▶ your network lets you know when someone is leaving a job so you can fill the gap before the job is advertised.

Another reason for taking a direct approach is that many employers do not fill all their vacancies! Research evidence points to a well-established annual problem – a shortfall in certain areas.

---

**Employers can't get enough**

---

Every year employers find it difficult to find enough good candidates to fill the following positions:

1 in 6 scientific and technical jobs;
1 in 6 engineering jobs;
1 in 6 research and development jobs;
1 in 8 management trainee jobs;
1 in 10 IT/computing jobs;
1 in 14 buying, marketing and selling jobs.

---

# NETWORKING – THE HIDDEN JOB MARKET

The notion of approaching someone you don't know and asking for help and advice leaves most of us feeling uncomfortable. Such apprehension is a quite normal reaction to risking, at best, embarrassment, at worst, outright rejection.

However, think for a moment how you feel when someone asks you for help. Don't you find that you want to offer some help and advice, even feel quite proud that they approached you? Anyway, networking is not the same as contacting total strangers.

---

### ACTIVITY 14.1    Identify your network

Use the following headings to identify contacts you already have.

**Family and friends**
Immediate family
Other relatives
Neighbours
Friends
People you are at university with – their friends and family

**University**
Professors
Lecturers, in your subject and nearby
Your tutor
Postgraduates
Careers advisers
Research assistants, postgraduates

**Clubs/leisure activities**
Church/religious groups
Sports clubs – other members (their friends and families)

**Work**
Term-time work – your manager, contacts, colleagues
Summer placement – line manager, colleagues

**Professional contacts**
Bank manager
Doctor, dentist
Solicitor
Landlord
Student adviser
Professional societies
Recruitment agencies

---

Look at this list and identify those you feel most able to contact initially. When you have developed your skills and experience, you can broaden your approach.

A network can give you:

- ▶ advice about career options;
- ▶ a realistic picture of a profession or job;
- ▶ ideas you may not have considered;
- ▶ a good understanding of a role/business;
- ▶ advice about your CV;
- ▶ introductions to other people;
- ▶ referrals to people who may have a job to offer you.

## HOW TO NETWORK

'My name is Emma Newton. George Evans from Sell. Co. suggested that I call you. I am interested in developing a career in marketing. George mentioned you have a lot of experience working in that field and in recruiting staff.'

Depending on your relationship, you can write or phone people on your list. If you phone, be clear about what you are asking for – one or more of the items listed above might be a good starting point.

Start by mentioning the name of your contact and how/why you have been referred.

'I wonder if I could ask for a few minutes of your time for some advice about my CV and how to get started? Could we arrange to meet up at some point soon/in the next week or two?'

You could use this approach to ask to work-shadow someone for a few days, help with a project and gain work experience. Once this contact has met you, they may be able to find or create a job for you or be happy to give you a referral to someone else who can.

Don't forget that an increasingly large number of employers use networking to reach undergraduates, often speaking to teachers and tutors. Doors may open more easily than you think. You can use this networking approach throughout your undergraduate days to gain career-relevant experience. It can help you decide on your career and find out inside information about different employers. Add networking to your list of personal skills.

# THE SPECULATIVE APPROACH

You can contact an organization 'on spec' by sending a CV and covering letter. Sending out bulk mail and a standard letter to a large number of people, even using mail merge techniques, has questionable results. It's generally far better to select and individualize letters to a smaller number of carefully targeted individuals.

## HOW TO DO IT

Your letter should outline your skills, what you can offer, what problems you can solve, relevant experience and, indirectly, perhaps your willingness to arrange a short-term contract. After all, some temporary jobs turn into permanent jobs. See the next chapter for examples of speculative letters.

You will need to do some basic research into each organization, and phone them to ask for the name of the person responsible for recruitment. You should then telephone them a short while after they will have received your letter, asking to discuss it and your CV with a view to arranging a first meeting.

When you get through:

► begin with a brief summary of your letter – they are unlikely to have it to hand;

► respect the fact that you are talking to a busy person – don't waste their time;

► try to build an initial rapport – get them to talk as well;

► if you encounter a secretary, be polite – they are very powerful people – and tell them you are expecting to speak to Mr/Ms X, but if X is busy, ask them to look in the diary and suggest a suitable time to speak to them.

Once you have met your speculative contact, they may be able to find or create a job for you or refer you on. This method is particularly useful for ensuring work experience for summer holidays and can lead to a permanent job in due course.


## SUMMARY

► Develop your own jobhunting strategy based on the type of job you are targeting, your resources (especially time) and your analysis of the competition.


## SIGNPOSTS TO MORE HELP

www.jobworld.co.uk

A useful site for jobs in IT, finance, management consulting, manufacturing and engineering.

www.monster.com

US-based job site but has useful career centre and CV make-over tips.

www.stepstone.co.uk

For jobs in UK and Europe plus career and job-hunting advice.

## A winning application conveys one message: 'I am the person you are looking for.'

**In this chapter, you will:**

☐ learn about the varieties of application;

☐ find out how to make a winning application;

☐ discover guidelines for handling questions on standard and employers' application forms;

☐ be able to draw ideas from worked examples;

☐ see how to match yourself to the selection criteria;

☐ get some hot tips on stylish presentation.

**In the activities:**

**15.1** Are you the person they want?

**15.2** Match your personal profile to the job

**15.3** Presentation – how to achieve a professional finish

# VARIETIES OF APPLICATIONS

The world of graduate work is changing rapidly. Many of the traditional routes into typical graduate jobs are still open, but there are new ports of entry and new procedures. The Standard Application Form (SAF) is still in use and can now be downloaded from: www.prospects.csu.ac.uk/pd/dwnload/saf.htm. However, in many cases it is now being eclipsed by the growth of the tailor-made employers' application form (EAF). This chapter focuses on the skills and knowledge needed to complete both types of forms.

Many small and medium-sized enterprises (SMEs) prefer you to apply using CV and covering letter rather than a form – the golden rule is to check what is required. Rapid expansion of the Internet has brought with it new on-line varieties of job application, not just for jobs in IT and myriad on-line recruitment agencies. The on-line versions generally require a CV rather than the tailor-made employer application forms, so this topic is included in Chapter 16.

The same rules apply to applications for work experience and placement opportunities. In most cases, employers now use the same selection criteria, and they recognize work experience is a sneak preview of your potential suitability for a full-time role after graduation.

# MAKING A GOOD APPLICATION TAKES TIME, ENERGY AND THOUGHT

Making an application is a big step. Many forms may appear to have been designed along the same lines as a medieval instrument of torture, extracting blood, sweat and tears! You can help yourself make the whole process a worthwhile activity by ensuring that you have the right preparation, planning and execution. Making a good application takes time, energy and thought, but the effort will be worth it. You can set yourself apart from the droves of eager candidates who will be keen to get through this first round.

---

**What other students say about making applications**

'An absolute nightmare, far too long and time-consuming!'

'Many forms have taken me literally hours and hours ... you have to be really interested in the job to bother.'

'Making applications takes so long that, after having a go at three or four, I decided to put the whole job search thing off until after I have graduated.'

'I learned a lot about myself as I reflected on my time at school, work experiences and hobbies. I got quicker at filling them in. I used the same bank of stories and examples over and over, just changing the emphasis according to the questions asked.'

'I worked in a sort of syndicate group with friends interested in the same organizations and careers. We helped each other get the hang of it.'

---

Employers face a very difficult problem in selecting employees. They have limited time and resources to cope with the large number of students and graduates that apply for their jobs. Competition is fierce, with over 100 applicants for many jobs. Employers only want a face-to-face interview with candidates who have true potential. Have you got what they are looking for?

# JOB APPLICATIONS IN CONTEXT

Any activity concerned with actually making a formal job application should have already involved you in undertaking substantial background research. After this point, it becomes much more explicitly a process of two-way communication. Just to review, you should by now have developed an understanding of:

▶ yourself – your **SHAPE**, that is, your Skills, Hopes, Ambitions, Personality and Experience;

▶ the job or role, especially the skills and personal attributes required;

▶ the employing organization;

▶ the industry or sector generally.

Your knowledge of these will help you ensure that there is a good match between your skills and job expectations and your prospective employers' requirements.

This matching principle is the solid foundation on which you can build your marketing strategy. The essential prerequisite of any marketing campaign is to know your product (you) and your customer (your potential employer). If you are actually at the application stage for a specific job, you may find it helpful to stop and check that you have an accurate picture of what the employer is looking for. Activity 15.1 provides you with an opportunity to do just that.

Make sure you list everything. The glossy graduate recruitment information should give you a steer. If application is by EAF, the questions set will also give you good clues as to what the organization sees as important.

## DO YOU HAVE WHAT THEY ARE LOOKING FOR?

If not, reconsider whether or not it's worth applying. You may be better devoting your time and effort to jobs where you clearly meet the criteria.

If you do broadly meet the criteria, keep the notes you have made in Activity 15.1 for the next stage of completing the application form, where you link the job spec to your own personal profile.

Gather together all the information you have about the job or role you are interested in. Some organizations actually provide a job description (especially in the public sector) or person specification. This is rarer in the private sector. However, most employers do want you to have a clear picture of what they are looking for – it streamlines the process for everyone.

On a large piece of paper – A4 at least – write down everything you know about the job requirements by the various attributes.

| Attributes | Stated as essential | Desirable |
|---|---|---|
| Education and qualifications | Such as specific A levels, minimum UCAS points | Certain course modules |
| Skills | Technical, IT, language, handling machinery | Driving licence |
| Work experience | Previous related employment, placement experience | Related term-time working, demonstration of interest in the career |
| Personal attributes | Qualities stated in the job advert, such as motivation, independence, achievement, orientation, teamwork | Other qualities you know are needed in this job/ career/ industry |

# LIES, DAMNED LIES AND JOB APPLICATIONS?

In most organizations, there is some distance between the actual job advertised and those organizing the recruitment and selection process. This can lead to a Chinese whispers effect, so the real job on offer may end up being very different to the one advertised in the glossy brochures by HQ. Employer branding strategies can also build up your expectations of an organization and the jobs on offer – the reality can be disappointing. This is not necessarily intentional deception on the part of the employer.

Selection is a two-way process, so you may even contribute to some of the problems of the selection yourself. This may be a deliberate impression management approach or wholly unintentional.

## SINS OF EXAGGERATION AND OMISSION?

Manipulating the truth and giving a false impression can involve exaggeration of facts, omission of facts or plain lying. Students and graduates do this for a number of reasons. Some believe it is acceptable because everyone else does it, suggesting that integrity is out of date. Most of us would probably draw the line at total outright lies about qualifications, but how much 'hyperbole' is permitted? Is it true that everyone lies on their CV?

Recent research does indicate that qualifications are often enhanced, both in terms of grades and numbers. The SAF form makes such massaging tricky as they specifically ask you to list the dates and grades of all the examinations that qualified you for your course, whatever the outcome. Facts can be massaged, duration of jobs stretched, periods of unemployment reframed as self-employment, research or further study. Job titles and responsibilities may be enlarged. False claims, therefore, can abound.

### Why do it?

There are huge pressures to perform and achieve. These can be internal pressures and desires to gain access to a particular career or employing organization. Exaggeration is usually underpinned by a belief that telling the truth would not be good enough. This view is reinforced by a belief that everyone else is doing it.

You may have a false self-image, exaggerate strengths, overlook weaknesses. Some may even suffer from the reverse problem and not present themselves favourably enough! You may unwittingly give misleading answers to questions posed on the forms because the questions are confusing, leading or difficult.

## TOWARDS AN ETHICAL FRAMEWORK FOR JOB APPLICATIONS

You may be interested to know that the Association of Graduate Recruiters (AGR), the NUS and the careers service (AgCAS) have produced a code of practice for all concerned. You can find a copy of it in the *Prospects* directory, available from your local careers advisory service.

## APPLICATION FORMS AS WEEDING

The function of the application form in the mind of the employer is to act as a screening device to sift out unsuitable candidates at the first hurdle. Employers vary in the numbers of applications they allow through to interview stage. The selection ratio (the proportion that go on to interview) can be anywhere from 10 to 70 per cent. Some employers or careers attract enormous numbers of applications. This has resulted in a trend towards self-screening stages, on-line or by letter, to deter those without the necessary qualifications from bothering to apply.

The initial sifting of formal applications may be undertaken by the employer or, commonly, by an agency specially recruited to undertake the early screening stage on the graduate recruiter's behalf. Consequently, the application form is a crucial part of jobhunting success. The initial sift will usually be based on biographical information contained in the form, including, but not limited to, past academic attainments and anticipated results.

Most employers mark your application form with their assessment of your suitability with brief reasons. You may be rated according to a system similar to the one shown below:

A – strong candidate – definitely invite to next stage of the selection process;

B – good candidate – possibly invite to next stage of the selection process;

C – acceptable candidate, but does not adequately meet selection criteria – not to be taken further;

D – unacceptable candidate – reject.

Some organizations use computer scanning techniques and may produce an arithmetical assessment. If you are rejected and want to know why, these assessment methods enable the organization to give you the feedback you need.

# MAKING WINNING APPLICATIONS

The golden rule for making a winning application is that you start with a good match between your personal profile (your **SHAPE**) and the employer's requirements. Before putting pen to paper, you will have completed your self-assessment, produced your personal skills profile and thought about your work experience and skills as a package.

## WHAT GOES INTO AN APPLICATION FORM?

The application form and CV have a great deal in common – they are both your main means of selling yourself to the selector. Both the SAF and the EAF are directed to specific topic areas and themes or questions. They are usually at least five pages long and some take on marathon-like proportions.

Standardized forms need not mean standard answers. This is your opportunity to be creative, imaginative and set yourself apart. You must also ensure you press the right buttons, especially when completing the growing number of competence- or criteria-based application forms. You need to answer each question fully and properly. Your objective is to ensure that you have presented clear evidence that you possess all the qualities and skills they want.

Think through the following sequence:

► identify the job requirements;

► create your own career **SHAPE** profile;

- check that these match;
- reassess your profile – is there anything you can add;
- does anything need to be omitted?;
- do you have any better stories or examples? – try brainstorming;
- can you reframe any past experiences to make them more relevant?

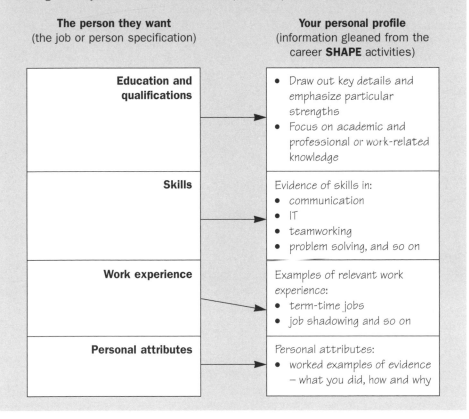

**ACTIVITY 15.2  Match your personal profile to the job**

You can do this exercise by placing the chart you completed in Activity 15.1 on the person they want alongside your **SHAPE** profile created in the activities you completed in the first four chapters. Use a highlighter pen to check that you have made reference to every key selection criterion – identify the gaps and fill them.

The key to making a great application for a job is to ensure you match your personal profile to the job. You can do this very practically by creating a job profile chart and matching this to your own career **SHAPE** or personal profile, as shown below.

**The person they want**
(the job or person specification)

**Your personal profile**
(information gleaned from the career **SHAPE** activities)

| Education and qualifications | • Draw out key details and emphasize particular strengths<br>• Focus on academic and professional or work-related knowledge |
| Skills | Evidence of skills in:<br>• communication<br>• IT<br>• teamworking<br>• problem solving, and so on |
| Work experience | Examples of relevant work experience:<br>• term-time jobs<br>• job shadowing and so on |
| Personal attributes | Personal attributes:<br>• worked examples of evidence – what you did, how and why |

## SO, WHAT SHOULD AN SAF APPLICATION FORM INCLUDE?

### Basic details

The first page of the SAF (and most EAFs) requires the essential biographical details – Personal details, Education, Qualifications. This is usually the least painful part of the process. You should really produce a master copy in your personal portfolio for handy reference.

### Work experience, interests and achievements

The personal details section is usually followed by some blend of questions about employment and work experience and your interests and achievements. In an SAF, you are invited to explain your achievements in relation to both work and spare-time activities and hobbies.

Many forms also ask a specific question about your preferred geographical location and level of mobility. Take this question seriously – some employers require you to be mobile to fit in with, for example, a rotational training scheme. Check this out. It is OK to say you would prefer to be in London – your prospective employer will want to know and may be able to accommodate your wishes. Employers are interested in what you did, but even more interested in what you achieved or learned from the experience. In your answers, focus particularly on the learning outcomes. Choose stories and examples that illustrate how well you fit their requirements.

Sell yourself, but make sure your arguments are properly targeted. Try to ensure you present a balanced view of yourself, mixing team things and independence, being competitive but also sociable and fun. A worked example is given in Figure 15.1 to demonstrate what I mean.

The information you provide in answers to questions about work or other activities has multiple purposes. If you get through this first stage, it will be a basis for the interview.

### Specific evidence

Most modern application forms include a number of questions about how you have behaved under certain circumstances in the past. The Deloitte & Touche graduate recruitment brochure 1999 gives the reason for these, which is that 'your previous patterns of behaviour are good evidence of likely future trends'. Many recruiters now think this way.

The SAF refers to this part of the application form as 'Specific evidence' and homes in on three key areas. These are discussed because they are core questions, included in some way on most forms you will be filling in. Behavioural or competence-based questions are designed to provide you with an opportunity to give evidence that you meet the selection criteria. Examples should reflect a balance between your studies, work experience, interests and other activities.

## Employment and work experience

Please describe briefly any work (whether paid or unpaid) which you have undertaken. Highlight (*) the two most relevant and note what you achieved.

| From – To month/year | | Employer | Job title and responsibilities | Achievements |
|---|---|---|---|---|
| 07/99 | 09/99 | Sainsbury's | Product supply assistant<br>Logistics<br>Quality control<br>Product availability | Learned to use SAP<br>Developed customer service awareness<br>Helped cost-efficiency |
| 09/98 | 07/99 | Café Vert | Waiter (part time)<br>Serving customers<br>Receiving payments | Promoted to senior waiter<br>Communication skills<br>Numeracy<br>Handling money<br>Customer relations<br>Hygiene regulations |

## Geographical location

Do you have a strong preference for a particular location? If so, give details.

I am fully mobile but would prefer to work in London.

## Personal interests and achievements

Use the space below to describe **with dates (year)** any spare-time activities. Include organizing, leading or group activities. Those requiring initiative, creativity or giving intellectual development are also of interest.

**University Hockey Society**
Club Secretary – organization, personal discipline, planning
Competitions – teamwork (or leadership), competitive
Social life – sociability, sense of humour, outgoing

**Industrial Society**
Full member – business awareness
Site visits – motivation, initiative
Campus lectures – personal development

FIGURE 15.1 **Example of balanced presentation in a SAF (standard application form)**

## Specific Evidence

The following questions are designed to encourage you to provide evidence of specific abilities. Your examples can be taken from your education, work experience, placements or spare-time or other voluntary activities but do not write solely about course-work.

### Planning, implementation and achieving results:

Describe a challenging project, activity or event which you have planned and taken through to a conclusion. Include your objective, what you did, any changes you made to your plan and state how you measured your success.

**Tips**  This question is basically designed to draw out examples of behaviour in the two key competences of planning and achieving. The selector will be looking for:

- your ability to set goals for yourself and others;
- how you kept focused on the objective and avoided distractions;
- your adaptability, ability and willingness to change to meet different situations;
- being able to think strategically and analytically;
- proactive and results-oriented.

---

### Influencing, communication and teamwork:

Describe how you have achieved a goal through influencing the actions or opinions of others (perhaps in a team context). What were the circumstances? What did you do to make a difference? How do you know the result was satisfactory?

**Tips**  The selector will be looking for:

- ability to accurately assess who are the key people to influence;
- recognition that you have used different styles and approaches with different people;
- ability to influence without causing resentment, know the dangers;
- a good listener, can choose and select an appropriate form of communication;
- recognition of the different roles needed for a team to work well;
- awareness of anti-team behaviour and ability to avoid it;
- goal and achievement orientation – results do matter!

(You may find the section on teamworking in Chapter 4 helpful.)

---

### Analysis, problem solving and creative thinking:

Describe a difficult problem that you have solved. State how you decided which were the critical issues. Say what you did and what your solution was. What other approaches could you have taken?

**Tips**  The selector will be looking for:

- ability to break a problem down into its main elements in a logical way;
- being vigilant in looking for underlying causes, making deductions from the evidence;
- evaluation of the options and making decisions;
- recognition that there were other options, how you decided against them;
- ability to come up with novel and innovative ideas;
- being able to look at things differently.

**FIGURE 15.1**  *Continued*

## Specific skills

You may be asked to give details of any other skills you have. Here, include IT skills and give details of the programs and applications you can use. Having a driving licence and languages should also be included.

## Career choice

Employers want to know why you believe you are suited to a career in X. Most students and graduates do very badly when answering this question on the application form and at interview, so it's worth spending some time thinking about what you will say. Make sure you cover the following points in your reply:

► what attracts you to the career;
► how this career/job matches with your personal profile and interests;
► particular familiarity with the job – work experience, connections, your research;
► what is special about this particular job;
► what is attractive about this employer.

You will be asked questions about your availability. Be honest, because this information is designed to help the employer to offer you an interview that doesn't clash with other arrangements, interviews or exams.

Most organizations now include an equal opportunities monitoring form, which is intended to ensure that recruitment procedures do not discriminate. These go to personnel departments and do not play a part in the selection procedure.

You are usually asked to name two referees. One should be academic, the other preferably someone professional who you know from work or via your other activities. Choose someone who knows you well and respects you. Make sure you ask them first, don't do it retrospectively! If you get through to interview, you should give your referees a copy of your application form so they can choose to comment on salient facts about you.

Finally, sign the form, fill in the declaration and date it. For a truly organized and professional finish, try to make sure the date on the application form matches that on the covering letter. Take a copy of the finished masterpiece for your records before sending it, investing in first class post when you do.

## WHAT ABOUT EAF FORMS – HOW DO YOU HANDLE TRICKY QUESTIONS?

What delights have EAF forms got in store? The seven basic principles of completing your application form (see pages 172 and 173) should serve you well, whatever the question. Here are a few examples of typical EAF questions drawn from the 1999 crop:

**'Please describe your most outstanding non-academic achievement'**  *(Shell)*

**'How would your friends/colleagues describe you in five words.'**  *(Shell)*

'Please analyze fully the main consequences of the increase in global communications (use your own analysis – we do not expect you to research this area).'     *(Shell)*

'Who encouraged you to apply to Deloitte & Touche?'     *(Deloitte & Touche)*

'Describe an experience when you have had to cope with a changing situation. Help us to understand how you dealt with it.'     *(Rank Hovis McDougall)*

'Tell us about a project or activity you have been involved in that has been particularly interesting. Describe your personal contribution and the impact the activity had on you.'     *(Arthur Andersen)*

'Describe a situation where you have had to persuade and challenge other people's opinions.'     *(Tesco – Excel Programme Application Form)*

Thinking through answers to questions posed by organizations that are in a similar sector or industry as the one you are applying to can also help you prepare for interview. This gives a good indication of the way different employers think.

---

**ACTIVITY 15.3    Presentation – how to achieve a professional finish**

Fill in a spare form following the seven golden rules of applications for a stylish and professional look.

▶ **Follow the instructions**
You would be amazed at the number of applicants who don't. In an SAF, for example, you are asked to *print* your personal details and to list your most recent qualifications first. Many people miss these details and write as normal and list their qualifications chronologically. Demonstrate your attention to detail by noticing all the instructions given. This is part of the assessment.

▶ **Have a dress rehearsal**
Make sure you have a spare SAF (or a photocopy where it is an EAF) and use that for a dry run. However tempted you feel to shortcut this process, resist!! Never, ever go straight for the finished version. I know you may have essay or exam preparation deadlines looming, but it is a false economy.

▶ **Complete the whole form**
It may be tempting to just write 'See attached CV', but never do this. If the form is being computer scanned, this can result in its immediate rejection. If the information sought is not in the required slot, you go into the bin. Second, it is annoying for the person selecting you. Just think of them, wading through endless reams of paper. Turning over several pages to find the appropriate bit of your CV can be a total turn off. Don't risk it. Also, what would this say about how motivated you are to get the job. Avoid giving the impression of having a short cut, easy life mentality.

*continued*

### ▶ Writing

If you are blessed with attractive, neat handwriting, you are already ahead. If not, take action now. You can improve your handwriting by practising; pay attention to letter size and spacing, too. Keep it straight by putting lined paper underneath. If it is hard to read, try writing more slowly and think about the pressure you use – this often increases when you feel anxious. Use a good pen, try experimenting with real ink or gel roller balls. Find out which helps you most.

Some European-based organizations actually employ handwriting experts to study the writing styles of applicants as part of the selection process. Graphology is based on the notion that handwriting reveals something about your personality. Graphologists pay attention to the things I have described above – the line and formation of letters, pressure.

Dotting the i's and crossing the t's takes on a whole new meaning! For example, people with loads of energy often place the i dot well to the right. People with a bad temper apply substantial pressure and often cross their t's very heavily. If you are making an application to a French company, you should take handwriting analysis seriously. Recent research indicates that around 50–75 per cent of employers use it to select managers and executives! The number of UK employers to have adopted handwriting analysis is less clear. Some studies suggest that around 5 per cent of the big graduate recruiters use it, but many try to keep its use confidential.

This perhaps explains why employers object if you get someone else to fill in the form for you – just be careful who you ask!

### ▶ Grammar and spelling

There are certain words that are hard to spell. The most common errors involve driving licences (beware American/English Spellcheckers). Get someone else to check your grammar and spelling – it is very hard to spot your own errors.

### ▶ Proofreading

It is not possible to proofread yourself. Do it, then do it again and always ask a friend to help you. Do not rely on your own judgement, unless you are the English Language expert of the block in which case you can market your proofreading skills and add this to your work experience portfolio.

### ▶ Fragile, handle with care

Handle application forms with respect. Avoid coffee/beer stains and fingerprints. You would be amazed at how even the smell of cigarette smoke can linger and be a big turn-off to a health-conscious graduate recruiter. Don't risk it!

# ON-LINE APPLICATIONS AND THE INTERNET

The Internet is an increasingly useful means of finding job vacancies, but it is still a relatively immature arena with a number of problems and pitfalls. These are discussed in more detail in the next chapter about writing. The key points are summarized below. Access to personal information is not easily restricted. Be cautious about including personal details, such as home address, phone number. Never post up details of when you will be away on holiday.

The technology for designing and screening your application is improving all the time, but many systems have problems identifying crucial data. Many of the databases used by employers use text-based processing systems, which can be very limited in their ability to extract important information. A more refined type of technology based on artificial intelligence is available but not yet widely applied due to extra costs. This can mean you get screened in for unsuitable jobs and screened out for others.

On-line applications are usually accompanied by guidelines: read them. They may tell you to use particular abbreviations or buzzwords. Follow the instructions to get the best benefit you can from the system. If you want to know more about finding jobs on-line, go to Chapter 7 and read under the heading. 'Job vacancies on the Internet – what it can do and what it can't'.

## AND FINALLY ...

This is the moment you have been longing for – the application form is complete! Invest in a good-quality A4 envelope and resist the temptation to turn your work of art into a concertina and – send it first class. Now all you can do is wait.

## SUMMARY

▶ Making an application on either an SAF or EAF requires considerable skill and thought.

▶ You will need to adhere to the matching principle that guides this book. Review your career shape and see how it compares to those required by prospective employers.

▶ The way that job applications are structured makes it hard to evade the truth. For example, you are usually asked to give the results of all exams you have taken, not just those you passed.

▶ You will need to pay special attention to competence-based application form questions – these require you to give evidence of occasions when you demonstrated particular skills and abilities.

▶ This chapter has also outlined ways to handle questions about career choice and provided guidelines for handling tricky questions.

▶ Use the section on producing a professional finish as a checklist to help you produce a winning application.

# SIGNPOSTS TO MORE HELP

## Further reading

The following are available from most higher education careers advisory services.

Phillips, C. (1997) *Making Wizard Applications*, GTI series.

AgCAS (1997) 'Making applications' – 24-page booklet covering CVs and application forms.

## Advice

Your local careers advisory service will provide help for undergraduate and postgraduate students. Many of them also provide help and advice to graduates under a national agreement. Contact your local office for details of your entitlement.

There are also useful mini articles in the graduate directories, such as *Prospects* and *Get*, and detailed occupational advice in the AgCAS booklets and in the Ivanhoe Career Guide (www.insidecareers.co.uk).

## Appendix

See the section entitled Careers decisions, jobhunting skills and information.

**Your CV is both a reflection of your past and a signpost to your future.**

**In this chapter, you will:**

☐ find out what a CV is;

☐ learn how and when to use a CV;

☐ develop a CV strategy;

☐ discover what should appear in CVs for students, graduates and first job changers;

☐ find types of CVs with examples;

☐ be given insider tips on CV content and presentation;

☐ find out about alternative CVs and 'attachments';

☐ learn all about covering letters.

**In the activities:**

**16.1** Do you need to update your CV?

**16.2** Designing your own CV

# WHAT IS A CV?

*Curriculum vitae* literally means 'the course of life'. The traditional view of a CV suggests that its purpose is to provide a prospective employer with a clear, concise picture of your suitability for a job or role within their organization. There is far more to it than that of course. In many ways, a CV is a unique document because it attempts to provide evidence of past achievements and simultaneously reveals your hopes and ambitions for the future. A CV is essentially aspirational.

The future orientation of the CV reflects the optimism that so often permeates the graduate recruitment literature to which you are responding. Organizations have aspirations too! The CV does not exist in a vacuum, rather, it is derived from the language, etiquette and expectations of the graduate recruitment arena. Your CV cannot contain the whole truth about you – if it is well constructed, it will provide a foretaste to whet the recruiters' appetite, leaving them wanting more.

Writing a CV is another point in the selection process where you must reflect on your past life experiences, your achievements and point towards your hopes for the future. You may have already completed the self-assessment exercises in Part 1 and considered your career **SHAPE**, so you are now well placed to move to this key stage of the process.

Just like the SAFs and EAFs, your curriculum vitae, or resumé, is of huge importance in your quest for a great graduate job. It needs to achieve the perfect balance between truly representing who you are and being sensitive to exactly what the employer is looking for. This is part of the matching principle that you encountered first earlier and that runs throughout this book.

Your CV is your main marketing tool to convince the buyer that you are the one who will meet their needs. This is the moment to really sell yourself, to highlight all your best features and show how you will be of benefit as a future employee.

## A WORD TO FIRST-TIMERS . . .

This may be the first time you have written a CV, or at least the first time you have written one as an undergraduate or recent graduate. You may find this difficult to do. Writing a CV is very demanding – it requires you to really know yourself, then understand the job and employer. The time you spend doing this is very well invested because you are likely to need the skills of self-evaluation again and again in the years ahead – it is a good investment in your future.

## AND THOSE PRACTISED IN THE ART

If you are an undergraduate or graduate already involved in jobhunting, you may have written a CV, even quite recently. However, you and your quest for a great job will be constantly changing. Your recent experiences of work, a summer job, a chat in the pub … these things can all have a big impact on self-image and career aspirations. This is especially true for graduates who are seeking a second job, having found that the first one didn't meet their expectations.

Make sure your CV still represents you. Keep it up to date, check it against the best practice benchmarks outlined throughout this chapter. For now, though, check whether or not you need to update your CV by completing Activity 16.1.

<table>
<tr><td colspan="3">ACTIVITY 16.1  Do you need to update your CV?</td></tr>
<tr><td colspan="3">Date my CV was prepared _ _ / _ _ / _ _</td></tr>
<tr><td colspan="3">Since then, have you (please tick the appropriate boxes):</td></tr>
<tr><td>1. gained any further qualifications<br>(driving licence, for example)</td><td>Yes ❏</td><td>No ❏</td></tr>
<tr><td>2. gained any further skills<br>(IT, new applications, for example)</td><td>Yes ❏</td><td>No ❏</td></tr>
<tr><td>3. had any further work experience</td><td>Yes ❏</td><td>No ❏</td></tr>
<tr><td>(a)  term-time</td><td>Yes ❏</td><td>No ❏</td></tr>
<tr><td>(b)  holiday</td><td>Yes ❏</td><td>No ❏</td></tr>
<tr><td>(c)  placement</td><td>Yes ❏</td><td>No ❏</td></tr>
<tr><td>(d)  voluntary work or in student groups/sports and so on</td><td>Yes ❏</td><td>No ❏</td></tr>
<tr><td>4. refined your career focus?</td><td>Yes ❏</td><td>No ❏</td></tr>
</table>

If you have answered 'yes' to more than one question, it is worth reviewing your CV.

# HOW AND WHEN TO USE A CV

Use a CV as part of your jobhunting strategy whenever there is no clear instruction to use a form only. The well-known graduate recruiters are not the sole providers of graduate jobs. There are masses of jobs in smaller firms and organizations where the CV still remains the normal *modus operandi*. Use a CV when networking, making targeted applications or cold calling (see Chapter 14 for details of these jobhunting strategies).

Generally, you should not include a CV with an SAF. In addition, most employers who have gone to the trouble of designing their own application form (EAF) will not look favourably on graduates who attach a CV, especially – a real *faux pas* this – if you do this instead of completing the form. If in doubt, ask your prospective employer or careers advisor about protocol.

# DEVELOPING A CV STRATEGY

Another important question you must answer is how will you present yourself? There are no easy answers to this, of course – there is no one best strategy you should adopt, except to match your response to the particular employer and job.

The only exception to this rule is for anyone writing a *generic* CV – one that will be used for a broad range of job applications. The short-term advantage to you is the time saved; the downside is that this CV may just reflect a watered-down version of who you are. Worse still, generic, mass-produced CVs cannot be fine-tuned to communicate using the tone and language of individual job adverts.

# BUILDING A BRILLIANT CV

Constructing a CV can be a rewarding experience and, when completed, will feel like an achievement in itself. The basic ingredients of a CV are:

▶ well-chosen, relevant content
▶ superb presentation.

The following pages offer you guidelines, ideas and worked examples.

## WHAT GOES INTO A CV?

Apart from the basic biographical details, you have huge scope in deciding what to include in your CV and how to include it. The varieties of CV format are discussed below with examples. Here, highlight the six main areas that you should cover. The way you do it and the emphasis you give to each part depends on you and the job you are applying for. The basic building blocks of any CV are shown in Figure 16.1.

| Name |  |
| --- | --- |
| (Personal profile/career objectives – optional) | |
| Personal details | Skills and/or attributes |
| Education/qualifications and professional memberships | Interests/hobbies |
| Work experience and/or achievements Career history | Mobility References |

FIGURE 16.1  The basic building blocks of a CV

## CVs for students, graduates and job changers

The next sections set out best practice in designing your own CV. I recognize students and graduates seeking jobs are diverse – some of you reading this will be second or third or final year under-grads, some postgrads of varying sorts, some already graduated and some in work that is not meeting your expectations. I have tried to draw out the key points for readers in all of these situations below. I hope I have succeeded in giving you the right balance of guidance with scope for your own creativity.

## MAKING A START

First, resist the temptation to write '*Curriculum vitae*' across the top. It is a waste of precious space and won't score you any points, possibly the reverse.

You may have come across CVs that begin with a personal profile statement. These are a matter of taste. Personal profiles usually include three or four short sentences to give a gripping, thumbnail sketch of you. If you do want to put a personal profile in your CV, include a summary of your main areas of *knowledge* (expected degree), *skills* (technical and interpersonal) and *experience.* You may also wish to include a brief mention of your career goals here. This should be an exciting taster of what follows, leaving the selector wanting to read on and find out more about you. Be careful, though, not everyone likes personal profile statements. Don't risk overdoing it. A simpler (and less risky) alternative is to include a concise statement about your career aims.

## PERSONAL DETAILS

What information you provide in your CV is your decision. There are conventions that suggest certain personal information is essential, some at your discretion.

### 'Essential' items

► Surname;

► First name(s);

► Home and term-time addresses;

► Telephone number and e-mail address;

► Date of birth (but not in applications to the USA).

I have a small reservation about putting date of birth in the essential column. Although various agencies are working towards the introduction of anti-age discrimination in the UK, there is no legal protection. There have been one or two leading cases where organizational recruitment practices (such as those of the Civil Service) have been found discriminatory because of age limits, but this has usually been on grounds of indirect sexual discrimination.

### At your discretion

The information in the discretionary category is for you to include where you feel it provides evidence of your suitability over other candidates.

*Marital status*

If you are single, you can use this to convey independence, mobility and flexibility. If married, you could use this to emphasize reliability, teamwork, communication and negotiation skills.

*Dependants*

This is a matter of personal taste. Many include their dependant children or elderly relatives to demonstrate responsibility. If an organization has a high rate of staff turnover and is seeking individuals who are likely to stay around for a few years, this may be seen as a positive attribute. My own experience is that this is more of an advantage to male applicants than to females, due to enduring stereotypes and the social realities of who stays at home when dependants are sick.

## EDUCATION

Recruiters are always interested in your education and exam results.

### University education

Outline the institution at which you studied, the title of your degree and expected (or actual) result. List the subjects you studied, focus on topics of particular relevance to the job you are applying for. You may find it helpful to write yourself a summary of your subjects year by year. This can provide a helpful checklist if you intend to prepare tailored CVs rather than produce a generic, all-purpose one.

### Secondary

List your A levels (or Scottish/European equivalents) and grades.

Depending on your qualification profile, there are a number of approaches you can adopt. If you have a high-flying list of straight As, go ahead, flaunt it. If not, you need not list the details of every GCSE. For example, 8 GCSEs (Grades A–C) can cover a multitude of results! It is often helpful to emphasize that you do have a GCSE in Maths and English. You have more freedom here than in an SAF.

## WORK EXPERIENCE

This category can vary enormously, depending on your individual profile. A mature student with a prior track record or a part-timer presently in work would have more to include here than an undergraduate with minimal term-time or holiday work experience. You can choose a CV format that best suits your personal circumstances and the nature of the job.

If you are a mature student with many years of work experience and possibly the odd change of career direction thrown in, the challenge will be to distil out from all this the key points that are relevant to where you are heading now.

Whatever your work experience, you should aim to include the following information as a minimum:

► dates employed;

► employer;

► job titles plus status – full- or part-time, holiday job and so on

► your role and responsibilities.

My personal preference is for including some information about the skills you developed or what you achieved during this time. Employers are interested in people who learn quickly and get results! You may find it helpful to refer back to Chapter 5 for further information and ideas about assessing and describing past work experience.

## KNOWLEDGE, SKILLS AND ATTITUDES

Use the information at hand to decide how much emphasis to give to your level of job-related knowledge – languages, particular procedures, law and so on. It is increasingly common for employers to state the specific skills and attitudes they are seeking. Generally, these include a blend of:

► intellectual strength;

► problem solving;

► numeracy;

► communication;

► teamworking.

Common attitudes include:

► being highly motivated;

► commitment;

► enthusiasm;

► adaptable

► learn quickly.

A large number of graduate recruiters are now using 'competences' to select staff. These are descriptions of the personal attributes needed to do a job successfully – a mix of skills, attitudes and personality. Try to find out whether or not the organization you are applying to operates a competence approach. You can find out by looking at their recruitment materials. If in doubt, contact their HR or recruitment section and ask. They may not tell you exactly which competences they are looking for, but, speaking to them about the job may give you a good idea of how to target your CV and covering letter. You may also find that the words listed in Table 16.1 are a help as you try to describe yourself in CV language.

**TABLE 16.1  Action words for CVs**

| Communicating | Problem solving | Creating | Achieving |
|---|---|---|---|
| Addressed | Analyzed | Composed | Accomplished |
| Advised | Arranged | Conceived | Achieved |
| Bargained | Assessed | Created | Attained |
| Coordinated | Budgeted | Designed | Concluded |
| Counselled | Checked | Developed | Delivered |
| Demonstrated | Classified | Devised | Distributed |
| Directed | Collated | Discovered | Expanded |
| Encouraged | Composed | Established | Motivated |
| Guided | Conceived | Founded | Performed |
| Influenced | Conducted | Generated | Presented |
| Instructed | Decreased | Implemented | Processed |
| Interviewed | Defined | Initiated | Promoted |
| Led | Distributed | Instituted | Provided |
| Liased | Established | Introduced | Served |
| Marketed | Explained | Invented | Succeeded |
| Mediated | Identified | Launched | Transferred |
| Negotiated | Improved | Led | Overcame |
| Ordered | Investigated | Made | Won |
| Presented | Modernized | Opened | |
| Promoted | Planned | Originated | |
| Proposed | Prepared | Pioneered | |
| Provided | Redesigned | Planned | |
| Recommended | Reduced | Prepared | |
| Represented | Refined | Produced | |
| Resolved | Reviewed | Promoted | |
| Taught | Revised | Sparked | |
| Presented | Scheduled | Started | |
| Lectured | Settled | Transformed | |
| Trained | Simplified | Triggered | |
| | Solved | | |
| | Surmounted | | |
| | Synchronized | | |
| | Uncovered | | |
| | Verified | | |
| | Vetted | | |

# TYPES OF CVS

Although all CVs are composed of similar building blocks, they can be arranged in a wide variety of ways to create different effects. Think about the criteria that the selectors will be using as they sift through the applications for suitable candidates and use a format that will maximize your chances of success. The different styles offer you the opportunity to emphasize your strengths and put other features in the background (or out of the picture altogether). I have provided a brief summary of the features and benefits of the six main CV styles you can choose from.

## CHRONOLOGICAL

This is a traditional approach to CV writing that can be varied according to your preferences. The emphasis is on presenting factual data and an account of your education and work experience so far. The advantages of this type of CV are that it can be used off the peg for most jobs and provides all the information most employers want in a familiar way. The disadvantages are that it does not stand out in a competitive environment and may not emphasize your skills and personality sufficiently for some jobs.

## SKILLS-BASED

The skills-based CV uses the basic building blocks, but places emphasis on the work-related skills you have demonstrated and developed. This approach is particularly suited to responding to advertisements that indicate specific skills are required.

## COMPETENCE-BASED

The competences CV is a close cousin of the skills-based CV. You should only use the term 'competence' when you see it used in an organization's promotional material or web site – otherwise, stick to the term 'skills'.

## TECHNICAL

CVs for technical positions, such as in engineering, IT and telecommunications, should highlight the particular equipment and procedures you have been trained to handle. This means that technical CVs usually include a lot of details about the course of study and refer to the particular theories or approaches taught.

You may want to emphasize the facilities available for your studies to draw attention to your employability. Give precise information. You should also include details of any work experience – again, including precise information about equipment and systems used and what you achieved.

## EXPERIENCE-BASED

If you have substantial work experience, you can use this as a selling point in an experience-based CV. This type of CV can be designed to draw attention to evidence for your suitability for a post from a reverse chronological list of roles you have held in the past. The emphasis is on what you did and how you did it, not on the job titles *per se.* These CVs can be useful when you are very clear about the selection criteria. They can provide an immediate impression of someone who has a great deal of prior experience to bring to the job.

## ACHIEVEMENT-BASED

The focus is on what you have accomplished. This is the CV to use if the job you are applying for requires confidence and action. This is the CV that a results-oriented and determined individual uses! It can be very effective if used by the right person for an achievement-oriented role.

## ACADEMIC

If you are applying for a job in higher education, you may need to emphasize your academic qualifications, research training and any publications. You should refer to conferences you have attended and any papers given, too.

# CV PRESENTATION GUIDELINES

## KEEP IT CONCISE

Your CV should be no longer than two sides of A4. However, you can allow three pages if you are a mature student or have substantial work experience and achievements to outline.

Screening of most CVs is done quickly, so if the key points are on a sixth page, forget it. The selector probably fell asleep during the fourth!

## CLARITY

Make sure the reader can find the information they need at a glance. Don't make them play hide and seek for evidence of your suitability. Use plain English and avoid jargon. Don't assume that the selector will understand abbreviations. Use a sanserif font (ones without tails and curves at the ends of letters) they are easier to read and copy well. The font size should be 10–12 point, with occasional use of a larger point size for headings or your name.

## GOOD APPEARANCE AND DESIGN

Use a good, aesthetically pleasing layout. Leave a margin on the left-hand side so the selector can make notes if they want to. Create attractive spaces around the text. Make it look professional.

## PERSONALIZE EVERY PAGE

CVs may be separated from your covering letter to make screening easier. Make sure that you include your name on every page, perhaps using a header or footer. This has the added advantage of helping the interviewer remember your name if you get to the next stage.

## QUALITY MATERIALS

Use top-quality paper, preferably 100 gsm. Cheap paper is often transparent and can ruin the professional image you are trying to create. Use a laser-printed original, not a photocopy. The organization may well produce a copy in-house if you go forward for interview and a photocopy of a photocopy can be very hard to read. Recruiters have different preferences, but most dislike coloured paper. Pastels, bright and especially fluorescent paper is generally out, unless you are going for a high-profile media or design job where unconventionality is required. Note, however, that many colours are virtually impossible to photocopy.

## SPELLING, GRAMMAR AND PROOFREADING

Get someone else to check your grammar and spelling. Reading through it backwards can help you spot errors that you missed. If you have a spellchecker facility on your computer, make sure it uses the appropriate dictionary. Then, print it off and read it carefully forwards and backwards as often errors show up that you did not spot reading it on screen.

Remember, you cannot overdo the proofreading stage.

# LEARNING POINTS FROM OTHER PEOPLE'S CVS

The next few pages set out two different CV formats. Study these, find out which suits you best, then use it as a framework for your own CV.

## TRADITIONAL, CHRONOLOGICAL CV

This type of CV sets out the information in reverse chronological order.

This focuses the reader on the most recent information. If you have substantial work experience, you should put that first. Otherwise, place your degree prominently and highlight key course modules.

It is usual to produce a two-page CV and that should be the maximum unless, for example, you are writing an academic CV and have a long list of publications to include.

In Figure 16.2, Imran has highlighted both his degree subject and some key modules from the course. This can provide very helpful insights for a prospective recruiter, especially if your degree course title is unfamiliar.

Also, notice that the chronological list of work experience is clear about the responsibilities he had and includes action words that emphasize his achievements. You could also do this using bullet points, which makes it easy to scan read. A useful way to get yourself noticed.

The section on interests helps you to see the social side to Imran, but he has also drawn attention to his teamworking skills, sociability and drive as he has described them.

It is common for undergraduates' CVs to include one academic reference and one personal or character reference, perhaps from your term-time workplace. Imran has chosen to provide references 'on request' which is quite acceptable for most applications.


## SKILLS-BASED CV

A skills-based CV draws attention to the particular skills and abilities needed for a particular type of job. This approach is excellent for applications for a specialist role, but works just as well for more general managerial jobs.

In Figure 16.3, in order to emphasize her employability, Alison has given a considerable amount of prominent space in her CV to the skills section. You could also add interpersonal skills, such as teamworking, to your list. The key is to reflect the criteria highlighted in the job advert.

The 'Career to date' section gives a positive frame of reference to a recruiter, again emphasizing her readiness for work. This section is often called work experience, employment or achievements. Alison has chosen a CV structure that allows her to draw attention to all the evidence of her long-standing career interest and practical achievements together.

In order to keep this kind of CV to just two pages means that the section on her education is very concise.

The 'Enthusiasms' section gives a fresh perspective on hobbies and interests. You notice her considerable talent, but her sense of humour comes through as well, conveying something of her personality.

# Imran Gooljary

## Career objective: to be a human resources management consultant

## PERSONAL DETAILS

*Address:*        30 Larch Grove
Denton
Trowbury
TR7 6XP

*e-mail:*        i.gooljary@freeserve.co.uk

*Telephone:*        Home: 020 7445 4331
Mobile: 0420 262299

*Date of birth:*        09/09/1977

*Nationality:*        British

## EDUCATION/QUALIFICATIONS

1996–99        **Manchester School of Management, UMIST**
BA (Hons) Business Studies, awarded 2:1 2.i

Subjects studied included:

- human resources management;
- international business;
- economics;
- finance;
- industrial relations and employment law.

1989–96        **Denton Secondary School, Trowbury, Essex**
A levels     English (B), history (B), economics (C)

GCSEs     Nine subjects (six As, three Bs), including
maths and English

FIGURE 16.2   Example of a traditional, chronological CV

**RELEVANT WORK EXPERIENCE**

| | |
|---|---|
| Summer 1998 | **Final-year project, 1998** |
| | Summer holiday research project for Super-Market Co. examining the existing staff training programme. |
| | Work responsibilities involved large-scale consultations with HQ and sites and making recommendations to central office. This helped me develop an analytical approach to problem solving. |
| | |
| Summer 1997 | **Summer placement with Bridge Consulting, London** |
| | I conducted a staff opinion survey in conjunction with senior consultants. I processed questionnaire responses and presented the findings to the client. I also created a new client database. In order to be successful, I had to be adaptable, flexible and enjoy a challenge. |
| | |
| 1998–99 | **Quayside Café Bar, Salford** |
| | Part-time waiter and barman |
| | Main duties were serving customers, handling money. Working as part of a small team. |
| | In 1998, spent one week shadowing the Café Manager, attending meetings at HQ. Attended a number of company training courses on safety and food hygiene. |

**PROFESSIONAL QUALIFICATIONS**

Graduate of the Institute of Personnel and Development (Grad.IPD)

British Psychological Society's Certificate of Competence in Testing, Level A and Intermediate Level B

**OTHER SKILLS**

► Windows '95/'98 environment – word processing, spreadsheets, DTP, database, Internet
► Interviewing and research
► Conversational French, basic German
► Qualified to administer ability and personality tests (Certificate from the British Psychological Society)
► Clean driving licence

**INTERESTS**

**Sports**

I am very keen on watersports and have been a member of the university windsurfing club since 1996 and was chairperson during 1998. Windsurfing requires a lot of personal stamina and fitness as well as teamwork – and a sense of humour. I also joined the subaqua club and am presently learning to dive.

**Travelling**

I love travelling and have visited many European countries, including Germany, Switzerland and Poland. This has given me the opportunity to improve my language skills.

**REFERENCES**

To be provided on request

FIGURE 16.2 continued

# Alison Draper

## Science Researcher

**Address**  70 Wavertree Avenue, Shepherds Bush, London W14 3EX

**Phone**  Home: 020 7740 7276
Mobile: 07863 271686 + voicemail

**e-mail**  Home: ali.draper@talk.net

**SKILLS**

**Camera operation**  Regular use of DV cameras, shooting own film, and also for 'Cambridge Red' TV channel
City & Guilds Still Photography course: awarded two distinctions (1993–94)

**Editing**  Edited own short film; trained with Media 100; familiar with AVID

**Radio training**  Trained in using mixing desks, mini-disc recording equipment

**Driving**  Clean driving licence (since 1994)

**Computing**  Fully familiar with both Mac and PC set-ups
Regularly use the Internet
Proficient with MS Office and Claris Works; excellent keyboard skills

**Languages**  Conversational French, basic German and Spanish

**Music**  Can read, transpose and script music
Grade 8 piano and clarinet; Grade 5 theory of music

**CAREER TO DATE**

| | | |
|---|---|---|
| September 1999– | **BBC Science** | **Trainee researcher**: currently researching for *Tomorrow's World* |
| February 1999 | **National Science Week** | Wrote, presented and produced **short film** – *A Beginner's Guide to Geological Time* – as part of an interactive mobile exhibition for local schoolchildren; also on the student team responsible for genesis, organization and **production of the exhibition**, and acted as **publicity officer** for the project |
| 1998-99 | **'Cambridge Red' TV** | On **production team of a weekly student show** on local cable channel. Responsible for coordinating production of short features and culture/arts magazine pieces, as well as creative input for programme content, scripting, filming, presenting and editing |
| 1998 | **Varsity** | **News reporter** for university student newspaper |
| September 1998 | **Yorkshire TV** | **Researcher** on Channel 4 Schools science series 'Scientific Eye' |

**FIGURE 16.3  Example of a skills-based CV**

| August 1998 | 'Television & Young People' Conference | Selected as delegate for conference, the youth wing of the Guardian Edinburgh International Television Festival; included workshop with Uden Associates, **filming and editing a short documentary** on Hibernian FC (within 30 hours!) |
| July 1998 | XYTV | **News researcher** with small independent, working on *First on Five*, scientific strands for **Channel 5 News** |
| July 1998 | 'Media Calling' | **Training course**: Institute of Contemporary Christianity, London, involving camera experience, interviewing techniques |
| June 1998 | *The Daily Telegraph* | National Young Science Writer Awards: **finalist** |
| July 1994 | Central TV | **Work placement**, included local news reporting, editing and studio work |
| April 1994 | *Rotherham Advertiser* | **Work placement** at local newspaper with **photographers** |

**EDUCATION**

**1995–99**

**Cambridge University**
**BA Hons/MSci Natural Sciences**
**Awarded 2.1**

Part I: Chemistry, physics, geology, maths, history and philosophy of science

Part II: Geological sciences
*courses included climatology, volcanic activity, cosmology, oceanography*

Part III: Geological sciences
*included independent research project on volcanic eruption on Montserrat, leading to publication of results in scientific journal, in June 2000*

**1988–95**

**Wickersley Comprehensive School, Rotherham**

**5 A Levels** Grade As: physics, chemistry, maths, general studies
Grade B: further maths

**9 GCSEs** All grade As (include English, French and German)

**ENTHUSIASMS**

I have a passion for independent **travel**, both as part of my degree subject and outside it. I've travelled throughout Britain and Europe on fieldwork trips; I also spent summer 1996 travelling around Mexico, and **teaching** in a slum area in Mexico City.

I'm a committed **Christian**. As part of this, I am actively involved in my local church, and have also for several years been on the **youthwork team** on a **summer holiday mission**, working with children in North Wales.

A keen **photographer**, my favourite medium is **black and white film**, allowing me to develop and print my own work.

I enjoy most **outdoor pursuits**, especially hiking and climbing anywhere mountainous and rocky – my passion for geology extends beyond my degree!

**Music** is one of my main interests – from singing, playing piano or clarinet in various orchestras and groups, to listening to almost anything, especially jazz.

I love **creative design** – from making my own greetings cards, to producing designs for tablecloths, wallhangings, bedspreads and clothes.

**FIGURE 16.3 continued**

# ALTERNATIVE CVS AND 'ATTACHMENTS'

I have outlined the traditional approach to writing CVs above. It would be tedious not to at least mention the range of alternative CVs in use by some creative and adventurous students and graduates. My definition of 'alternative' is a broad one – anything that represents a departure from the norm counts.

A CV may be viewed as alternative by virtue of its *content* – for example, the inclusion of quotes about you from your boss or recent work colleagues.

I was once tempted to use a leaving card I was given at the end of a year teaching a communications skills course for social workers. Each of the students had made a template of their own footprint and written a personal message of farewell to me, setting out what they had learned and what they were taking with them from the course.

CVs can be alternative by virtue of the *medium* chosen to convey the message. I have encountered graduate CVs sent inside a well-known superstore's own plastic bag, on video, cassette and even attached to a (used!) sports shoe.

Many employers ask for, and expect, you to take samples of your work to the interview. This is common for design, media, landscape, architecture and other such work.

Why wait for the interview? You can make a big impact by sending samples of your work along with your CV. One journalism student in Salford sent her CV along with a 250-word article in the style of the house magazine to show what she could do.

I once did this when applying for a job that involved designing a new staff support service. I sent a draft strategic plan and timetable for rolling out the new service along with my CV. I was the only applicant to do something different and it got me noticed!

I have often considered attaching my CV to a helium-filled balloon and sending it in a box marked 'Private' with the graduate recruiter's name on. Most graduate recruiters say they would definitely invite anyone who did that to interview out of pure curiosity! Worth a try if it reflects your personality and the company culture.

Such approaches are not for everyone, but are worth thinking about.

# COVERING LETTERS

You should always send a covering letter with your CV. The letter will be the first opportunity you have to make a positive impression, so it is important to get it right.

The purpose of the covering letter is to help the CV find its way in the organization to the right person. This is true whether the CV is being sent in response to an advertised position or as a speculative approach.

## CONTENT

In the case of applications made in response to an advert, you should ensure that you say:

▶ why you are interested in the job;

▶ why your skills and qualifications meet their requirements;

▶ what is attractive about the organization.

For administrative purposes, mention the contact person and reference numbers you are given in the advertisement. Many organizations monitor the effectiveness of their advertising and will appreciate a brief comment about when and where you noticed the advertisement.

Don't then just lift text out of the CV – try to express the essence of it without repeating it.

Get someone else to look at the advert (if possible) and compare it to what you have written – are there any glaring omissions? How does your letter come across?

End optimistically – say that you would look forward to having an opportunity to meet them and discuss your application further!

## PRESENTATION

▶ Word process your letter rather than write it by hand, unless you have very neat, attractive writing.

▶ Use the same type of paper and font style for both your CV and the covering letter.

▶ Keep it concise and clear.

- ► Proofread it carefully on-screen and printed out.
- ► Keep a copy for your records, then send it off, as with application forms, in an A4 envelope, first class – be professional!

Figure 16.4 is an example of a well-written, well-presented covering letter.

---

Linda Palmer
35 Queensway
Birch-in-the-Fields
Reading RG4 5JU
Tel: 0118 274 6372
Email: L.Palmer@talk.net

Ms Fryers
Plasma Pharmaceuticals
Human Resources
Room 7F13
Grassington,
Macclesfield SK8 3BH

26 March 2000

Dear Ms Fryers,

**Re: Appointment of graduate trainee, reference PLMA/S4/036**

I read your advertisement for a graduate trainee in *Marketing Week* (24 March 2000) with great interest and would like to be considered for the post. I would love to work in a progressive organization like Plasma Pharmaceuticals – I made a special study of the pharmaceuticals sector for my final-year dissertation.

Please find enclosed my current CV, which I believe shows that there is a good fit between your stated requirements and my qualifications, experience in marketing and brand management and my personal profile.

My first degree was in sociology at the University of Sussex, where I was awarded a 2:1 honours Degree in 1999.

I have just graduated from the University of South London with a postgraduate qualification in business studies. This course has provided me with a thorough grounding in all aspects of accounting and finance, marketing, business strategy and international management.

My work experience includes many aspects of marketing, with recent success in a product launch during a summer placement with SmithKline Beecham.

I would be delighted to be given an opportunity to meet you to discuss my application further,

Yours sincerely,

Linda Palmer

Linda Palmer

---

**FIGURE 16.4  An example of a good covering letter**

# SUMMARY

▶ Your CV should provide an employer with a clear, concise picture of you and your aspirations.

▶ Try to achieve the right blend of optimism and accuracy.

▶ Base your CV design on an accurate self-assessment, but target everything you say to match with what the employer is looking for as well.

▶ Choose a CV style that reflects your personality, does justice to your particular strengths and fits well with the culture of the organization you are applying to.

▶ Pay attention to presentation – first impressions are important.

▶ Make sure your covering letter adds value to your application.


# SIGNPOSTS TO MORE HELP

### Careers advisory service

▶ Many careers advisers will provide help in writing and checking your CV – ask locally.

▶ The *Prospects* and *Get* directories include samples of undergraduate CVs.

▶ See the AgCAS information booklet 'Making Applications' (CSU, Manchester).

▶ See the careers advisory service booklets 'How to write a CV' (available for £3.50).

▶ Many careers advisory services have a local on-line jobhunting service called CVplus – ask locally.

▶ Advisers can help you produce CVs to use on-line.

▶ They can also help and advise on producing CVs for use in Europe.

### Books

Perkins, G. (1995) *Killer CVs and Hidden Approaches*, Pearson Education, London.

Perret, J. (1996) *Job Hunting after University or College*, Kogan Page, London.

### On-line

A number of sites offer CV advice, plus examples. In particular visit the following sites:

www.prospects.csu.ac.uk

(traditional UK graduate recruitment site linked to the *Prospects* directory)

http://www.careermosaic.com

(international job vacancy site, plus advice on CVs and electronic resumés).

# how to succeed at interview

## How familiar are you with employment interview techniques and etiquette?

**In this chapter, you will:**

- [ ] come to understand interviews;
- [ ] find out what the employer wants from the interview;
- [ ] work out what you want to get out of the interview;
- [ ] see how to guarantee failure;
- [ ] learn all about the art of impression management;
- [ ] find out how interviews are structured;
- [ ] see how to prepare for interview questions;
- [ ] learn about recruiters' interview techniques.

**In the activities:**

**17.1** Your interview objectives

**17.2** Develop telephone interviewing skills

**17.3** Practical preparations checklist

**17.4** Interview self-assessment

# INTERVIEWS – THE DOOR TO NEW OPPORTUNITIES?

Many graduates see going for an interview as an ordeal, a necessary evil in the pursuit of work. Indeed, the graduate recruiters you meet have great power. They are the gatekeepers, able to open or close the door to the job you want. Reading this chapter will help you be fully prepared for any challenges that the interview stage will throw your way.

## FIRST INTERVIEWS

First interviews usually follow an initial screening stage based on your application. This is not always the case, however. For example, at recruitment fairs an interview may take place following a brief chat over your CV.

First interviews sometimes follow a brief telephone interview or an ability test used as part of an employer's screening process. Interviewing is a time-hungry activity for all concerned and so, increasingly, employers are attempting to make the process as cost-effective and efficient as possible.

If you have been shortlisted for interview, you are already viewed as potentially suitable for this post. Only around one in five candidates get this far!

## SECOND INTERVIEWS

If you are applying for a traditional milk round job with a well-known graduate recruiter, you are very likely to end up having a second interview, possibly at an assessment centre (see Chapter 18). However, some companies don't run assessment centres, especially if few graduates are being employed or the job is a direct entry one rather than a milk round-style advance recruitment. Under such circumstances, second interviews may be looking in more detail at your specialist or technical skills. Second interviews also give an owner, director or senior partner a chance to look you over. This may be an informal interview, a casual drink or a 'trial by knife and fork' in a local restaurant.

The rules of interview success are:

► anticipate the questions you will be asked;

► prepare convincing answers;

► deliver your replies to questions professionally.

# UNDERSTANDING INTERVIEWS

An interview has been defined as 'a controlled conversation with a purpose'. It is a complicated social process with an unwritten, secret code of conduct. Peter Herriot, a well-known careers writer described it like this:

> 'The selection interview is a rule-governed social interaction with clearly defined reciprocal roles allocated to both parties. ... It is considered appropriate for the interviewer to take charge of the situation and to ask questions of the applicant. The applicant is expected to wait until invited to do so before asking questions.'
>
> *(adapted from Herriot, 1984)*

The interviewer will have a vested interest in the outcome – they will either be working with you directly or may be held accountable later if things go wrong, so this can be a stressful time for the interviewer as well.

You need to know and understand interview etiquette. The interviewer will have an expectation of proper candidate behaviour. If you act 'in role', it will be perceived as appropriate behaviour and you are more likely to be viewed favourably. If you act 'out of role', this is likely to cause a negative reaction – a bad interviewee is assumed to be a bad applicant. Understanding the interview etiquette at this level can help you prepare well and subtly handle the interviewer without them knowing!

---

**CASE STUDY   Lucy: final-year French language student at the University of Manchester talks about interview etiquette**

'I can vividly recall my worst moment ever at interview. I had decided I wanted to be "myself". I had got through to a first interview with one of the top five business consultancies. I found the questions hard to answer because I hadn't thought enough about what they would ask. There were long silences. Then I was asked "And how do you describe yourself?" "What did I reply? Mad".

I saw the interviewer's face drop in amazement. I had blown it. Digging myself in even deeper I went on to explain "My friends call me Hot Banana". I learnt the hard way that to succeed at interview you have to avoid making your interviewer feel awkward or embarrassed.

---

# WHAT DOES THE EMPLOYER WANT FROM THE INTERVIEW?

During an interview, your prospective employer will be using a range of techniques to discover more about you. They will be aiming to find answers to the following questions.

▶ Will you be able to do the job?

▶ Will you fit into the department or section where you will work?

▶ Are you enthusiastic and motivated?

▶ Will you be flexible and work well in a team?

Your ability to do the job is an important part of the equation. It is only one of several factors, however. You will notice that a great deal of emphasis is put on ensuring that you will match the prevailing company or organizational culture, can be managed and are highly motivated. Many employers now specify the particular skills and personal attributes or competences they are seeking in their adverts. Knowing exactly what the employer is looking for is essential to effective preparation.

## WHAT DO YOU WANT TO GET OUT OF THE INTERVIEW?

An interview should be a two-way street. It is not just about the employer deciding whether or not you are suitable for them. Many graduates are very dissatisfied with the jobs they obtain. The interview offers you an opportunity to think about your expectations and then probe the employer to find out if they can deliver.

---

**ACTIVITY 17.1    Your interview objectives**

Here is a checklist of objectives you might want to set for the interview process. Tick the ones that apply to you.

☐ To get the job – no matter what.

☐ To collect information about the organization.

☐ To find out more about the job and the training programme.

☐ To gain practice in interview techniques.

☐ Other personal reasons, which are:

_____

---

## HOW TO GUARANTEE FAILURE

You will fail to be offered the job or get through to the next stage of the process if you fall into one or more of the following traps:

► you have poor knowledge of the organization;

► you have poor interview skills;

► you do not match the job;

► you have a nightmare interviewer.

You can take action now to ensure that you avoid the first three pitfalls – read the rest of this chapter! You can even learn some tactics to help you take charge of the nightmare interviewer scenario.

# TYPES OF INTERVIEWS

Interviews for selection purposes can take a number of forms. Contact the organization's HR/personnel department as soon as you are offered an interview and ask them to explain who will be interviewing you and the approach they intend to take. Many organizations will explain the selection criteria in some detail if you ask. They regard this as evidence of intelligent resourcefulness!

## PERSONAL INTERVIEWS

You may encounter an individual, one-to-one interview. The person interviewing you may be from the personnel department or a manager or professional from the area you have applied to work in. These tend to appear informal and chatty, but be on your guard. The interviewer may follow a traditional, unstructured approach or a more modern, structured format (see below for more details on these techniques). This type of interview has the potential for individual bias – this could be either for or against you!

A slight variation on the individual interview is the 'individual/sequential' approach. Here you are interviewed on a one-to-one basis by a series of different people – usually someone from the human resources department (HR) and a line manager or technical specialist.

A further variation is the 'joint interview' where two people interview together, each with a different (usually planned) role, exploring different aspects of the job.

Less common for most graduate jobs, but one you may encounter, is a 'panel interview', and, rarer still, a 'selection board', comprised of several staff members or interested parties.

## TELEPHONE INTERVIEWS

Telephone interviews are becoming common in some areas of graduate recruitment, especially as a time-efficient way of screening candidates. The questions are likely to cover typical first interview issues and you should prepare accordingly. The main problem with not being able to see the interviewer is having to communicate without the usual body language signals and non-verbal responses.

If you have never experienced telephone interviews, you can practise by using Activity 17.2.

If you feel too embarrassed doing this with someone else, you should at least go through the exercise alone. It will give you a head start over other candidates.

## STRESS INTERVIEWS

You may think that all interviews are stressful, but some interviewers set out to place you in a challenging or difficult situation to see how you react. These are quite rare for most graduate jobs. I have encountered one student who was invited to sit down and then the interviewer just said 'Impress me'. For another, the interviewer said 'See this pen on my desk? Sell it to me'.

As an interview is a reflection of the way in which people are treated once they are inside the organization, at least the stress interview provides you with a useful insight – take your skills elsewhere!

# GET READY FOR YOUR NEXT INTERVIEW

## INTERVIEW FORMATS

Good interviewers know what they are looking for and how to find it. Prior to the interview, the employer should have undertaken an evaluation of the job advertised. The organization will usually have generated some assessment criteria – the skills, abilities and attitudes they know will lead to success in doing the job (see Chapter 13). Most interviews have a familiar structure of four stages:

▶ a start;

▶ a middle – a sequence of questions, carefully timed;

▶ an opportunity for you to ask questions;

▶ an end.

## A START

The employer intends to put you at your ease and help you relax. They understand that being interviewed can be nerve-racking and they want to help you do yourself justice.

The impression you make in the first few minutes will be crucial to a successful outcome. The interview stage is not the only time in the selection process where image is important. You need to make a good first impression many times, such as at company presentations, recruitment fairs, when networking and at first and subsequent interviews and/or assessment centres.

## Making the right impression

Impression management can be defined as a set of techniques employed to control the image other people have of you. Successful politicians do this all the time, but is there a place for impression management in the work of jobhunting? The answer depends on your perspective. Some view attempts at image management as a form of interpersonal manipulation. It *can* be deceptive if it is used to massage the truth, and this raises some important ethical issues about jobhunting generally, mentioned in Chapters 15 and 16.

I suggest that you can use impression management ethically as part of a toolkit. Figure 17.1 sets out an impression management toolkit for you to think about and use as part of your repertoire of communication techniques. Of course, it is not just job candidates who employ impression management techniques – organizations do it as well. They invest £100,000s every year in ensuring that the right image comes across in graduate brochures. Organizations have aspirations too!

## Using impression management in interviews

Figure 17.1 shows the four main ways in which impression management strategies can be adopted during an interview to promote success. These involve:

- ▶ appearance and body language
- ▶ assertiveness
- ▶ self-protection
- ▶ self-promotion.

*Appearance and body language*
Scholarly research shows that the first four minutes of your initial meeting with another person are critical to their assessment of you. If you pay attention to some basic rules about interpersonal psychology, you will help yourself to make a favourable impression.

Communication skills are the essential tools for building and developing a relationship with your interviewer. You have two key dimensions – your words and your body language.

Words have an impact that relates to both their content and the style of their delivery. Your body language and appearance are powerful factors in conveying any message.

You should aim to project self-confidence, assurance and motivation.

| Appearance and body language | Assertiveness |
|---|---|
| • Appropriate dress and grooming<br>• Good posture, but relaxed<br>• Eye contact<br>• Facial expressions<br>• Smiling | • Self-confidence<br>• Asking the interviewer questions<br>• Willingness to meet a challenge<br>• Taking the initiative in the discussion<br>• Leading the interviewer towards favoured topics |

**IMPRESSION MANAGEMENT**

| Self-protection | Self-promotion |
|---|---|
| • Giving good explanations<br>• Justifications<br>• Minimizing negative experiences or results<br>• Avoiding problem areas or weak spots | • Positive framing of attributes<br>• Choice of appropriate personal stories and anecdotes<br>• Focus on the positive<br>• Emphasis on what you have achieved and learned |

**FIGURE 17.1  How to make a good impression at interview**

---

**First impressions count!**

A massive 55 per cent of communication depends on body language, 38 per cent on how you speak and only 7 per cent on what you actually say!

The first minutes count – the so-called 'primacy effect'.

Interviewers carry unconscious stereotypes of what constitutes an 'insider', so you need to ensure you meet these unspoken expectations. You need to demonstrate you will fit in – send the message 'I belong here'.

People who succeed in interviews operate within an interviewer's comfort zone.

---

*The handshake*

The use of touch can be a powerful symbol of a relationship being built. There are hidden dimensions, relating to gender and culture. However, the ideal interview handshake will convey a warm greeting between two people on equal terms. It should be firm and brief.

It is advisable to wait until the interviewer offers their hand to you. An overtly heavy-handed greeting can convey either aggression or nerves. If you know you perspire when under stress, wash your hands just before the interview to avoid that sticky 'wet fish' effect.

*Seating position and posture*
Follow the **SOLER** principle:

**S**eating position – some find sitting at a slight angle reduces the sense of confrontation;

**O**pen body position – don't fold your arms as this makes you seem very unapproachable;

**L**ean slightly forward – this shows interest, attention;

**E**ye contact – a warm and interested, not a fixed stare, is what is needed;

**R**elax – well, try to!

Research indicates that eye contact alone carries powerful messages. More eye contact demonstrates confidence and equality. Don't overdo it, though.

*Appearance*
Most conventional writing on dressing for interview success follows the matching model approach. Find out exactly what insiders wear and emulate that as closely as possible. This approach is ideal if you are sure you want the job.

However, you may be unsure. You may have a distinctive personal style of dress, short/long hair and sport rings or studs in various prominent places. If you do not feel ready to peel off these symbols of your individuality as the price for getting a job, that's fine. If this is required, it is probably a good indication that you are looking at the wrong sort of job or employer. Find something that does allow you to retain your individuality.

How you dress for interview is a reflection of your aspirations for the future. It also reveals a huge amount about your self-image and your understanding of what is required to fit in. For most professional or business jobs, the best advice is to choose the best-quality suit, shoes and briefcase you can afford, beg or borrow. Choose a style that suits you and allows you to concentrate on your performance.

---

**CASE STUDY  Lynn, speech therapist working in the NHS – how to create the wrong impression**

One of the candidates Lynn interviewed turned up in odd socks. She said this about it:

'I just could not get over the fact that he was wearing socks that didn't match. What did this say about his attention to detail, his attitude to his patients. What would he be like to work with? I just knew he would be turned down, it was too much of a risk.'

---

**CASE STUDY  Emma, trainee solicitor – coming up smelling of roses ... not!**

Emma is a music student at Leeds University, but, during holidays, works as a receptionist for a well-known firm of solicitors. One young hopeful student came to an interview for an appointment as a trainee. He had overdone the aftershave so badly that the fragrance lingered in the reception area for a full hour after he had left. The interview experience had literally brought tears to the interviewing panels' eyes. Their comment to Emma:

'There is no way we are employing somebody who smells like that.'

---

*Assertiveness*

There is scope in every interview for you to influence the direction, tone and content of the discussion. Your level of self-confidence and suitability for the job will be reflected in your willingness to lead the interviewer towards information you have provided in your CV.

*Self-promotion*

An important skill for interview success is the ability to emphasize the skills, abilities and experiences that demonstrate you will fit into this workplace and culture. You need to promote all your strengths and talents. I discuss handling tricky questions in more detail later in this chapter.

**Self-protection**

In interviews, you will always encounter questions that probe your limitations and weaknesses. I do not suggest that you attempt to portray yourself as superhuman – instead, try to develop a positive approach to describing limitations, going for a 'silver lining' effect. You should aim to give a truthful but optimistic view of yourself. Don't overdo this positive re-framing though your prospective employer deserves to be answered truthfully. A 'weak spot' now many just be a 'training opportunity' later on!

# A MIDDLE – QUESTION TIME

A good interview will be well planned. The questions should all have a purpose and be linked to the job or person specification. Some writers distinguish between straight and trick questions. I think it is more helpful to think of all interview questions as potentially tricky – they are intended to probe and challenge you. Your reactions are likely to be determined by your level of preparation.

A really useful source of information for interview preparation is the employer files held in many university careers advisory services. In these, past and very recent interviewees record their experiences of the interview and assessment process with the intention of helping you through this minefield. You will find all kinds of inside information.

The six most likely areas of questioning are:

▶ about yourself;

▶ your academic or educational record;

▶ your work experience;

▶ your career direction, interest in this job, motivation;

▶ your knowledge of the organization;

▶ your personal achievements and non-academic activities.

## About yourself

You may have noticed that many EAFs ask you to describe yourself. These are very popular in student/recent graduate interview scenarios. Be prepared to answer questions such as the following.

*What kind of person are you?*

*Can you describe yourself in just three words?*

*Describe yourself in five words?*

*Give me a thumbnail sketch of yourself?*

Employers also like to ask you to highlight strengths and weaknesses or ask how you think other people see you. Here are some examples of these kinds of questions.

*What do you think are your main strengths?*

*How does your college tutor see you?*

*How would your fellow students describe you?*

*What weaknesses do you think your referees will highlight?*

Always aim for the silver lining effect when highlighting faults. For example, 'I am too hardworking'. You may also find it helpful to return to Chapter 4 and reread about the good and bad sides of various temperaments associated with Belbin's team roles.

## Academic or educational record

You may be asked direct questions about your A levels or expected academic results. To stretch you even more, there may be questions about the subject you are studying or that test your general thinking skills.

Here are some 'straight' questions.

*What made you choose to study physics, astrology, business, outer Mongolia ... ?*

*What did you enjoy most/least about your studies?*

*What aspect of your studies had the biggest impact on you personally?*

And now for some 'tricky' questions – watch for the twist.

*Why would anyone want to study sociology?*

*Do you regret choosing Egyptology?*

*Your course has not included any business studies ... don't you think that this will place you at a disadvantage in our organization?*

*What part of the course did you really struggle with?*

## Work experience

Students and graduates now have widely varying levels of work experience. Your past performance at work will be of great interest to an interviewer, who might ask the following questions.

*What did you achieve in your summer placement at ... ?*

*How would you describe the organizational culture?*

*What were your main responsibilities?*

*What were the three main lessons you learned while working at ... ?*

*What was most interesting about your work assignment?*

*What was the thing you found most difficult?*

You may also be asked questions about your relationships with work colleagues and managers.

*How did you get on with your boss?*

*How would you describe their management style?*

*What would you have changed about them?*

*Looking back, is there anything you would do differently if you had an opportunity?*

You may encounter questions about how you solved problems in the past or what you would do in some hypothetical situation in your job (see more on this under the headings Situational interviewing and Behavioural interviewing later in this chapter).

## Career direction, interest in this job, motivation

You are likely to be asked how you found your career direction and what particularly interests you about this role. The most frequently asked question in any first interview is the following.

*Why do you want this job?*

Make sure you can answer that one! Also, a similar one.

*What do you think will be most satisfying about this job?*

Be prepared for questions such as these, too.

*Are you applying for other jobs in this field?*

*Who else have you applied to?*

*What stage are you at in applying for other jobs?*

*Are you applying for jobs that are very different to this one?*

## Knowledge of the organization

Most modern employers want people who will be committed to their goals. You are therefore likely to be asked the following questions or similar ones.

*What do you know about this organization?*

*What do you most admire about our products or services?*

*How do you feel the media handled the recent problems we had in …?*

*What are the key issues facing our organization at present?*

You will make a good impression if you can name specific examples, compare products, services, culture to those of competitors. It also looks good if you can name the chief executive or a board member who said or wrote something recently.

Depending on the sector and type of products, you may also be asked very direct questions about topical issues.

*Can you outline your personal views on (for example, animal testing, genetically modified food products, weapons, defence systems, handling waste products)?*

Your replies to questions in this category are often crucial to your success.

## Personal achievements and non-academic activities

You will be expected to say something about your non-academic interests and work experience. In particular, this is your chance to describe your drive, energy, tenacity, leadership, teamworking and other skills. Interviewers are interested in the way you have used your time to gain the most from holidays and so on.

*What are your major interests outside university?*

*How did you get involved in the Hiking/Swimming/Wine-tasting/Computing Club?*

*Which newspaper do you read most often? (Watch out for the follow-up question.)*

*Do you have a favourite columnist? Which one and why?*

*Have you travelled far? Where did you go? Why? What impact did your journey have on you?*

## Questions you should not be asked

Questions that may discriminate against you on grounds of your sex, race, ethnicity, sexuality, political or religious beliefs, such as the following, should not be asked.

*Do you have any children and, if so, who is going to look after them when you are at work or they are sick?*

*Will you mind having a male/female boss?*

*Are you planning to start a family in the next few years?*

*What is your race/ethnic origin?*

*What is your religion?*

*Are you affiliated to a particular political party?*

*What is your opinion about trade union membership?*

*What is your sexual orientation?*

*Do you drink or smoke heavily?*

## AN OPPORTUNITY FOR YOU TO ASK QUESTIONS

This is also part of the interviewer's assessment of you. You need to use the opportunity to both find out information you need and to make a further good impression. Searching intelligent questions will reflect well on you. Make sure you have prepared some suitable questions in advance. Good examples could include those on the following points:

▶ clarification of the nature of the job;

▶ to know more about the team or department you are working in;

- show an interest in the actual products or range of services the company offers;
- the opportunities for training and development – is it tailor-made for each jobholder, is there a graduate scheme?

However, avoid asking questions about pensions and perks. Don't ask questions that will trip up the interviewer and make them feel foolish. If they have told you that they are from personnel, they are unlikely to answer detailed, complicated, technical questions. No one likes to be deskilled.

## AN END

Given that most interviewers see several candidates, they will be aware of time boundaries. You will do well to respect this and quickly pick up any ending signals. The interviewer should tell you the next stage in the process and when you will hear the result from this interview before you leave.

Thank the recruiter for this opportunity, say you have enjoyed meeting them and respond if offered a departing handshake. Afterwards, write and thank them formally. The interviewers could become an important part of your career network.

# EMPLOYERS' INTERVIEW TECHNIQUES

Organizations are very keen to make good choices in selection. In recent years, there have been a number of developments in the field of interviewing, especially the rise of so-called 'scientific' approaches to interviewing. Read about these below to be fully prepared for your next interview.

## THE TRADITIONAL INTERVIEW

In the management literature about interviewing techniques, the traditional selection interview is often described as unsystematic and unstructured. In the typical traditional approach, the interviewer would ask different questions of different candidates. This approach is criticized for offering no basis for fair comparison between applicants. The problems are often further compounded by having no selection criteria, poor interviewing techniques and being open to both conscious and unconscious bias.

The most well-known form of bias is the 'halo and horns' effect. This effect occurs when the interviewer assesses one aspect of a candidate favourably and then transfers the good impression to their interpretation of everything else the candidate says and does. Almost anything can trigger a halo effect – you may have the same name, appearance or aftershave as someone they admire or else have attended a school or university they have had positive experiences of. The 'horns' effect is a 'halo' in reverse – assessment is skewed negatively.

Concerns about unlawful discrimination have led many organizations and interviewers to become more disciplined and adopt a more structured form of interviewing.

## THE STRUCTURED INTERVIEW

### The basic structured interview

The halo and horns effect and other criticisms have led to the creation of new interview techniques, based on notions of statistical reliability and validity. These approaches are scientific and, consequently, considered to be fairer. Whether or not this is actually the case is in dispute.

There are many variations on the theme of a structured interview. In general, this means that they are based on objective assessment criteria. The criteria themselves have been drawn from a careful analysis of the job being advertised. In most cases, the human resources department (where there is one) will have produced a specification that outlines the essential and desirable qualifications and qualities required to do the job well. In most cases, candidates will all be asked the same questions or a number of questions from a pre-planned list. The interviewers will know what sorts of replies will indicate future success in the job.

### Behavioural interviewing

A growing trend in graduate recruitment is to include a proportion of behavioural questions. This is based on a belief that your past behaviour is the best predictor of your future performance. The interviewer will ask you to describe how you handled a particular incident that they consider relevant to the job. If you have filled in an SAF, you will already be familiar with these types of questions. Here are some examples.

> *Describe a challenging project, activity or event you have planned and taken through to a conclusion.*
>
> *Describe how you have achieved a goal by influencing the actions or opinions of others.*
>
> *Describe a difficult problem you have solved.*

The interviewer assesses your answers according to a specially designed behaviour rating scale. The quality of your responses can improve greatly with preparation and practice.

### Situational interviewing

The situational interview is designed to find out how you would respond under certain hypothetical circumstances. An example for a marketing position would be the following.

> *What would you do if you arrived for an appointment with a potential customer and found that he had double booked and could not see you?*

The interviewer would assess your answer according to a specially designed rating scale that had been designed by experts in that type of work. This is your opportunity, for example, to show how much you understand and appreciate customer care.

# THE IMPERFECT ART OF SELECTION INTERVIEWING

Interviewing is an imperfect selection device as there are many potential sources of error and bias, as shown in Figure 17.2. This can either work in your favour or against you, depending on the circumstances. Do your best to find as much common ground as possible, be aware of the interviewer's perspective and the issues that affect their decision making.

# YOUR INTERVIEW STRATEGY

### How to prepare

The time and effort you give to preparation will be a good investment. It will build up your confidence and greatly enhance your ability to handle the questions posed. Preparation should cover three areas – practicalities, knowledge and interview skills.

## PRACTICALITIES

Many first traditional milk round interviews are held on campus, often at the local careers services offices or in suitable university accommodation. Some interviews are held at a larger regional centre or hotel. If you are applying for a job outside the traditional graduate employment framework, you are very likely to be invited to the organization's local offices or HQ, depending on the job.

Think about your practical travel arrangements and what you need to take with you.

## KNOWLEDGE

Make sure you have read up about the job and are familiar with everything you said in your CV and covering letter. Make sure you have done your homework in terms of knowledge:

▶ about yourself;

▶ about the employer;

▶ about key issues in that field of work;

▶ about competitors, markets and globalization.

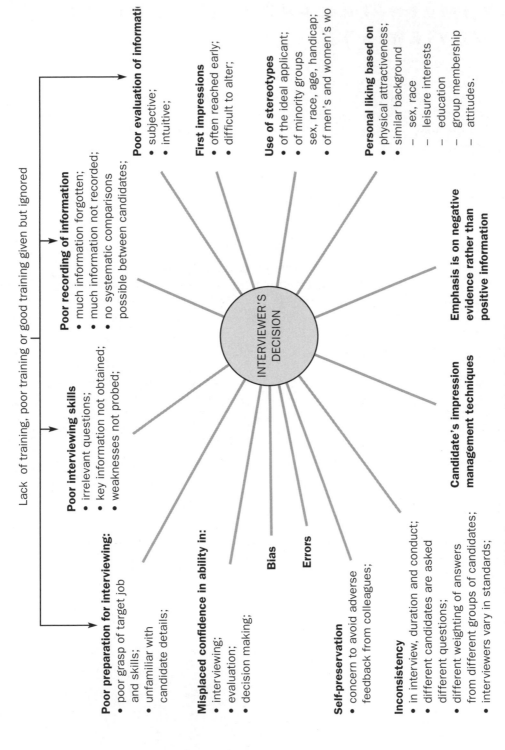

Lack of training, poor training or good training given but ignored

**Poor preparation for interviewing:**
- poor grasp of target job and skills;
- unfamiliar with candidate details;

**Poor interviewing skills**
- irrelevant questions;
- key information not obtained;
- weaknesses not probed;

**Poor recording of information**
- much information forgotten;
- much information not recorded;
- no systematic comparisons possible between candidates;

**Poor evaluation of informati**
- subjective;
- intuitive;

**First impressions**
- often reached early;
- difficult to alter;

**Use of stereotypes**
- of the ideal applicant;
- of minority groups sex, race, age, handicap;
- of men's and women's wo

**Personal liking based on**
- physical attractiveness;
- similar background
  - sex, race
  - leisure interests
  - education
  - group membership
  - attitudes.

**Misplaced confidence in ability in:**
- interviewing;
- evaluation;
- decision making;

INTERVIEWER'S DECISION

**Self-preservation**
- concern to avoid adverse feedback from colleagues;

**Inconsistency**
- in interview, duration and conduct;
- different candidates are asked different questions;
- different weighting of answers from different groups of candidates;
- interviewers vary in standards;

**Bias**

**Errors**

**Candidate's impression management techniques**

**Emphasis is on negative evidence rather than positive information**

**FIGURE 17.2  Questionable influences on an interviewer's decisions**

Source: *Deception in Selection*, L. Whalley and M. Smith, 1998. Used with kind permission of John Wiley London

## ACTIVITY 17.3    Practical preparations checklist

**Travel**

▶ Make travel arrangements in plenty of time.
▶ Buy train/coach tickets in advance.
▶ Check all your connections will get you there on time.
▶ Allow plenty of time to get to your interview.
▶ Aim to arrive at least 15 minutes early.

**Appearance**

▶ Wear something smart, appropriate and comfortable.
▶ If it's new, wear it beforehand – try sitting down in it!
▶ Don't overdo the jewellery, tie, aftershave or perfume.

**What to take with you**

▶ A smart briefcase.
▶ A copy of your CV/application form and covering letter.
▶ Your letter of invitation and the location map or venue details.
▶ Notebook and a good pen.
▶ Money.
▶ Mobile (but switch it off during the interview);
▶ A portfolio of your work, if appropriate.

# SKILLS

Get some practice answering the questions you think you'll be asked. You can develop your skills in a careers advisory service session or with a friend in role plays. Many find that visualization helps. Use your imagination to practise the interview and how you will handle it. Many university careers advisory services provide interview training, workshops or an opportunity to run through potential questions.

# EVALUATE YOUR PERFORMANCE

**'The only true mistake is one from which one learns nothing.'**

*Oscar Wilde*

Every interview offers you the opportunity to learn something about your performance. Whatever the outcome of the interview, you will benefit most by spending a few moments reflecting on what you did well and what went badly. This will help you prepare effectively for next time.

Use the checklist below after your next interview.

---

**ACTIVITY 17.4    Interview self-assessment**

After an interview, note down your answers to the following questions.

How did you feel when you arrived for the interview?

_____

_____

How much preparation and planning had you done beforehand? Were there any gaps in your knowledge?

_____

_____

Which questions could you answer well? Why?

_____

_____

Make a note of any questions that surprised you. On reflection, how could you have answered them?

_____

_____

Write down anything different that happened. Was this your first situational or behavioural interview?

_____

_____

Were any inappropriate questions asked? (About your marital status, dependants, arrangement for childcare and so on.)

_____

_____

Were there things you had intended to say but didn't get the opportunity to? What can you do to take charge of the situation next time?

_____

_____

What will you do differently next time?

_____

_____

Make sure you ask them for feedback. What had impressed them? Where did you fall short? What did the interviewer suggest about the way you could have improved your performance?

_____

_____

# SUMMARY

## Ten golden rules of interview success

▶ Prepare well beforehand – do your homework.

▶ Make a good first impression – aim for a halo effect!

▶ Follow the secret codes of interview etiquette.

▶ Use appropriate body language, eye contact and body posture.

▶ Always be positive.

▶ Don't give long replies in any answer.

▶ Answer the question asked.

▶ Never offer any self-criticism.

▶ Never criticize a former boss or employer.

▶ Emphasize how much you have learned from each episode in your life.

**Studies show that around 75 per cent of all large organizations and a growing number of smaller ones (up to 40 per cent) are using assessment centres for graduate recruitment.**

**In this chapter, you will:**

☐ find out what happens at graduate assessment centres;

☐ find out how to prepare for, and practise doing, typical selection exercises;

☐ find out how you will be evaluated;

☐ learn how to be prepared, to cope with the unexpected;

☐ be one step nearer to a brilliant job!

**In the activities:**

**18.1** How to prepare for assessment centre interviews

**18.2** How to prepare your own presentation

**18.3** A tailor-made in-tray exercise;

**18.4** Practise the role of chairperson

**18.5** After the assessment centre

# INTRODUCTION

If you have been asked to go to an assessment centre, you have the best possible opportunity of securing a job offer. An assessment centre is usually the last part of the selection process and so only about 5 per cent of applicants ever see one. Follow the advice, develop the skills and get the knowledge in this chapter to maximize your chances of getting that job!

# WHAT ARE ASSESSMENT CENTRES?

There are several types and formats available, ranging from a couple of hours to a couple of days. Any combination of the following may form part of the programme in any order:

▶ interviews;
▶ ability/personality tests;
▶ group exercises/team games;
▶ case studies/problem solving;
▶ giving a presentation;
▶ in-tray exercise;
▶ social events;
▶ site visits/office or factory tour.

A survey of assessment centre practices in the UK shows that interviews, ability and personality tests and group exercises are the most common activities, while smaller firms are less likely to include an in-tray exercise (see Table 18.1).

A well-designed assessment centre will be based on exercises and activities that correspond to the type of work you will be employed to do.

TABLE 18.1  Content of assessment centre exercises in the UK

| Type of assessment centre exercise adopted | Small recruiters (%) | Medium recruiters (%) | Large recruiters (%) | Total sample (%) |
|---|---|---|---|---|
| Interview | 97 | 97 | 97 | 97 |
| Aptitude test | 89 | 91 | 91 | 91 |
| Personality test | 80 | 83 | 79 | 80 |
| Group discussion | 67 | 79 | 89 | 79 |
| Case study | 49 | 64 | 71 | 62 |
| Presentation | 54 | 59 | 61 | 58 |
| In-tray exercise | 19 | 38 | 48 | 35 |

Source: T. Keenan, 'Graduate recruitment in Britain: A survey of selection methods used by organizations', *Journal of Organizational Behaviour*, 16, pp. 303–17, 1995

If you have been invited to attend an assessment centre, the letter should outline the programme and give you an idea of timings. You would normally be provided with an explanation of the types of tests to be used and their purpose. Most employers will now also send you sample questions to help you prepare (for more details, see Chapter 19).

For those of you who haven't got to this stage yet (or for anyone who has applied to a secretive organization), examples of typical graduate assessment centre timetables are given in Figures 18.1 and 18.2.

---

**One-day assessment, with ability test screening**

10.30 Arrive, coffee
10.45 Welcome and introduction
11.00 Ability tests
13.00 Lunch with recent graduates with office tour
14.15 Interviews with senior managers for those who succeeded in the ability tests or
        ten-minute feedback/departure interview for those who didn't
15.15 Break
15.30 Group exercise
16.30 Depart

---

**FIGURE 18.1  Example of a timetable for a one-day assessment**

---

**Two-day assessment (one night)**

**Day 1**
18.00 Arrive at venue (usually a hotel)
18.30 Welcome and briefing session
19.00 Mutual introductions
20.00 Evening meal with recent graduates

Required to complete questionnaire and prepare for next day's activities

**Day 2**
09.00 Review of programme
09.15 Tests
10.15 Break
10.30 Group discussion
11.15 Individual interviews, discuss questionnaire
12.15 Preparation for group problem-solving task
13.00 Lunch with senior managers and line managers
14.00 Group problem-solving task
14.45 Individual presentations (10 minutes x 6 with break)
16.15 Debriefing session/presentation of graduate training scheme
16.45 Finish

---

**FIGURE 18.2  Example of a two-day assessment timetable**

Assessment centres (sometimes called selection centres) are designed by employers to obtain the best possible indication of your potential to do the job well. It is well known among recruiters that first interviews can be subjective and flawed for various reasons – they are influenced by first impressions, stereotypes and interviewer bias (see Chapter 17 for more on this). Although expensive to design and run, employers believe that assessment centres give them a true picture of your abilities and personality.

# WHAT EXACTLY ARE THEY LOOKING FOR?

Organizations have different cultures and jobs have different requirements. With most modern recruitment procedures, you will be measured against specific selection criteria. You may know these already, having done your research at the first interview stage. If not, you should be able to discern the key qualities the employer wants. Refer to the recruitment information – it may include a job description or, importantly, a person specification that sets out the skills and abilities the employer is looking for.

Many employers now use a competence framework and may have highlighted specific competences that are needed for this job. Examples include drive, teamworking, tenacity and so on. If you have not done so already, you may find it helpful to refer to the section on Person specifications and competences in Chapter 13.

It is important that you know what the selectors are looking for. However, some employers do try to keep their selection criteria secret, fearing that you will use impression management techniques and tailor your behaviour to suit expectations. More enlightened employers recognize that the process is a two-way one – openness about selection criteria is to be applauded.

# HOW IS PERFORMANCE EVALUATED?

It is helpful to know how your performance will be measured. Most participants are usually evaluated by a group of trained assessors who observe and carefully record what they see and hear. You can see a sample of the sort of evaluation sheet that might be used as your assessment record in Figure 18.3.

## WATCH OUT WHEN THE PEOPLE HOLDING CLIPBOARDS APPEAR!

The assessors will probably use a master sheet that records your performance for each activity. In group activities, the assessors are likely to be looking for communication skills, power to influence, teamworking, being assertive but not too dominant, listening to others, creativity, imagination and capacity to solve problems.

| Exercise: group negotiation | Positive evidence | Negative evidence | Rating |
|---|---|---|---|
| **Incisiveness** Gets a clear overview of an issue, gets to the heart of a problem, identifies limits to information | Candidate noticed production data for last quarter was missing | | 5 |
| **Imagination** Generates options, considers impact of different courses of action | Suggested 1 of the 4 options that emerged | | 4 |
| **Self-confidence** Expresses and demonstrates confidence in own ability, can admit when lacking in expertise | Admitted own lack of knowledge about TQM | Allowed lack of knowledge in one thing to affect overall contribution | 3 |
| **Sensitivity** Listens to others, adapts to other people, demonstrates empathy | Willing to support a good idea | | 5 |
| **Tenacity** Demonstrates determination to succeed, perseveres through obstacles | | Could have promoted own idea more | 2 |

Key:
5 Showed clear evidence of a high level of competence in the dimension and no substantial negative evidence
4 Showed evidence of competence in the dimension and little negative evidence
3 Showed more positive evidence of competence than negative
2 Showed enough negative evidence to be judged lacking in competence in the dimension
1 Showed substantial evidence of lack of competence in the dimension and no positive evidence

**FIGURE 18.3  Example of an evaluation sheet for rating an exercise**

Source: Adapted from *Assessment Centres: Identifying and developing competence* (2nd ed.), 1993, C. Woodruffe. Reproduced with kind permission of the publishers, the Institute of Personnel and Development, IPD House, Camp Road, London SW19 4DX

Next, let us look at the kinds of exercises encountered at assessment centres.

# INTERVIEWS

As mentioned above, most assessment centres involve an interview. The guidelines for these are the same as for other interviews (see Chapter 17). You will probably need to exercise greater care and prepare more thoroughly because second interviews tend to be more challenging than first interviews. The main features of second interviews are that they are:

- still related to specific selection criteria;
- more focused and questions may be more searching;
- often conducted by a more senior manager or a technical specialist, often alongside a human resources or personnel staff member;
- going to refer to comments and 'problem areas' or issues for further exploration highlighted by your first interviewer.

**ACTIVITY 18.1   How to prepare for assessment centre interviews**

- Refer back to your initial application form or CV and covering letter.
- If you made notes following your first interview, dig them out now and use them.
- Think about the questions you were asked, what were the gaps?
- Which areas do you expect to cover again, perhaps in more depth?
- What new questions do you think they will ask?
- Expect a challenging time!
- Make sure you do thorough and up-to-date research on the company (see Chapter 11).
- Read a good-quality newspaper before you attend, concentrating especially on issues that may affect your prospective employer.

## HANDLING A PANEL INTERVIEW

It is easy to feel thrown by having more than one person in front of you during an interview, especially the first time. Look at this positively, though – panel interviews can be fairer than the traditional one-to-one type when one person's bias can rule you out.

Listen carefully when you are introduced to the panel members – it is likely that one will be a technical or professional expert, another from personnel. You can craft your responses to suit their different interests. Don't be surprised when members take notes, just try to maintain eye contact with the person who asked the current question.

**Interviews in a nutshell**

- Expect a more challenging interview than the first.
- Know what you said on your application form or in your CV.
- Do your homework on the job and the organization.

# ABILITY AND PERSONALITY TESTS

Tests are of two main types – ability and personality tests.

## ABILITY TESTS

Ability tests explore what you can do, commonly measuring verbal and numerical reasoning. There are also more technical ability tests that assess your ability with two- or three-dimensional shapes, mechanical operations or diagrams, in various combinations.

Common features of ability tests are that:

▶ they begin with a chance to work on one or two sample questions;

▶ the answers are right or wrong;

▶ they are time-limited, usually designed so you will not answer all the questions;

▶ the questions start off easy and get harder.

There are several things you need to succeed in tests. Primarily, you should have matched yourself well to the skills needed for the job. You also need information about the different types of test, guidelines on how to do well and an opportunity to practise. In order to perform really well, you need to feel refreshed and alert, so don't be tempted by free beer in the bar the night before! For specific guidance and practice tests, see Chapter 19.

## PERSONALITY TESTS

Personality tests – sometimes called personality inventories – measure 'traits', or personal characteristics, such as your motivation, how you handle your emotions and how you interact with others. Prospective employers are interested in how these qualities will affect your performance at work and your ability to fit in with the company culture.

Common features of personality tests are that:

▶ they begin with a chance to work on one or two sample questions;

▶ there are no right or wrong answers;

▶ there is usually no time limit, although the test administrator will know how long the questionnaire usually takes to complete;

▶ many tests include questions that check you are answering honestly and consistently;

▶ your answers are used to produce a personality profile;

▶ some organizations provide feedback on your personality profile.

# GIVING A PRESENTATION

Giving presentations can be stressful. You can minimize the pain by doing lots of preparation and practising. Your presentation must be designed to take account of:

▶ what the recruiter is looking for;

▶ the audience.

The selector will be looking at:

▶ your style of speaking;

▶ confidence;

▶ logical planning;

▶ skills in handling the overhead projector or IT package;

▶ your knowledge;

▶ how you handle stress.

The three main elements of skill, knowledge and personality are all under scrutiny again! Presentation skills are very important in most professional and managerial roles, as well as in commercial, scientific and research positions. Very few jobs or roles escape this requirement.

▶ Say what you are going to say.

▶ Say it.

▶ Say that you have said it.

You may be told before going to the assessment centre that you are expected to give a presentation. Equally, you may not be warned about it – some organizations like to spring it on you – so it is as well to prepare yourself just in case. You should at least be aware of the basics of how to plan, prepare and give a talk. Many of the groupwork and problem-solving exercises require a short presentation of findings.

When preparing your presentation, you should follow the instructions given to you. Pay particular attention to the time allocated and whether or not you are expected to invite and answer questions. You should also be prepared to cope with a video recording being made of your talk. Your performance may be viewed and judged by other assessors as part of the selection process.

## STRUCTURE

### A good start

Introduce the subject and get everyone interested. In particular, outline the main content of the talk as this makes it easier to listen to. Try to personalize your presentation. For example, if you have been given the choice, say *why* you chose the topic.

If you are presenting the results of a team exercise, you should start by setting the problem in context and explaining the situation to your audience.

### A good middle

Move logically through your main points. You should have planned these in advance and know how they link together. If *you* don't have a clear picture of what you are trying to say, no one else has a chance. Do not try to make too many points, provide a clear structure.

If you are presenting the results of a team exercise, this is the moment to identify key problems and issues that arose.

### A good ending

Summarize and give a conclusion. For team presentations, explain how problems can be overcome and propose workable solutions. Keep to the time given – you may be cut abruptly short if you don't, so avoid this happening. Invite questions and stimulate a discussion, if appropriate.

## PRESENTATIONS AND STYLE

- ▶ Speak as if you are addressing the people at the back of the room – especially if that is where the assessors are sitting.
- ▶ Try to relax – if the talk is about you, remind yourself you know the material better than they do.
- ▶ Keep eye contact – it helps others feel involved and holds their attention.
- ▶ Don't read from the script parrot fashion – voice and eye contact are important.
- ▶ Change pace – include some animated (bits to keep them awake), slow down for reflection (don't exhaust them) and pause occasionally.
- ▶ Be aware of body language, especially posture and how you use your hands.
- ▶ Keep it personal – help them make connections with you, make them feel they have been there.
- ▶ If you do use visual aids, make sure they are of a good quality and in a suitable font size – check everyone can read them.

### The dos and don'ts of using visual aids

You may be expected to use an overhead projector, so practise beforehand – this will help both your skill and confidence.

*Dos*

▶ Overheads should be simple and clear – make sure the people at the back of the room will be able to read them and remember that it is better for your font to be too large than too small.

▶ Use concise bullet points rather than detailed text.

▶ The content of the visual aid should support what you are saying and keep in step with your slides.

▶ Don't try to use too many slides – less is more.

*Don'ts*

▶ Standing in front of the overhead or obscuring people's view.

▶ Turn around to talk to the overhead – talk to the audience and have a copy of the slide in front of you to refer to.

▶ Just repeating what you say on the overhead – add value by what you say.

It may be possible to bring along some ready prepared overheads or a PowerPoint presentation. Consider using a couple of job-related or organizational jokes – perhaps a picture from their latest company report or your favourite cartoon characters. Use your creativity.

However, some assessment exercises allocate all candidates similar basic equipment, such as blank overheads and a set of pens to ensure a level playing field. If you are going to attempt anything creative or novel, check it out with one of the assessment team beforehand. It's great to be seen as resourceful, but you don't want to be dismissed as a total maverick.

---

**ACTIVITY 18.2    How to prepare your own presentation**

Assume you are attending an assessment centre shortly. You have been told that the programme involves your giving a ten-minute presentation about a non-academic interest.

1.  What subject will you choose? Why?
2.  What will be your main approach to, or angle on, the topic?
3.  Think of around three to five interesting key points you want to make.

*Example*
**Subject**     Orienteering
**Main idea**   My obsession
**Key points**

▶ Why orienteering attracted me – the physical and intellectual challenge.
▶ My best experience – achievement, motivation, success.
▶ My worst moment – coping with challenges, overcoming obstacles.
▶ What I have gained – friends, personal development, leadership/teamworking skills.

Now, write out your presentation on just one side of A4 paper. Practise running through it against the clock – ten minutes goes by very quickly.

You could try presenting it in front of a mirror, to a friend or taperecord yourself. Alternatively, many careers advisory services now have video equipment that can really help you improve your presentation skills or you could ask to use the overhead projector equipment in a seminar room in your department.

# IN-TRAY EXERCISES

These are designed to test your ability to absorb a large volume of complicated information quickly, work out what would be priorities and make decisions. You will be given a large amount of information, a set of instructions and a time limit. The documents usually include a pile of letters, memos and phone messages, plus some background about the organization (contact lists, personnel files, budgets and so on).

The exercises are usually set in a work-related context. If you were applying, for example, for a marketing job with a food manufacturer, you may be given reports, statistics and letters about a forthcoming new product launch. Normally, you are asked to imagine yourself in the role of a manager returning to work after a two to three week holiday or to help out a colleague who has been taken ill suddenly.

The selectors are looking for evidence that you can prioritize information, discern which issues are important and make decisions quickly. Scenarios vary. Sometimes you will be told that your out tray will be emptied every 15 minutes or you can be interrupted by a sudden 'emergency', such as a staff dispute or accident. Be prepared for interruptions or a sudden 'newsflash'.

View an in-tray exercise as being in two parts, the actual exercise and then the follow-up discussion about it. You will usually be given a chance to explain your reasons for the decisions you made. This is an important part of the event – be logical, explain your rationale and stick to your argument. There are often several ways of handling in-tray material, so simply explain the rationale behind your approach.

It may help to know that in a business environment the following are always a priority:

▶ health and safety issues;

▶ keeping production lines working and making sure services are delivered to customers;

▶ union grievances and possible industrial action;

▶ PR issues, handling the media;

▶ handling customer complaints;

▶ responding to senior managers;

▶ issues concerning the environment.

You should also think about delegating tasks to others when possible as this demonstrates leadership and teamworking skills.

You can practise the skills needed for an in-tray exercise either alone or with a friend. It would be useful especially to do this activity with someone applying for similar jobs as you.

**Time limit is 45 minutes.**

Take a copy of a quality broadsheet newspaper or a recent professional journal. Quickly scan or read through the whole newspaper/journal, then decide which five articles would be of utmost priority to the following two people in the organization you are applying to:

▶ The chief executive or managing director;
▶ The Director of Marketing or Human Resources or Chief Engineer (or other senior role for the area of work you are interested in).

Provide a brief synopsis of the contents of the article, why you consider it important and recommend the action the organization needs to take. If you have done this with a friend, you can compare notes and practise justifying your decisions.

---

**In-tray exercises in a nutshell**

▶ Scan or read the material quickly to get an overview of the issues first.
▶ There may be several ways of handling in-tray material, just explain the rationale behind your approach.
▶ Be prepared for interruptions and surprises, stay calm.
▶ Be aware of the values and priorities of particular organization or business

---

# GROUP WORK VERSUS TEAMWORK

It is important to distinguish between groups and teams. A group is merely a collection of individuals who may participate together in a particular exercise or activity. Many assessment centres deliberately include group exercises to observe your interpersonal skills, assertiveness, ability to persuade others and, especially, your competitiveness.

A *group* can become a *team* when the individual members collaborate and work together to achieve a common objective. It takes time to build genuine, supportive teamwork relationships. You may be familiar with the notion that teams evolve through five stages:

▶ form
▶ storm – when they work out relationships, establish power and control, identify skills;
▶ norm – when they establish a status quo;
▶ perform;
▶ dorm (when the team is no longer effective).

A problem with teamworking at an assessment centre is that there is little time for the team to form properly – many never really get through the storming stage. You are likely to find yourself and/or others in the group trying so hard to prove their leadership, thinking or influencing skills that the team does not work on the actual task.

## UNDERSTANDING TEAMWORK

Meredith Belbin, a well-known expert on management teams, identified the problems that can occur when people don't collaborate – something he called the 'Apollo Syndrome'. Over a long period of researching team performance, Belbin noticed the tendency for teams composed of highly talented, intelligent people to perform less well than other teams. One of the main reasons was that they spent too much time and energy competing with each other, so many failed to accomplish the task set.

Make every effort to avoid Apollo Syndrome behaviour in teams you belong to. This said, some of Belbin's Apollo teams *did* do well. It is possible for talented people to work together, but only when they learn and follow the rules of teamwork and avoid the pitfalls.

What makes a good team? A team that succeeds in reaching its objectives will usually include individuals who respect, value and listen to each other. Good teams harness individual strengths and recognize the different roles people play.

### Team roles

Belbin's work has become well known in management circles, it will certainly raise your kudos if you know of his team role ideas. If you missed it earlier, refer back to the team types section in Chapter 4.

# GROUP EXERCISES

There are several different types, including:

- ▶ group discussions – leaderless and chaired;
- ▶ problem solving and case studies;
- ▶ team games.

## GROUP DISCUSSIONS

It is common for an assessment centre to include some form of group debate or discussion. These can be in the form of a leaderless discussion group or follow a format with each candidate taking turns at being in the chair.

## Leaderless discussion group

The purpose of a leaderless discussion group is to assess your negotiation and influencing skills – it is normally only used where this is a key part of the job. IBM was one of the first companies to develop this approach, and involved each candidate presenting a particular IBM 'employee' for promotion. They were each given a CV, were required to make a brief presentation about their nominee to the group and then join in a group discussion. This approach or variations of it are still widely used in graduate recruitment today. The IBM-style exercise places you in a realistic work setting, but the downside for undergraduates is that it may favour those with real work experience.

This type of discussion group takes many forms. Rob Feltham (1989) describes another version used by Shell, where candidates make up an editorial team for a newspaper. Various news items are identified as possibilities for headline status the following day and the group makes a choice following 'an unconstrained discussion'. Another popular approach is the 'balloon debate', where the task is to present a convincing argument as to why you (or the character you are given to play) should be saved or chosen in a given emergency scenario. Some companies avoid ethical dilemmas altogether by inviting you to present the most compelling argument for being given, for example, a bar of chocolate.

## Chaired discussions

Some assessment centre exercises allocate the role of chairperson to different candidates. This is so that everyone can have an opportunity to demonstrate leadership skills and can help overcome some of the natural competitiveness that occurs at a selection centre. Exercises similar to the leaderless discussion group ones described above are sometimes used, but everyone is given a ten-minute slot to chair the discussion.

---

### Chaired discussions in a nutshell

▶ Check everyone is aware of the rules, the time allowed and the discussion topic.

▶ Initiate the discussion, open the debate up, but remember that your key objective is to get everyone else talking.

▶ Listen to what others say, respect their opinions, never disagree immediately yourself, especially if you are naturally an ideas person – remember to take on board the responsibility of being the chairperson.

▶ Give everyone an opportunity to say something, notice who is contributing.

▶ Be sensitive to shy or quiet members of the group, actually help them to join in, invite their comments.

▶ Do not dominate the discussion yourself. Control anyone in the group who does begin to dominate. Do this by gently but firmly closing them down – 'And what do others think?' or 'Let's go round the table shall we?' often work.

▶ Try to be aware of the overall group dynamics – is there an approach or idea the group has totally missed?

---

> ▶ Be aware of the time and give a warning about two minutes before the end.
>
> ▶ Encourage the group to summarize and evaluate the discussion – have you reached a consensus?
>
> ▶ Depending on the nature of the exercise, you may wish to make a brief conclusion at the end. Finish within the time set.

### ACTIVITY 18.4    Practise the role of chairperson

Ask five or six friends to join in – they may learn something to their advantage! Ask one friend to watch proceedings and keep an observation sheet, using the guidelines given above. Run through the guidelines so everyone knows what you are aiming at.

Write down a couple of discussion topics on a piece of paper (common ones include 'Should foxhunting be abolished?' 'What is the impact of IT on the quality of life?' 'All accountants are boring – myth or reality?'). Agree a ten-minute slot and start the discussion.

When you have finished, ask your observer to give you some feedback on what you did well and where you made mistakes. When giving feedback, people should be specific rather than just generally critical and should only make comments that are intended to help you gain insight and do better next time. I find it often helps if you agree that the person observing has to have a go at being in the hot seat.

## PROBLEM SOLVING AND CASE STUDIES

As well as leaderless groups, it is also common to be given an exercise that requires you to work together and find a solution to a problem. These can be in the form of cases studies, sometimes referred to as 'situational decision making'.

Two typical examples are given below – one for the private sector and one for the public sector. In these exercises, you may be given a role such as director of finance, marketing, IT or human resources. In other cases, it is left completely open, so then you could take the lead (before someone else does) and point to the need to allocate roles and responsibilities in the team.

Here are examples of case study exercises.

▶ **Virgin beer**
  Richard Branson intends to launch a new product – Virgin beer. He has appointed you as his project team. You have 12 months before this product is due to go on sale. How will you achieve this objective. You have 60 minutes to prepare your strategy. Prepare a ten-minute presentation that outlines your strategy, timetable and rationale.

▶ **Cottage hospital to close**
  The local NHS Trust is closing a 40-bed cottage hospital as part of a rationalization programme. The Trust intends to replace the lost beds by building a new wing at the existing main hospital building. Planning permission has been granted for the extension, but the hospital needs to secure funding, negotiate the changes with staff and overcome local objections. How will you achieve this

objective? You have 45 minutes to develop your strategy. Prepare a 15-minute presentation that outlines your strategy, timetable and rationale. You are not expected to know about the formal procedures or legislative framework, but do highlight any assumptions you have made in coming to your decisions.

---

### Problem-solving and case study exercises in a nutshell

If you are allocated the role of leader you should demonstrate your understanding of the role – which is to plan, motivate, organize and control – in the following ways.

▶ **Planning** Explain the rules, plan your strategy.

▶ **Motivate** You shouldn't be too hard under the circumstances. A leader generates a 'can win' attitude and maintains a sense of humour.

▶ **Organizing** Discuss who should do what, invite the team members to identify their own strengths and preferences, only be directive if you have seen the others at work and are getting to know them a little.

▶ **Controlling** Keep everyone to their allotted task or role and be aware of the time.

**Example of a problem-solving exercise**
Join all four dots to form a single enclosed shape using only three lines.

(See the answer at the end of this chapter.)

As well as having a leader, teams need a range of other talents and skills to be successful. The **ENGAGE** model for overcoming problems includes some helpful problem-solving techniques such as force field analysis (see Chapter 6 to remind yourself about this technique).

As part of a team undertaking a problem-solving activity or case study, you could:

▶ offer an original or alternative idea or think of an interesting twist to something already suggested;

▶ pay attention to the facts of the situation and make sure that the team is considering all the information given;

▶ if the group is getting too bogged down with facts and data, point to the bigger picture;

▶ draw in anyone who doesn't seem to be involved – be aware of group dynamics;

▶ notice when the group gets stuck, making a suggestion that helps the group make progress.

---

## TEAM GAMES AND ROLE-PLAYING EXERCISES

Another variation of teamwork and groupwork exercises are team games. In these, you are invited to join in a team game – usually but not always competing against another team or the clock. Typical examples include being provided with a box of basic equipment (such as three newspapers, a bucket, string and a roll of sticky tape) and then having to construct a rocket, bridge or sculpture.

One very common game involves being given a construction set, such as Lego or kNex, and, again, having to build something. There is usually a twist, such as half the team being blindfolded or a rule imposed that the design instructions can only be mimed.

You may naturally prefer a different team role to that of leader, but it is important that you accept the role if it is assigned to you. There will be opportunities for you to demonstrate your other talents!

You should also be prepared for role-playing-type exercises. These require you to act out the part of a character, usually in a work-related setting. Some companies employ trained actors to play the role of a difficult customer or work colleague. Your task would usually involve role-playing a suitable response.

For all these games, follow the points listed above under the heading Problem-solving and case study exercises in a nutshell … and maintain a sense of humour!

## HOW TO DO WELL IN GROUP EXERCISES

All groupwork exercises are designed to test a wide range of skills and personal attributes. In particular, your ability to be a good teamworker and yet make an individual contribution will be assessed. Do not be too competitive, but add something and distinctive to the discussion.

Before attending the assessment centre, think about your strengths and weaknesses in team settings. Which of the Belbin team types do you most closely resemble? (See Table 4.1 on page 44.)

Try to be involved in the exercise, yet also try to remain detached and objective. Assess where the discussion is going – what ideas and approaches are being missed? Demonstrate the capacity to think both convergently and laterally.

---

**Group exercises in a nutshell**

- ▶ Be assertive, not aggressive. Demonstrate your skills, but do so while helping the group to achieve its objective.
- ▶ Avoid the Apollo Team syndrome of being too competitive and not achieving the goals.
- ▶ Don't dominate the group and block other people; go for value not volume.
- ▶ Never put down other team members. Instead, draw the best from their ideas; be a builder, not a demolition expert.
- ▶ Be willing to think 'outside the box'.
- ▶ Be positive – think about all the experience you can bring. Seminar groups, sports activities, even sharing a flat require teamwork, negotiation and influencing skills.

---

# THE SOCIAL EVENT

There will be many opportunities to socialize at an assessment centre, over coffee, but more so at mealtimes. The selectors will want to use this time to do one of three things:

▶ see how you mix with others;

▶ give you an opportunity to relax and unwind;

▶ enable you to ask probing questions of recent graduates and managers.

Be careful, though, the socializing may be part of the assessment. I know of a solicitor's practice that uses its recent graduate staff to provide refreshments and a guided office tour to candidates. Information gleaned in this informal setting is then discussed with the partners prior to any decisions about job offers.

Many employers do offer you a genuine opportunity to mix with employees who will not be part of the selection process. Just check.

Check the dress code beforehand or with other candidates – some change for dinner, others don't. Try to relax and enjoy these events, but keep your guard up – be polite and courteous to everyone, including bar staff and receptionists. You would be amazed at the internal grapevines that operate, especially when an assessment centre is run at a company's own premises. Watch your alcohol intake and don't let things get too informal with any of the other candidates or staff!

# AFTER THE ASSESSMENT CENTRE

Make a few notes about what you did well and what, if anything, went wrong. What can you learn about yourself, the job or the organization?

Some organizations will give you some feedback on your performance at the centre but, the quality and quantity of the information is variable. If you want to do a more thorough review, you can use the checklist in Activity 18.5.

Normally you will receive a letter within a week or so from the assessment centre with their decision. If they offer you a job, congratulations, but turn to Chapter 20 before you accept or reject the offer.

If a thin letter comes by second-class post in a dull brown envelope, you can reassure yourself that you *nearly* made it. If the decision comes as a surprise – you thought you had done well – as mentioned earlier, you can phone the organization and ask for feedback.

Note down your answers to the following questions.

How did you feel when you arrived at the assessment centre?

_____

_____

How much preparation and planning had you done beforehand? Looking back, were there any gaps in your knowledge?

_____

_____

Which activities did you do well at? Why?

_____

_____

Make a note of any activities that surprised you. On reflection, how could you handle these better next time?

_____

_____

Write down anything unexpected that happened. For example, was this your first assessment centre role play or in-tray exercise?

_____

_____

What will you do differently next time?

_____

_____

Make sure you ask for feedback. What had impressed them? Where did you fall short? What did the assessors suggest about the way you could have improved your performance?

_____

_____

# FURTHER INFORMATION

Feltham, R. T. (1989) 'Assessment Centres' in Herriot, P. (ed., 1989) *Assessment and Selection in Organizations: Methods and practice for recruitment and appraisal*, Wiley, Chichester.

Keenan, T. (1995) 'Graduate recruitment in Britain: A survey of selection methods used by organizations', *Journal of Organizational Behaviour*, 16, pp. 303–17.

Woodruffe, C. (1993) *Assessment Centres: Identifying and developing competence* (2nd ed.), IPD, London.

# SIGNPOSTS TO MORE HELP

## In this book:

▶ Chapter 4, on personality and teamworking

▶ Chapter 6, on overcoming obstacles

▶ Chapter 17, on interview success

▶ Chapter 19, on ability, personality and other tests

## In other career books:

▶ Hornby, M. (1994) *36 Steps to the Job you Want*, Longman, Harlow.

▶ Perrett, J. (1996) *Job Hunting after University or College*, Kogan Page, London.

▶ Phillips, C. (1996) *Second Interviews and Assessment Centres*, GTI specialist publications, London.

---

**Confessions of a graduate assessor**

▶ Don't assume that all the assessors know what they are doing. Some do, some don't. Some may even be employees who were only recruited last year themselves. They were put through this, so they may enjoy watching others suffer!

▶ Some will like being part of an assessment centre, others welcome it as much as a wart on the nose. Most people acting as assessors have busy jobs and targets to meet; they view graduate recruitment as a necessary evil.

▶ Watch out when the senior management team arrives. This usually means that there is at least one person at the assessment centre that the company really wants to win over. Watch who they sit with – that will be the person or people they are targeting.

▶ Do not leave the bar much before 11.30am – antisocial behaviour – but, equally, don't stay after around 2pm – the Bar Staff will complain about you. No one will make allowances for your hangover in the morning, and it is not the best way to prepare for ability tests or team games!

▶ Most assessment centres end with a wash-up session, when your results and performance are evaluated. On occasions this is done objectively. More often, though, the 'top brass' influence outcomes and objectivity goes out of the window. Make sure you know who really makes decisions and impress them shamelessly!

---

Answer to example of a problem-solving exercise

Think outside the box!

# how to succeed at selection tests

**Testing times ahead? Get the inside information and practice you need to win!**

**In this chapter, you will:**

☐ develop an understanding of selection tests;

☐ learn about different types of test;

☐ find out how to prepare for tests;

☐ focus on ability testing;

☐ see how to succeed at tests;

☐ learn about personality questionnaires;

☐ find out what to expect;

☐ learn how to prepare.

**Take the following practice tests:**

▶ verbal reasoning

▶ numerical reasoning

▶ abstract reasoning

▶ mechanical reasoning

▶ personality tests

# INTRODUCTION

Tests of any sort are enough to send a chill running down the spine. Most of us know only too well how much is at stake. In the case of selection tests, anxiety runs high, questions run through your mind – 'What will the tests reveal about me?', 'What will they be like?', 'How will they be conducted?', 'Will I succeed or fail?'

More and more companies are using ability, personality and other tests as part of the recruitment process for both work experience placements and graduate jobs. Investing some time in finding out what is involved and practising can give you the edge over other candidates.

The amount of information available to help you prepare is often very sketchy and the opportunities to practise are limited. This chapter is designed to give you all the information you need to be fully informed and prepared for any tests you may need to do.

# UNDERSTANDING SELECTION TESTS

Quite varied techniques are used to evaluate candidates in selection. A number of these – such as group discussions, in-tray and team exercises – have been described in the previous chapter. This chapter, though, focuses on the formal *psychological* selection tests that fall under a generic umbrella term 'pyschometric'. This term is generally used to describe a procedure that evaluates psychological functions, such as intelligence, ability, personality, interests and values. They usually involve a pencil and paper or are computer-based tests that are administered under standardized conditions. Your answers are analyzed to produce a score or profile. Results are usually quantified by reference to a scale derived from research. Your scores can then be compared to those of other people who have taken the test or tests before.

Such tests should be administered and analyzed by properly qualified staff. In the UK, the British Psychological Society (BPS) is responsible for issuing certificates of competence. Many leading test publishers also require test administrators to attend their own training courses before letting them loose on students and graduates. The BPS and firms of occupational psychologists are keen to maintain standards, both of the tests and the way candidates are treated. Be encouraged!

# WHY EMPLOYERS USE TESTS

Tests are used for a variety of reasons. One of these is that they are seen as objective, scientific and fair. Selecting candidates according to various measures of ability and individual temperament can help employers maintain their standards and company culture, especially when recruiting a large number of graduates from all over the UK or even worldwide. From the employers' point of view, they can also help streamline the recruitment process.

Tests have their critics, who oppose their theoretical basis (for example, they ask if intelligence or personality really can be measured objectively) and highlight problems with specific tests, questioning their validity or tendency to unfair discrimination (often on grounds of gender and race). You may well feel concern yourself at the idea of your intelligence and ability being measured and labelled 'objectively'. On a positive note, psychometric tests are not normally used as the only basis for selection – they are intended to complement other procedures, such as interviews.

# HOW TO PREPARE FOR TESTS

There are basically three things that you need to do well in tests:

▶ a positive attitude;
▶ information;
▶ practice.

## A POSITIVE ATTITUDE

It is all too easy to allow exam nerves to take over. Keep in mind that you have got to an advanced stage of selection – the organization is interested in you. Next, try to focus on the benefits to you of doing the tests – you may learn more about yourself. In the long run, finding out about your genuine strengths and weaknesses can help guide you to the right job and employer. Try to see the test as an opportunity, not a threat!

## INFORMATION

We all feel more anxious when we enter the unknown. The organization should give you practical details about the time and place of the tests, though they will not tell you exactly which tests you will take. As a minimum, you can prepare yourself by knowing generally what tests are measuring and how they work, the practical arrangements for testing and how you will receive feedback.

## PRACTICE

You can practise in a number of ways. Included is a set of sample questions for each of the main types of graduate recruitment test (the answers are given at the end of the chapter).

> **CASE STUDY   Gareth – my first selection test**
>
> 'I had applied to one of the top blue chip retailers for a place on their graduate trainee scheme. Everyone regards these as plum jobs and I knew I would be up against stiff competition.
>
> 'I had read the employer file at my careers advisory service and knew there would be at least three tests – one verbal, one numerical and a thinking/personality type. This was sort of confirmed in a letter. I was told there would be tests in the morning, followed by interviews in the afternoon.
>
> 'The tests did feel like another exam – we sat in silence and I could here the scratching of pencils and heavy sighing all around me. The time flew, I found the verbal tests quite easy, the numerical one was hard for me but I'm a typical history student! I knew the numerical test would be hard and I had tried to improve by swotting using some simple maths and statistics workbooks. Just reminding myself of what to do with equations, brackets and percentages helped me feel more confident.
>
> 'I got some feedback at the interview – I had done really well in the verbal tests and even managed above average in the numerical one.
>
> 'Again, the hard work I had done contemplating my navel paid off during the interview. The discussion about my personality profile was very interesting – overall, I seemed to have painted a pretty accurate picture of myself.
>
> 'I can highly recommend practising. Play to your strengths but minimize your weaknesses!!'

# TEST PROCEDURE

The contexts for taking the test may vary. Some tests are taken alone as part of an initial screening, but it is more common to include them alongside an interview or an assessment centre (see Chapters 17 and 18 for more information). Most tests will follow a similar format.

## ADVANCE INFORMATION

You will usually be invited to attend by a test letter. Most employers tell you in advance that you will be tested and will give a broad outline of the abilities they will measure. Some employers send you a short test takers guide that sets out the testing procedures and gives you a couple of sample tests. If you have any special needs – for example, regarding mobility or diet – you will be asked to let the employer know beforehand so they can make the necessary arrangements.

## ARRIVING FOR THE TEST

Organizations understand that this may be a nerve-wracking time. They usually try to put you at your ease, provide refreshments and a comfortable waiting area.

## TEST ADMINISTRATION

In order to maintain their reliability and validity, tests are usually administered in what may seem like a cold, standardized way. The testing room may resemble a traditional exam environment, with formal seating arrangements – be ready to battle the chill factor! The test administrator should outline the rules of play – how long you have to complete the test, how to fill in the questionnaire or use the computer and so on.

If you wear glasses and have left them in your coat pocket, don't worry. There is always time built in for you to sort out practicalities. You will be given an opportunity to look at, and try, a sample test question and have time to ask for clarification if you don't understand anything.

You then take the test and hand in your completed answer paper at the end, again under standardized conditions and you will not be allowed to escape with any test booklets to show to your friends. These are kept locked away to protect the integrity of the test or tests.

## FEEDBACK

The amount of feedback you receive varies enormously according to the type of test and the willingness of the organization. I know of students who have enjoyed lengthy phone calls discussing their performance and others who have received little or no feedback at all.

As a candidate for testing, you can expect:

▶ to be treated with respect;

▶ to have the tests explained and give your consent to the process;

▶ test results to be handled confidentially and sensitively;

▶ people administering the tests to be fully qualified and competent;

▶ to be given feedback on your performance.

# TYPES OF TESTS

Without getting into all the technical complexities, tests are one of two main types:

▶ aptitude, ability and intelligence tests;

▶ tests of personality, also called tests of temperament or personality inventories.

# APTITUDE, ABILITY AND INTELLIGENCE TESTS

Various ways of understanding the notions of intelligence and ability have already been discussed in Chapter 4. Modern theories of intelligence accept that there are different dimensions or aptitudes, such as numerical, verbal and spatial skills. You may be musical, have great dexterity or a brilliant sense of direction. Most of us are good, even superb, at some of these and weak (useless?) in others.

## GENERAL INTELLIGENCE

Full-blown, general or global intelligence tests are very long, complicated and expensive to administer. Very few graduate employers are likely to give you 'the works'. Many use shortened tests that focus on a particular aspect of intelligence that they feel is important if you are to be a success in the job you are applying for.

The four most common types of tests for graduates focus on verbal and numerical ability. There are other types of tests, usually targeted at applicants for technical jobs. These include non-verbal reasoning tests, spatial ability, mechanical ability and diagrammatic reasoning. These tests usually last around 20-40 minutes each, often appropriately referred to as a 'battery'!

Some organizations have commissioned specialist tests, designed for certain occupations, such as IT, actuaries, accountants or to test for knowledge of a foreign language.

## VERBAL ABILITY TESTS

There is a massive range of tests, even within just the 'verbal ability' category. Verbal reasoning tests measure the ability to see relationships between words. They often require a blend of both reasoning and good vocabulary. They also require that you work quickly because the tests invariably have time limits. These sorts of tests are used in occupational fields that require written and oral communication, such as business, management, education and most professions. There are three very common types of questions – on analogies, synonyms and antonyms.

# PRACTISE TAKING TESTS

You now have an opportunity to practise taking a number of tests. These questions are reproduced from *Prepare for Tests at Interview for Graduates and Managers*, by Robert Williams (1999) (ISBN 0–7005–1601–8, published by NFER–Nelson Publishing Company Ltd, Darville House, 2 Oxford Road East, Windsor SL4 1DF). As the book title suggests, the tests are specially designed for graduate and managerial level, so their difficulty provides a genuine benchmark for the real thing.

Following normal test procedures, you are given a sample test with a worked answer, followed by further questions. The answers are all provided at the end of the chapter.

# VERBAL REASONING TESTS

## Finding words that are related in a logical way – analogies

**Example**

Circle the correct answer.

**Q1** **Wasp** is to **sting** as **lion** is to ...
A. fierce
B. roar
C. bite
D. tail
E. mane

The answer to Q1 is (C) bite, as that is how lions attack. You may have been tempted to answer (D) tail, but this misses the key concept of inflicting pain. The key skill here is to find how the two words are connected. Here are some more to try.

**Q2** **Animals** are to **hybrid** as **metals** are to ...
A. mixture
B. alloy
C. compound
D. blend
E. element

**Q3** **Word** is to **abbreviate** as **book** is to ...
A. edit
B. shorten
C. abridge
D. amend
E. compress

**Q4** **Fathomless** is to **deep** as **infinitesimal** is to ...
A. short
B. large
C. small
D. long
E. narrow

**Q5** **Drought** is to **rain** as **stalemate** is to ...
A. draw
B. progress
C. hindrance
D. cessation
E. inequality

## Finding words with the same meaning – synonyms

A second type of verbal intelligence tests asks you to identify a word with the same meaning from a list (usually of five alternatives). These types of questions may advantage certain groups and possibly disadvantage others. Today, care is taken to eradicate gender or ethnic bias as far as possible.

### Example

Of the five multiple choice alternatives suggested, select the one that is closest in meaning to the word in bold.

**Q6** The **ascetic** hermit dwelt in a hut on the mountain top.
 A. austere
 B. religious
 C. penitent
 D. reclusive
 E. indigent

The answer to Q6 is (A) austere. Some of the other words may be used to describe a hermit. However, you must follow the test instruction, to identify the word that is closest in meaning to 'ascetic', not another word to describe a hermit.

**Q7** On the flight to New York, she sat next to a very **garrulous** woman.
 A. sullen
 B. attractive
 C. convivial
 D. loud
 E. talkative

**Q8** At the school assembly, the headmaster sternly declared, 'Honesty is a **tenet** of this institution.'
 A. rule
 B. principle
 C. tradition
 D. secret
 E. solemn

**Q9** The king filled his court with **sychophants** and fops.
 A. courtiers
 B. flatterers
 C. loyalists
 D. advisers
 E. dandies

**Q10** Investing in the nuclear power industry proved to be the entrepreneur's most **astute** decision.
 A. calculated
 B. risky
 C. controversial
 D. lucrative
 E. shrewd

## Finding words with the opposite meaning – antonyms

Verbal reasoning tests may also ask you to find a word with the opposite meaning.

### Example
Select the multiple-choice option that is the *opposite* in meaning to the word shown in bold. Circle the correct answer.

**Q11 mean**
  A. generous
  B. average
  C. miser
  D. median
  E. good

The answer to Q11 is (A) generous. If you have answered (B), (C) or (D), you have wrongly chosen words of *similar* meaning. The key to success in these tests is to pay careful attention to the instructions! Why not try the remaining practice questions, remembering this advice.

Select the multiple-choice option that is the *opposite* in meaning to the word shown in bold.

**Q12 sincere**
  A. faithful
  B. hypocritical
  C. genuine
  D. suspicious
  E. unkind

**Q13 evergreen**
  A. myrtle
  B. flower
  C. deciduous
  D. fern
  E. yellow

**Q14 innocuous**
  A. vaccinate
  B. amicable
  C. harmful
  D. ostensible
  E. effusive

**Q15 benevolent**
  A. kind
  B. empirical
  C. demagogue
  D. uncharitable
  E. eminent

## TIPS FOR SUCCESS IN VERBAL ABILITY TESTS

▶ Take a watch and keep an eye on the time. Move through the questions as quickly as possible. Don't worry if you cannot finish all the answers – you are rarely expected to!

▶ Don't allow yourself to get stuck on one problem – move on to the next.

▶ Read the instructions carefully – are you being asked to find the *same* or *opposite* meaning?

▶ Pay attention to detail.

▶ Keep checking that you are marking your answers against the correct answer box – make sure the numbers match.

▶ Remember that these verbal tests are only measuring a narrow field of your ability. They do not look at your sense of humour, creativity or your ability to influence.

## HOW TO IMPROVE YOUR PERFORMANCE IN VERBAL ABILITY TESTS

The verbal sections of intelligence or ability tests have a lot in common with quick crosswords commonly found in newspapers. You can improve your performance by:

▶ doing such crossword puzzles – they help improve both your vocabulary and develop the reasoning process;

▶ playing scrabble;

▶ buying a specialist crossword or puzzlebook, available from most newsagents;

▶ testing your own general knowledge – watch quiz programmes and answer as many questions as you can;

▶ stretching your vocabulary – use the reference tools in your word processing package, especially the Thesaurus.

There are also many tests used that explore your powers to think critically. They might test for your ability to:

▶ evaluate the validity of inferences drawn from a series of factual statements;

▶ distinguish between strong and weak arguments;

▶ identify unstated assumptions or presuppositions.

# CRITICAL THINKING TESTS

## Comprehension and critical thinking

Many graduate and managerial roles require employees to extract relevant information quickly from written documents and make judgements based on that information. The following four examples give you an opportunity to test your own powers of comprehension.

### Example

The comprehension questions below consist of a passage of text, followed by two statements about the information contained within the passage. Identify which of these statements is *correct* and which is *incorrect*. Only use the information provided in the passages. Assume that the information is correct in the passages, even if you know otherwise.

### Comprehension passage 1

> Editors are not just glorified spellcheckers. They have to ensure that the text is grammatically correct. They have to check that the typesetters and artists have produced material that is in line with the specifications that they were given. An editor must clarify that all the artwork and tables are in the correct places. It is also vital that they check that every aspect of a product adheres to company standards. They liaise with many internal and external contacts, including authors, product managers and production controllers.

Is the following statement (A) correct or (B) incorrect? Please circle the correct answer.

**Q16** Product managers and production controllers must liaise closely with external contacts.
   A. correct
   B. incorrect

The passage only refers to the role of the editor liaising with product managers and production controllers. The statement made in Q16 cannot be substantiated from the information provided in the passage, so the answer is (B), incorrect, based on the information in the passage alone.

### Further questions about comprehension passage 1

Are these statements (A) correct or (B) incorrect? Please circle the correct answer.

**Q17** Editors can ignore company standards when they consider it appropriate.
   A. correct
   B. incorrect

**Q18** An editor must check that artwork is in the correct position.
   A. correct
   B. incorrect

**Comprehension passage 2**

Cinema recently celebrated its hundredth anniversary. A multimillion-dollar business, cinema is the United States' second largest industry, second only to aeronautics. However, today's blockbuster Hollywood films, with their dazzling computer-generated special effects, would not have been possible without the pioneering work of Edward Muybridge in the late nineteenth century. An English photographer, Muybridge photographed sequences of animals and humans running and walking. He invented a device called a succession, creating an illusion of movement. Films today are shot on 35mm film and shown through a projector, which operates in a similar manner to Muybridge's invention. A typical feature-length film uses 2.5km (1.5 miles) of film, which runs through the projector at a rate of 8 frames per second. Although Muybridge's experiments did not feature sound, plot, colour or movie stars, his vision paved the way for an entire industry.

Are the following statements (A) correct or (B) incorrect. Please circle the correct answer.

**Q19** Feature films today can use several kilometres of film.
  A. correct
  B. incorrect

**Q20** Edward Muybridge has a place in cinema history as a pioneer.
  A. correct
  B. incorrect

# NUMERICAL ABILITY TESTS

Numerical ability tests measure the ability to perform mathematical reasoning tasks and may feel like a conventional exam. Questions explore your ability to handle basics such as addition, subtraction, multiplication and division. The purpose of most of these tests is to measure reasoning skills rather than mathematical ability. In some tests you will be allowed to use a calculator. There are several types of questions set out below with examples.

## TEST PRACTICE ACTIVITY

## General number sequence

Many tests include a general number sequence, in which you have to work out the missing digit. Such tests may begin with a few easy problems and then introduce more complexity. It is worth remembering that they may involve more than basic addition, subtraction, division or multiplication.

### Example
Choose the correct answer from the five multiple-choice alternatives provided (A, B, C, D, E), circling the correct answer.

**Q21** 3  9  36  ?  1080
    A. 130
    B. 131
    C. 180
    D. 181
    E. 360

In Q21, the numbers follow a pattern of multiplication of $3 \times 3$, $9 \times 4$, $36 \times 5$ and $180 \times 6$, so the answer is (C), 180.

Work out the number sequences in the following questions.

**Q22** 1664  824  404  194  ?
    A. 89
    B. 365
    C. 44
    D. 45
    E. 46

**Q23** 7  18  47  ?  322
    A. 100
    B. 123
    C. 127
    D. 137
    E. 143

**Q24** –3  –1  3  9  ?  27
    A. 13
    B. 14
    C. 15
    D. 17
    E. 23

**Q25** 75  300  150  100  300  ?
    A. 200
    B. 150
    C. 100
    D. 75
    E. 33.3

## Numerical reasoning in a work context

Within the workplace, numerical information can be encountered in a number of formats. You may be required to understand and interpret graphs, pie charts and tables. Use the following sample questions to get a feel for the type of approach these tests usually take.

### Example
The simple and compound interest figures for the different rates, added on to £100.00 after 5 years, are shown in the table below.

| Yearly rate (%) | Simple | Compound |
| --- | --- | --- |
| 7 | £35.00 | £40.26 |
| 8 | £40.00 | £46.93 |
| 9 | £45.00 | £53.86 |
| 10 | £50.00 | £61.05 |

**Q26** What would the total compound interest be on £200.00 at a rate of 8 per cent over 5 years?
A. £107.72
B. £93.86
C. £87.19
D. £80.52
E. £88.00

The 8 per cent compound interest in the table shows that £100.00 earns £46.93 in interest after 5 years. The total compound interest on £200.00 at a rate of 8 per cent over 5 years will be twice this amount, making:

2 × £46.93 = £93.86.

The correct option, therefore is (B).

**Q27** How much extra is earned in compound interest, compared to simple interest, on £300.00 at 9 per cent over 5 years?
A. £18.86
B. £13.29
C. £26.58
D. £27.28
E. £53.86

The table shows the population of six countries, together with their population density.

| Country | Population (millions) | Population density (people per km²) |
|---|---|---|
| Australia | 17.8 | 2 |
| Canada | 27.8 | 3 |
| Japan | 125.0 | 33 |
| Sweden | 8.7 | 21 |
| UK | 57.8 | 239 |
| US | 257.8 | 28 |

**Q28** What is the total area of Japan in square kilometres (in 10,000s)?
A. 264.0
B. 37.8
C. 206.0
D. 26.4
E. 378.0

**Q29** What is the difference between the populations of Canada and the US combined, and Japan and Australia combined?
A. 115.0
B. 132.8
C. 142.8
D. 257.8
E. 267.8

**Q30** If the Japanese population increased by 4 per cent annually over the next 2 years, what would its population be in 2 years' time?
A. 135.20
B. 135.25
C. 135.40
D. 135.35
E. 135.30

# NON-VERBAL AND ABSTRACT
# REASONING TESTS

The overall purpose of non-verbal tests is to find out how well you can understand ideas and solve problems that are not expressed in words or numbers.

These tests include:

▶ non-verbal and abstract reasoning;

▶ spatial reasoning;

▶ diagrammatic reasoning;

▶ mechanical reasoning.

'Non-verbal reasoning' tests measure your ability to appraise various sequences and patterns. Typical questions give a series of three designs that change in a predictable way. You are then asked to choose the correct figure to complete the pattern or fill in a missing box from a range of alternatives.

Patterns are usually built up from several elements that change or rotate logically. The key to success is to recognize the elements and the different sequences being followed.

## TEST PRACTICE ACTIVITY

## Non-verbal and abstract reasoning

### Example
Identify the logical patterns within the sequences of squares in each grid, then decide which of the multiple-choice options is the most appropriate for the empty square in the grid and circle your answer on the answer sheet overleaf.

**Q31**

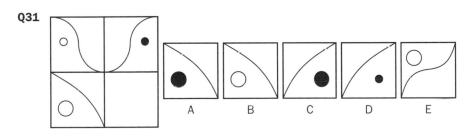

In Q31, the curved line of the top left-hand box is mirrored in the top right-hand box, and the small white circle is reversed to become a black dot. When the same pattern principles are repeated on the lower box, the correct shape is pattern (C).

Practise non-verbal reasoning by trying the following questions.

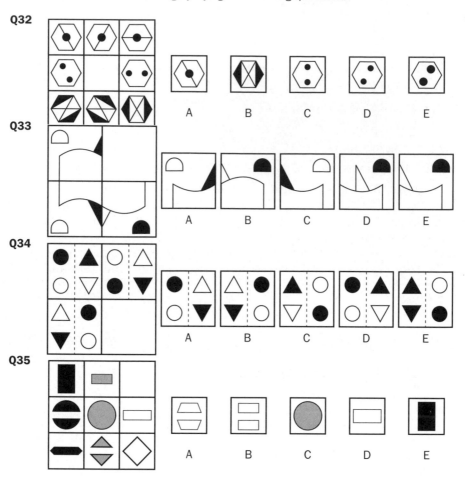

Answer sheet for questions 31 to 35

| Q31 | A | B | C | D | E |
|-----|---|---|---|---|---|
| Q32 | A | B | C | D | E |
| Q33 | A | B | C | D | E |
| Q34 | A | B | C | D | E |
| Q35 | A | B | C | D | E |

## HOW TO IMPROVE YOUR PERFORMANCE IN NON-VERBAL AND ABSTRACT REASONING TESTS

▶ Make sure you identify each element to the puzzle, then assess the sequence being followed.

▶ If you find the figures difficult, look at the answers and work back to find the sequence.

▶ When taking the tests for real, don't allow yourself to get stuck on one problem. Leave it and move on.

## SPATIAL REASONING AND SPATIAL RELATIONS

These tests measure how well you can visualize (form mental pictures) of solid objects from a flat paper plan. They try to answer the question 'How well do you think in three dimensions?'

Tests of spatial ability are similar to abstract reasoning questions, but usually consist of three-dimensional rather than two-dimensional puzzles.

Spatial relations tests consist of patterns with colours, shading or designs. You need to follow the same principles as with abstract puzzles. Try to break the puzzle down into its constituent parts and work out each part of the sequence separately.

# DIAGRAMMATIC AND MECHANICAL REASONING TESTS

There are many specialist tests targeted to test whether candidates have specific skills or can do particular jobs. A common example of technical tests are tests of mechanical reasoning. These tests explore your grasp of the common principles of physics, such as gravity and motion. They measure your understanding of the ways in which simple tools and machines move and operate. There are also special tests for diagrammatic reasoning and IT.

Many employers have commissioned tests to be designed to meet their own organizational requirements according to specific job-related skills. These are very common in accountancy, actuarial services and in specialist professions such as air traffic control. Keep in mind that tests are chosen to reflect the skills and abilities needed to do the job well. If you are suited to the job, the tests should not present huge problems!

## TEST PRACTICE ACTIVITY

## Mechanical reasoning

Examples of typical mechanical tests suitable for graduates and managerial positions are given here. Take a look at the mechanical problems and choose which of the five multiple-choice answers provided is correct.

**Q36** A crowbar is used to lift a load (below). Which crowbar makes lifting the load easiest?

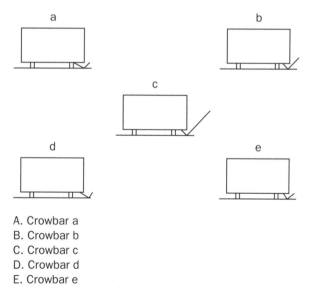

A. Crowbar a
B. Crowbar b
C. Crowbar c
D. Crowbar d
E. Crowbar e

The longest crowbar will make lifting the load easiest, so the answer to Q36 is (C).

**Q37**  Which person exerts the least pressure on the platform?

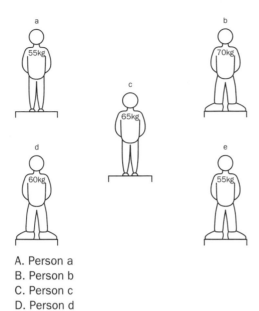

A. Person a
B. Person b
C. Person c
D. Person d
E. Person e

**Q38**  If wave 1 met wave 2 travelling in the opposite direction, which wave would result?

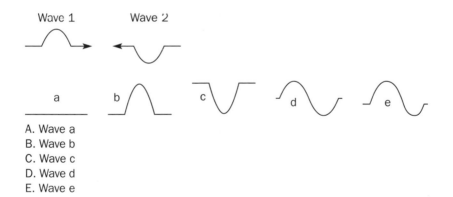

A. Wave a
B. Wave b
C. Wave c
D. Wave d
E. Wave e

**Q39** The five solid objects below are made from the same material. Which object has the lowest centre of gravity? (All objects are the same height.)

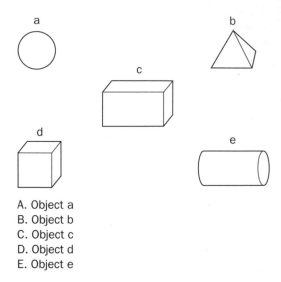

A. Object a
B. Object b
C. Object c
D. Object d
E. Object e

**Q40** Below are cross-sections of five aircraft wings. Which wing will produce the greatest lift?

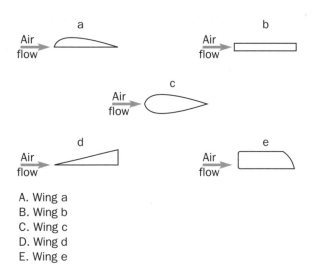

A. Wing a
B. Wing b
C. Wing c
D. Wing d
E. Wing e

# WHAT NEXT?

I hope you have found taking these sample tests useful.

You now know what is involved. You may have identified particular strengths and weaknesses. Use the tips for improving your performance to raise the standard of your answers to the questions. This will increase your confidence, reduce anxiety on the test day and so improve your performance.

# TESTS OF PERSONALITY AND PERSONALITY INVENTORIES

As we saw in Chapter 4, personality can be defined as 'people's characteristic tendency to behave, think and feel in certain ways'. Personality tests or inventories measure traits that may affect your performance at work, such as motivation and how you interact with others. In the graduate job scene, personality is often seen as an important indicator of whether or not you will be suited to a particular job and fit in with the organizational culture. Some tests measure the strength of your vocational or career interests.

The use of personality tests is more controversial than the use of ability tests. Critics point to ethical problems of assessing human nature in this way. Others believe that the underpinning theories are at fault – for example, by placing too much emphasis on temperament and too little on situation or circumstances. A more practical objection is that they are too inaccurate – far below the levels of reliability and validity offered by ability tests. Keep these criticisms in mind whenever you are asked to discuss the results of your tests.

These tests involve answering a set of questions and these are used to generate a profile or picture of your personality, your answers are interpreted to show how you score on each personality trait along a range compared to other people. A set of personality factors that are used frequently is shown in Figure 19.1 – in this case, 16 separate traits are used.

Your answers to the questionnaire will reveal whether you are, for example, more cool and emotionally distant (typical of introverts) than warm and attentive to others (typical of extroverts). The particular way of creating your profile differs from test to test, but most do provide a quite detailed measure of your score for each trait. If you look at each of the 16 personality traits listed in Figure 19.1, you will probably know roughly which side of the mid point you are on for each one. For example, are you very shy (far left), slightly shy (just left of the mid point), sometimes bold (just right of the mid point) or very bold and thick-skinned (far right)? It is important to note that most people will have a personality profile that includes scores on both sides of the mid point. So, a very shy person may also be very calm and self-reliant. Equally, another very shy person may be easily upset and reactive. Your profile is unique to you.

| | | | |
|---|---|---|---|
| Cool, emotionally distant | | ⇐ v ⇒ | Warm, attentive |
| Concrete thinking | | ⇐ v ⇒ | Abstract thinking |
| Easily upset, reactive | | ⇐ v ⇒ | Calm, stable |
| Avoids conflict | | ⇐ v ⇒ | Dominant, forceful |
| Serious, careful | | ⇐ v ⇒ | Lively, spontaneous |
| Non-conforming | | ⇐ v ⇒ | Dutiful, role follower |
| Shy, timid | | ⇐ v ⇒ | Social, bold, thick-skinned |
| Objective | | ⇐ v ⇒ | Subjective |
| Trusting, unsuspecting | | ⇐ v ⇒ | Wary, sceptical, shrewd |
| Self-assured | | ⇐ v ⇒ | Self-doubting |
| Traditional | | ⇐ v ⇒ | Experimenting |
| Group-centred | | ⇐ v ⇒ | Self-reliant |
| Flexible, tolerates disorder | | ⇐ v ⇒ | Self-disciplined, perfectionist |
| Related, patient | | ⇐ v ⇒ | Tense, driven |

**FIGURE 19.1  Personality traits that are used to create personality profiles**
Source: © Used with kind permission of ASE: NFER–Nelson Publishing Company, Windsor

## TYPES OF PERSONALITY TEST QUESTIONS

Most personality questionnaires have no set time limit. In all other respects, they are administered under the same conditions as ability tests. The questions differ in that there are no right or wrong answers – except, of course, that you know there are selection criteria that suggest some qualities are more desirable than others. A tense, bad-tempered and disorganized individual is hardly likely to thrive as a manager!

### The basic 'yes' and 'no' questionnaire or inventory

The simplest type of questionnaire asks questions that require straightforward 'yes' or 'no' answers. These are rather transparent. For example, 'Do you ever drink too much?', 'Do you have many nightmares?', 'Would you call yourself an anxious person?' You may encounter these types of question, but more common are the rather more subtle approaches that are harder to work out.

### Most like you/least like you

Some questionnaires will ask you to tick the answer that is most like you and put a cross against the one that is least like you.

### Example
I am a person who …

❏ enjoys parties
❏ often feels angry
❏ keeps things tidy
❏ is competitive

## The rating scale approach

Many questionnaires ask you to rate yourself on a scale from 1 to 5 regarding a number of statements. You are either asked to mark the questionnaire or fill in the appropriate box if you are given a separate answer sheet.

### Example
Please circle the response that most closely represents you by each statement:

|  | Strongly disagree | Disagree | Unsure | Agree | Strongly agree |
|---|---|---|---|---|---|
| I am a person who enjoys parties | 1 | 2 | 3 | 4 | 5 |
| I get angry quite often | 1 | 2 | 3 | 4 | 5 |
| I always keep things tidy | 1 | 2 | 3 | 4 | 5 |
| I am a competitive person | 1 | 2 | 3 | 4 | 5 |

Personality questionnaires can be short or long. The better tests generally have more questions, with 100–120 being quite normal. These should only take you around 30–40 minutes to complete. Some shorter versions are also used.

## HOW DO THE RECRUITERS VIEW PERSONALITY TESTS?

Designing and selling graduate selection tests is big business worldwide. These tests have made a significant impact on the graduate jobhunting scene, but let's keep things in perspective. Many recruiters view the whole process of testing (especially personality assessments) with a healthy degree of scepticism. The results of your personality test should be considered to represent only part of the picture – information on your CV and what was discussed at interview or observed during an assessment centre exercise filling in the rest.

## BEING SOCIALLY DESIRABLE!

In personality tests, there is plenty of scope for answering the questions in a way that you think is desired or expected.

Most tests have a built-in honesty check that measures the extent to which you massage your replies to make a good impression. Watch for questions such as 'Have you ever told a lie?' or 'Do you ever lose your temper?', 'Do you ever gossip?' Even the most moral, calm and discreet of us would have a problem saying 'no' honestly.

### Faking – is it worth it?

*Arguments for*
The advantages to you are that you demonstrate what you believe to be desirable qualities. You may even be able to change and adapt your personality so you do eventually conform to the picture you have portrayed.

Some employers see social desirability as a quality in itself. You may be demonstrating to them that you are an adaptable sort of person who is willing to fit in with what the organization wants – a sort of chameleon effect. You may have a lot to offer.

*And against*
You may end up being selected for a job you are not suited to, you may feel a fraud and could reinforce doubts that you are worth while as you are. Why pretend you are something you are not?

## HOW TO DO WELL IN PERSONALITY TESTS

▶ Know yourself well.
▶ Try to like yourself – if you don't, take action now, looking at the relevant text on personality in Chapter 4 and overcoming obstacles in Chapter 6.
▶ Be positive.
▶ Think about the qualities the job requires and be aware that a variety of roles can be fulfilled successfully by very different people.

# SIGNPOSTS TO MORE HELP

### Available from careers advisory services:
▶ *Prospects HE* – a self-reporting computer program-based personality/careers guidance questionnaire
▶ Psychometric test practice booklets
▶ Saville and Holdsworth Limited (SHL) practice tests (cost around £4.00 each from careers offices).

### Go on-line
www.shlgroup.com
SHL has a very useful, interactive career assessment service.

### Helpful books
Williams, Robert (1999) *Prepare for Tests at Interview for Graduates and Managers*, NFER-Nelson Publishing Company, Windsor.

Cohen, David (1993) *How to Succeed in Psychometric Tests*, Sheldon, London.

Parkinson, Mark (1997) *How to Master Personality Questionnaires*: The essential guide. Kogan Page, London.

A more comprehensive list is provided at the end of the Appendix.

# ANSWERS TO TEST PRACTICE QUESTIONS

## Finding words that are related in a logical way – analogies

| Questions | Answers |
|-----------|---------|
| 1 | C |
| 2 | B |
| 3 | C |
| 4 | C |
| 5 | B |

## Finding words with the same meaning – synonyms

| Questions | Answers |
|-----------|---------|
| 6 | A |
| 7 | E |
| 8 | B |
| 9 | B |
| 10 | E |

## Finding words with the opposite meaning – antonyms

| Questions | Answers |
|-----------|---------|
| 11 | A |
| 12 | B |
| 13 | C |
| 14 | C |
| 15 | D |

## Comprehension and critical thinking

| Questions | Answers |
|-----------|---------|
| 16 | B |
| 17 | B |
| 18 | A |
| 19 | A |
| 20 | A |

## General number sequence

| Questions | Answers |
|-----------|---------|
| 21 | C |
| 22 | A |
| 23 | B |
| 24 | D |
| 25 | E |

## Numerical reasoning in a work context

| Questions | Answers |
|-----------|---------|
| 26 | B |
| 27 | C |
| 28 | B |
| 29 | C |
| 30 | A |

## Non-verbal and abstract reasoning

| Questions | Answers |
|-----------|---------|
| 31 | C |
| 32 | D |
| 33 | E |
| 34 | C |
| 35 | B |

## Mechanical reasoning

| Questions | Answers |
|-----------|---------|
| 36 | C |
| 37 | E |
| 38 | A |
| 39 | B |
| 40 | A |

# accepting the offer and clinching the deal

Congratulations – you have got the job! Before you accept, though, ask yourself:

▶ are any strings attached?;

▶ is there scope for negotiating better terms and conditions?

In this chapter, you will:

- ❏ find out about accepting a job offer;

- ❏ learn about your contract of employment;

- ❏ gain insight into the terms and conditions of employment;

- ❏ importantly, see how you can clinch the deal, negotiating to your advantage;

- ❏ see how to then accept the job;

- ❏ come to understand the 'psychological contract';

- ❏ find out about sources of further information, including web sites.

# A HEAVIER THAN USUAL THUD

The long-awaited moment has arrived, and the envelope lands with a heavier than usual thud on the doormat. You open it to read that your application has been successful. Your job offer is a reality at last! You may, of course, receive the news by telephone – for many jobs an employer wants a quick decision. If you turn it down, they may want to move on quickly and offer the job to their second reserve.

Here, I outline key issues and the formal procedures involved in making and receiving job offers. I shall also help you think about the 'package' you are being offered and the scope you may have to negotiate the best deal possible.

It is important to state at the outset that this material cannot provide comprehensive and detailed coverage of all aspects of contemporary employment law. European and UK employment legislation is a highly complicated and specialist field, but, more pertinently, it is changing so fast that information included here would soon be out of date. However, I do include signposts to regularly updated sources of employment law information below and in the companion web site for anyone interested.

# RECEIVING A JOB OFFER

Once you have recovered from the initial euphoria, there are several issues to consider. You will be interested in key aspects of the job offer, such as starting salary, holidays and any perks in the package being offered. First, though, take a moment to find out if the offer has any strings attached.

## 'OFFER SUBJECT TO...'

The offer is likely to be conditional. The following are the six areas that your prospective employer will be concerned about.

### References

Many job offers are conditional on receiving satisfactory references. Not all employers bother to follow up references, but some do. Those that don't would probably agree with the following comment made by leading human resources management writer and consultant, Michael Armstrong in his book *A Handbook of Personnel Management Practice* (Kogan Page, 1996):

> **Personal referees are, of course, entirely useless. All they prove is that the applicant has at least one or two friends.**

You are entitled to ask about the timescale involved and can get in touch with referees and ask them to reply quickly.

## Health

You may be asked to complete a self-report questionnaire about your health. Some organizations go a step further and require you to have a medical examination with their own doctor or by arrangement with a local GP. Under the Data Protection Act 1998, you are entitled to see the medical report if you wish, subject to certain procedures being followed.

Medical examinations involve varying degrees of thoroughness. Your prospective employer will probably send you a form outlining the type of examination they wish you to be given. You should ask for details from the organization if you want to know more. The medical examination is often linked to pension and life assurance arrangements. An increasing number of UK companies include pre-employment urine screening to test for drug or alcohol use.

## Security

Some jobs, such as those that involve working with children, require a police check by law. Jobs with the Civil Service, government bodies and some private-sector organizations (especially involving military equipment) may also require more in-depth security clearance.

If your role involves responsibility for money, you may be investigated for credit-worthiness. The past few years have seen a rise in private investigation and 'fidelity bonding' agencies, which specialize in pre-employment checks.

## Exam results

If you are applying prior to graduation, your job offer may be subject to your exam grade. Do not despair, though – even if you fail to reach the usual 2:1 standard, the employer may still be interested in you. You can contact them with your results to see. Some employers may require you to pass your driving test as a condition of employment, though.

## Relocation

The job offer may be dependent on your agreeing to relocate. This can mean a one-off relocation to work at a given operational site, office or service centre. You may receive a 'disturbance allowance' – the ultimate irony if you are moving from college to live in London, which is the aspired work destination of most students in the most recent survey by High Fliers Research Ltd (1999).

A second type of relocation requirement is more usually included in your terms and conditions of employment – a mobility clause (see below).

## Eligibility for employment

Your offer of employment will be subject to your eligibility. This may be clear-cut if you are either a UK citizen or citizen of an EU member state. Work permits and a visa may be necessary – depending on your status, you may need to check this out.

# ACCEPTING A JOB OFFER

An employer will usually confirm the offer of employment after satisfactory references have been obtained and other conditions, such as passing the medical, have been met.

You should not rush to formally accept a job offer. Instead, check it carefully. Once accepted, this forms your contract of employment and is binding. It is far better to ask questions about the job and terms and conditions now than after acceptance.

> **'Employers will be flexible in the setting of deadlines for the acceptance of offers. Short deadlines may limit the ability of students to make informed decisions and prejudice the recruitment activities of other employers. This in turn may lead to students accepting offers and then reneging on them.'**
>
> *(Code of Practice 1995, AGR, AgCAS and NUS)*

I think it is perfectly reasonable to write a letter of personal acceptance subject to discussion about the details of the contract of employment.

An important factor to remember about the employment relationship is that, generally it is the employer who has the power to dictate the contractual terms. However, in many cases it is possible to 'talk up' your package. Next, we shall consider the key issues regarding your contract of employment – what it should include and how you might negotiate the best deal possible. Discussions about terms and conditions of a contract of employment only relate to individuals who become employees.

# YOUR CONTRACT OF EMPLOYMENT

The implications of employee status, the formation of a contract of employment and the main statutory employment rights were outlined earlier in Chapter 12. You should re-read that chapter as background preparation for your negotiations for a full-time job after graduation.

# WRITTEN STATEMENTS OF TERMS AND CONDITIONS

The terms and conditions of your employment are probably the focus of keenest interest. You have a legal right to a written statement, but, unfortunately, the employer does not need to issue this for up to two months *after* the beginning of your employment. That is far too late for any nasty surprises or disappointments. This section helps you to clinch the best deal and be as well informed as possible.

Please refer back to Chapter 12, which gives details of the terms and conditions that you are entitled to know about. See how much of this information you already have. Are there any gaps? If so, act now, contact the organization and ask for the information you need.

# NEGOTIATING THE BEST DEAL YOU CAN

Conventional wisdom suggests that you must accept the offer as it stands. In practice, many employers are flexible and will listen to your requests seriously. Some aspects of the employment contract may not be open to negotiation, especially if the organization operates a rigid reward system with salary and holiday linked to pay scales. Read through the terms and conditions listed below to see if you have any scope for negotiating your package.

## STARTING DATE

This may be flexible. Many organizations recruit all year round and may be able to delay your start date. Some employers are willing to consider substantial deferrals – of months or even up to a year. You will need to present a compelling case, though, or compromise and cut down on your time out.

## SCALE, RATE AND METHOD OF CALCULATING PAY

Your starting scale may be fixed or within a band of possibilities. Ask! The design and operation of pay scales is very complicated, often including an element related to your individual performance or, in the private sector, to company profitability.

It is also important to find out how often your pay is assessed. One job may have a lower starting salary than another, but have greater prospects for speedy increases if you do well. Is there any possibility of overtime payments for going beyond the contracted hours of working or are you just expected to work as long as it takes to get the job done?

## HOURS

These may be fixed across the organization or relate to your role. You may want to negotiate starting earlier, or finishing later (don't worry, in most graduate jobs it will be both anyway!)

## HOLIDAYS

There may be an organizational pecking order of holidays, starting with the least senior or most recent having, for example, 20 days (plus the 8 statutory bank holidays) only rising to 25 with promotion or long service. In such cases, an organization won't offer flexibility. You may be able to negotiate 'hidden holidays' by agreeing 'time in lieu' of long hours (say up to a day or so a month).

## PERSONALLY TAILORED PACKAGES

Many organizations now offer a graduate package, which includes salary, holidays and often other perks, such as car leasing schemes, private heath care, health or sports club membership and discounts on company products. You may be able to negotiate a personally tailored package – sometimes regarded as 'cafeteria benefits'. This is because you pick and mix the package to your own preferences within a certain pre-set 'value'.

## TRAINING AND PERSONAL DEVELOPMENT

The graduate training scheme may be a set programme or tailor-made according to the specific job. In addition, you may be able to gain agreement to study for externally accredited professional membership, Diploma in Management or even for an MBA. It's worth discussing your aspirations early and finding out what the possibilities are. Some organizations agree to fund your studies and offer reasonable paid release for study and exams.

# 'SPECIAL' TERMS, CONDITIONS AND RESTRICTIONS

Increasing numbers of employers include special clauses or restrictions. Try to find out if any of these apply to you.

## ON JOINING THE ORGANIZATION

**'A friend of mine has just been offered 'serious money' to join a small local IT firm writing tailor-made software programs'.**

'Golden hellos' or 'golden handshakes' are a means of attracting you to accept a particular post, especially in sectors such as IT, where there is a shortage of candidates with the necessary skills.

Many organizations will offer incoming employees financial and practical help, finding accommodation and so on. If the move is expected within four weeks or so of accepting the job, this would often include a package of hotel accommodation, meals and other expenses.

## TO STOP YOU LEAVING . . .

Some organizations also attach 'golden handcuffs', which are usually a lump sum or other inducement to stay for a specified period or complete a project. Given the highly mobile nature of some jobs and the lucrative benefits of career hopping, this is becoming an increasingly common practice.

## 'OPT OUT' CLAUSES

> 'I have been offered a job with a leading management consultancy in London, but they want me to agree to 'opt out' of my right not to work more than 48 hours in the average week.'

Some employers ask employees to 'opt out' of their statutory rights, as given under the Working Time Directive. The employer may want you to be available to respond to customers or cover for colleagues. This is very common in many fast-moving customer service sectors, such as management consultancy. The employer is entitled to ask you to opt out but you do not have to agree. Even if you sign the opt out clause, you can change your mind, provided that you give your employer three months' notice.

## 'MOBILITY CLAUSES'

Certain graduate trainee schemes involve a rotational system where you move between sites to gain experience. In some cases, the requirement to be mobile is included in express terms, but in many it is implied in the promotional material and job adverts. Employers must act reasonably, and it may be seen as reasonable if you are warned beforehand! There may be scope to reduce the number of hours you do if you can demonstrate prior knowledge or experience.

## LEAVING THE ORGANIZATION AND BEYOND

> 'I have just been offered a job in a local advertising/PR agency, but my contract includes a clause that I cannot work for their competitors if I leave.'

Get legal advice. This sounds like a 'restraint of trade' clause and the courts tend to look on them with disfavour. Your employer would have to demonstrate that the clause is reasonable – many such clauses are invalid. Check it out as such clauses could have a detrimental effect on your future career.

Some organizations require you to sign a clause that you will not take clients with you if you leave (for example, management consultants, accountancy firms and solicitors' practices). Again, take care to read the small print – these clauses can restrict your future career options. If in doubt, seek legal advice.

# THE PSYCHOLOGICAL CONTRACT

The concept of the psychological contract was mentioned earlier in Chapter 11. It is the set of unwritten expectations that operates between employees and employers. In an ideal world, the contract of employment would give room to include the expectations and assumptions being made on both sides. Problems can occur when there is a mismatch between your expectations and the reality of the job and/or organizational life.

You can do a lot to ensure your expectations are realistic by researching the organization and job as thoroughly as you can and asking detailed, probing questions throughout the selection process and after you have been offered the job. Make sure you use the information in this chapter to your advantage!

# SUMMARY

▶ Fantastic – you have a job offer! First, check there are no strings attached. If there are conditions, can you fulfil them?

▶ Your contract of employment is at the heart of your relationship with your future employer, so be sure you have as much information as possible before accepting the offer. This will helps you to avoid disappointment and nasty surprises later on.

▶ Some aspects of the employment contract may be negotiable. You may have to respect existing pay scales and holiday allowances, but, nothing ventured, nothing gained! Many aspects of the overall package can be individually tailored.

▶ Watch out for special terms and conditions that may have financial penalties or commercial restrictions attached if you leave.

# SIGNPOSTS TO MORE HELP

See Chapter 12.

### Factsheets

There are useful DTI factsheets on terms and conditions, sex discrimination and equal pay, maternity rights, the national minimum wage and many more.

Many university student union offices produce their own information leaflets and update them annually.

### Books

Pitt, G. (1996) *Employment Law*, Sweet and Maxwell. London.

Rousseau, D. (1995) *Psychological Contracts in Organizations: Understanding written and unwritten agreements*, Sage, Newbury Park, California.

## Web sites

www.dti.gov.uk/guidance.htm

A government site with comprehensive, up-to-date information and contacts.

www.tuc.org.uk

The Trades Union Congress site has regularly updated information on employment rights, plus details of a telephone advice service.

www.eoc.org.uk

The Equal Opportunities Commission site has data, contacts and telephone advice details.

www.incomesdata.co.uk

Incomes Data Services is an organization that produces a range of surveys of interest, including the *Directory of Salary Surveys, Pay in the Public Services* and *Company Car Policies.*

> **'What we call the beginning is often the end. And to make an end is to make a beginning. The end is where we start from.'**
>
> Little Gidding, 5. Four quartets from collected poems by T.S. Eliot 1909–1962© 1969. Faber and Faber, London.

**In this chapter, you will:**

❑ find out about making transitions – they can be emotional rollercoasters;

❑ prepare for starting work;

❑ be given an induction checklist: identify everything you need to know;

❑ learn what you can do to make it a success;

❑ find out how to deal with the boss;

❑ discover how to deal with colleagues.

**In the activity:**

**21.1** Get ready for work

# MAKING THE TRANSITION FROM BEING A STUDENT TO BEING AN EMPLOYEE

Starting a new job is a big step. It is one of life's big transitions, especially if it is also your first full-time job after graduation.

If you have been a part-time student or have prior work experience you already have some experience of 'starting work'. Even so, organizations do not always provide the same quality of support and induction to part-time or temporary staff that they give to incoming full-timers. Every organization and job is different, so you may even need to 'unlearn' things from your past as you enter something new.

Most of us start a new job with mixed feelings – anticipation (especially of that first payslip) and some apprehension.

Life could well be described as a sequence of changes and transitions. Just think of the ones you have already negotiated – childhood, secondary school, A level student, leaving home. Some readers may have made even more – building intimate relationships, parenthood, career changes. These changes may have had a major impact on your character, personality and self-image.

Starting work is no different – your experience of work, achievements and work relationships will exert a powerful influence on how you continue to develop in the months and years ahead.

Starting work promotes changes in five main areas:

► how you understand the world – new horizons, new insights;

► where you see yourself in it – new self-image;

► what you do day by day – new role and responsibilities;

► how, why and where you relate to others – status, freedom and control;

► your finances – payment of debts, spending capacity.

This chapter provides you with plenty of information and ideas about how to be prepared for work. This will give you confidence and help you make a good impression from day one.

The next section looks further at the notion of change and making transitions. This is followed by some practical advice about the sort of information you can expect to receive (or ask for!) prior to starting work and on your first day.

# THE EFFECTS OF CHANGE

Many researchers and writers have noticed a familiar pattern in the levels of morale and self-esteem during periods of change. This is shown in Figure 21.1.

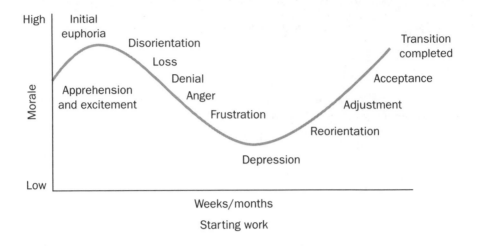

High | Initial euphoria

Disorientation

Loss

Denial

Apprehension and excitement

Anger

Frustration

Depression

Morale

Transition completed

Acceptance

Adjustment

Reorientation

Low

Weeks/months

Starting work

**FIGURE 21.1  Making transitions – an emotional rollercoaster**

---

**CASE STUDY   Matthew, 26 – graduate trainee**

'I was thrilled to start my first job. The first few days were a constant round of meetings and introductions. I was pleased and excited to have my own workstation, secretary and was thrown in the deep end. Nothing could have prepared me for the tiredness, though. I feel shattered – the concentration, learning the ropes, meeting new people, early starts and late finishes, wanting to make a good impression.

'I actually went to bed early midweek for at least the first two months – my plans to visit friends now dotted around the country went down the pan. It took me at least four months to find my feet.'

---

# HOW TO PREPARE FOR WORK

Your future employer should provide a substantial amount of information to help you settle in to work quickly. They are keen to make a good impression and a well-oriented employee is a productive employee! They want you to hit the ground running.

## PRE-EMPLOYMENT

Think about the information you already have about the organization. The job advert, information exchanged during the selection process, any brochures. You will receive starting instructions, telling you when and where to go on your first day and who to ask for. You may by now also receive details of your terms and conditions.

Everyone is different, and feels comfortable with varying levels of uncertainty. Is there anything that is bothering you about starting work that you can reasonably ask about in the weeks before you start? Don't hesitate to ask, contacting the Human Resources or Personnel Department.

# YOUR FIRST DAY

**Organizations vary enormously in the quality of their welcome.**

Every first day will be unique, depending on the style and approach your organization adopts. Some organizations run special programmes designed specifically for an incoming group of recent graduates.

Essentially, you should expect:

▶ a good reception – to be welcomed and expected by your future boss or someone from human resources or personnel;

▶ introductions – to key people, such as your boss, section or line manager, human resources staff, colleagues;

▶ information – it may feel like an avalanche of paper, in the form of procedure manuals, policies, company handbook, information about trade unions, a welcome pack and so on.

An inventory of the typical contents of a welcome pack or induction handbook are shown below.

| **Domestic information** | Geography of the site<br>Cloakrooms and lavatories<br>Canteen facilities<br>Rest and first aid rooms<br>Car parking, travelling arrangements<br>Time recording |
|---|---|
| **Health and safety** | Fire exits and fire drills<br>Basic safety rules, no smoking zones and so on<br>Accident procedures<br>Protective clothing<br>Occupational health service<br>Security alerts |
| **Pay** | Pay systems, including performance-related pay<br>Bonus schemes, including employee shareholding and so on<br>Savings schemes<br>Allowances (shift, overtime, standby, and so on)<br>Sick pay<br>Deductions<br>Explanation of payslip<br>Actual pay-out procedure |

**FIGURE 21.2 Typical contents of an induction handbook**

| | |
|---|---|
| **Other conditions of service** | Hours of work, flexitime, rest breaks<br>Annual leave, absence from work, extra-statutory holidays<br>Pension scheme and life insurance<br>Car and other expense claims<br>Disciplinary procedures<br>Grievance procedures<br>General rules and regulations |
| **Working matters** | Use of telephones, faxes, photocopiers<br>Workplace security procedures<br>Internal mail, including e-mail<br>Use of pagers<br>Use of company transport<br>Data protection procedures<br>Equipment maintenance<br>Energy conservation procedures |
| **Welfare and other benefits** | Sports and social facilities<br>Staff purchases<br>Suggestion scheme<br>Access to personal welfare counselling<br>Mortgage assistance, loans |
| **Trade unions and employee involvement** | Trade union membership or recognition policies<br>Who's who – shop stewards, safety representatives<br>Joint consultative systems – quality circles – briefing group system<br>Pay bargaining systems – national and local agreements |
| **Employee development** | Appraisal schemes<br>Training schemes<br>Assistance with professional studies, study leave, OU arrangements and so on<br>Promotion opportunity policy<br>Qualification incentives |
| **Equal opportunities** | The organization's policy on standards of behaviour expected of employees<br>Rules regarding sexual and racial harassment |
| **The organization itself** | The organization's mission statement and core values<br>Operational and other objectives and policies<br>Organizational structure – roles of constituent companies, departments, functions<br>Managerial and supervisory hierarchy and who's who<br>Scale – numbers employed, annual turnover, capital and revenue budget and so on<br>Processes, production methods, functions<br>Public relations policies |
| **The industry or sector** | Nature and size of the industry or economic sector<br>National/industrial organizations |

**FIGURE 21.2  continued**

The list in Figure 21.2 might look turgid and deadly dull, but you need to know about it if you want to be effective quickly. Remembering people's names and what they do, procedures and so on is a great way to make a good impression.

---

**ACTIVITY 21.1    Get ready for work**

Look at the information you may be given. Go back through the checklist given in Figure 21.1.

How much do you already know?

_____

_____

How much can you find out in advance?

_____

_____

What will wait until after you have arrived?

_____

_____

(Many practical and procedural matters can wait until you arrive, but taking a few steps in the right direction might help.)

---

# INDUCTION

There are various ways of understanding the word 'induction'. On the surface, it can be viewed as simply a means of helping you adjust to your new role, find out about policies, roles and conventions. The organization has statutory duties to tell you about health and safety issues and will want to explain broader issues, such as how performance is measured or how grievances and problems are resolved.

However, it is also commonly understood that induction is an important part of the way the organization 'socializes' you. You will probably be informed about their business strategy, values and beliefs. Given that you have been selected with care, these should not come as a surprise and you should feel well matched. Induction is a time when you begin to learn more about the culture and goals of the organization you have joined. It is helpful to distinguish between the welcome you receive on day one and induction, which is really more of a process than a single event.

## THE INDUCTION PROCESS

Your introductory programme may be structured or informed, short or long, individually tailored or part of a group. It is only the start, however. The three key features of the induction process are your relationship with your boss, the training you receive from the organization and, in some organizations, support from other staff, either a senior mentor or other recent graduates.

## THE ROLE OF THE 'BOSS' IN INDUCTION

Your manager will be charged with the duty of helping you to settle in quickly and learn how to function effectively at work. They may be expected to act as a role model for you, coach, direct and guide. The boss will also be keen to ensure you understand what you are expected to accomplish and to do this to the highest standards and with maximum efficiency. Your manager is accountable for the team and department and will have their own performance targets to meet.

## THE ROLE OF TRAINING

Most induction training includes elements about organizational policies and procedures. However many induction programmes offer personal development courses as well. These could include business awareness, time management, meetings, presentations. These combine elements of personal development with showing you 'how things are done around here'.

Your boss will be particularly keen for you to attend those courses that make you a really effective part of the team.

## MENTORS AND BUDDIES

Another part of the induction process may include the offer of support and advice from someone outside your immediate work sphere. Mentors come in various shapes and sizes, but are usually senior managers from different parts of the organization to yourself. Roles and objectives of the mentor vary, but they usually offer you a chance to ask questions about the organization, your job and career prospects in confidence.

If well organized, a mentoring system can provide you with knowledge, contacts, support, a sounding board for ideas and a fresh perspective on problems. Another approach is to offer you contact with a graduate who joined a year or so previously to be a 'buddy'. You may make these acquaintances naturally, but a formal link is helpful if there are no other new graduates near to your daily workplace.

# WHAT YOU CAN DO TO MAKE YOUR FIRST JOB A SUCCESS

There are several things you need to do well in order to make a success of your first job. Some relate to your own level of satisfaction, some to satisfying your manager and colleagues. Let's start with making a good impression on them.

- learning how to work;
- dealing with the boss;
- dealing with colleagues;
- accepting the reality of work – office politics, inefficiency.

## LEARNING HOW TO WORK

This will involve a blend of being technically competent and following accepted organizational norms. You can:

- prepare by improving your practical skills – find out what IT packages, e-mail and so on are used and make sure you can operate the key ones beforehand;
- know what you are good at and acknowledge areas for development – your boss and organization will work to help you identify training needs, so demonstrate your willingness;
- follow good practices and when you need it, ask for help (but not too often).

## DEALING WITH THE BOSS

How you handle your relationship with your boss will be a product of their style of leadership and your style of relating. Organizations and individuals differ – managers may be open or distant, controlling and directive or have a more open approach. You can:

- understand your manager's style and approach – respect it;
- try to understand the pressures and demands on your boss – show you have good business sense and want to pull your weight;
- if possible, try to create open and frank levels of communication;
- not complain about them or criticize them openly – at least not at work.

---

**CASE STUDY  Management consultant, graduate entry, male, aged 25**

'I can't describe the pressure and responsibility I have been given. Everyone works endless hours, very few leave before 9pm at night and I have often worked through the weekends. My boss is hardly a boss at all … at least not what I expected. We are on first name terms, I am left to plan my own work schedule and have control of budgets worth over £250,000. This is a real test, I am learning a lot and at times the adrenaline buzz is amazing. It won't last, though. I'll give myself two years, then I'll need to get out – if you don't, you burn out. Still, I'm glad I've done it – now I know what I'm made of!'

---

## DEALING WITH COLLEAGUES

If you are working with other graduates or those who entered the organization at a similar level, you may find them open, supportive and friendly. Some graduates come in at a relatively senior level and are viewed as 'stuck up'. You may have some work to do in gaining the respect and approval of non-graduate colleagues, especially if your predecessors have fulfilled their worst expectations.

You can make your colleague relationships successful by:

► being friendly and warm;

► being respectful of their knowledge and skills;

► demonstrating that you want to pull your weight and contribute;

► recognizing that there are many routes to personal development – university is only one of them, so don't underestimate other people;

► being shrewd – watch your back!

## ACCEPTING THE REALITY OF WORK

You will soon discover what sort of a place this is really like to work in. Accept that tensions, rivalries and bungling inefficiencies are part of life in every organization. You may also discover that the promised challenging and stimulating role also involves a large number of boring tasks. The opposite can also happen – you can feel out of your depth with responsibility and are faced with unrealistic deadlines and a heavy workload. Life is unfair and working life often doubly so.

As you settle in to your first job, there will be other skills you need to develop. I hope you have found that this chapter has pointed you in the right direction for a good start.

I hope you have enjoyed reading and using this book. I wish you great success and satisfaction in your first and all your future jobs.

Shirley Jenner

# bibliography

Alston, A. and Davies, A. (1996) *The Penguin Careers Guide*, Penguin, Harmondsworth.

Armstrong, M. (1996) *A Handbook of Personnel Management Practice*, Kogan Page, London.

Association of Graduate Recruiters (2000) *Graduate Salaries and Vacancies*, AGR, London.

Barclays Bank (1999) *Fifth Annual Graduate Survey*, Barclays, London.

Bolles, R. N. (1999) *What Colour is Your Parachute?*, Ten Speed Press, California, USA.

Buffton, B. *The Which? Guide to Choosing a Career*.

Boyatzis, R. (1982) *The Competent Manager. A model for effective performance*, New York, Wiley.

Coe, T. (1992) *The Key to the Men's Club: Opening the doors to women in management*, Institute of Management, London.

CSU (summer and winter 1998) *Graduate Market Trends*.

CSU (spring 1999) *Graduate Market Trends*.

Davidson, M. J. and Cooper, C. I. (1992) *Shattering the Glass Ceiling*, London, Paul Chapman Publishing Ltd.

Deal, T. and Kennedy, A. (1982) *Corporate Cultures*, Penguin, Harmondsworth, London.

Earnshaw, J. and Cooper, C. (1996), *Stress and Employer Liability*, IPD, London.

Feltham, R. T. (1989) 'Assessment Centres' in Herriot, P. (ed., 1989) *Assessment and Selection in Organizations: Methods and practice for recruitment and appraisal*, Wiley, Chichester.

Handy, C. (1993) *Understanding Organizations* (4th ed.), Penguin, Harmondsworth.

Harvey, L., Moon, S. and Geall, V. (1997) *Graduates' Work: Organizational change and student's attributes*, Centre for Research into Quality, University of Central England, Birmingham.

Harvey, L., Moon, S. and Geall, V. (1998) *Work Experience: Expanding opportunities for undergraduates*, Centre for Research into Quality, University of Central England, Birmingham.

Herriot, P. (1984) *Down from the Ivory Tower*, John Wiley and Sons Ltd., London.

Higher Education Statistics Agency (1999) *First Destinations of Higher Education Students in the United Kingdom for the Academic Year 1997/98*, HESA, London.

Higher Education Statistics Agency (1999) *Students in Higher Education Institutions, 1997/98*, HESA, London.

High Fliers (1999) *Graduate Careers: The fifth annual survey of final year undergraduate students at the UK's leading universities,* High Fliers Research, London.

Hopson, B. and Scally, M. (1993) *Build Your own Rainbow,* Pfieffer, USA.

Hornby, M. (1994) *36 Steps to the Job you Want,* Longman, Harlow.

Incomes Data Services (1998) 'Pay and Progression for Graduates 1997/1998', *Management Pay Review,* IDS, London.

Industrial Relations Services (November 1998) 'Graduate recruitment and sponsorship: The 1998 IRS survey of employer practice', *Employee Development Bulletin 107,* IRS, London.

Keenan, T. (1995) 'Graduate recruitment in Britain: A survey of selection methods used by organizations', *Journal of Organizational Behaviour,* 16, pp. 303–17.

Lazarus, R. S. (1976) *Patterns of Adjustment.* McGraw-Hill, New York.

Marchington, M. and Wilkinson, A. (1996) *Core Personnel and Development,* IPD, London.

Mullins, L. (1996) *Management and Organizational Behaviour,* Pitman, London.

National Union of Students (1995) *Survey of Student Employment* (quoted in the *Times Higher Education Supplement,* 8, 16 July 1999)

National Westminster Bank (1999) *Student Money Matters Survey,* NatWest, London.

Pearson, R., Perryman, S., Connor, H., Jagger, N. and Aston, J. (1999) *The IES Annual Graduate Review 1998–1999. The key facts,* Institute for Employment Studies Report 345, Brighton.

Perrett, J. (1996) *Job Hunting after University or College,* Kogan Page, London.

Purcell, K. and Pitcher, J. (1996) *Great Expectations: The new diversity of graduate skills and aspirations,* Institute of Employment Research/Department for Education and Employment/CSU, Manchester.

Purcell, K., Pitcher, J. and Simm, C. (1999) *Working Out?,* Institute of Employment Research/Department for Education and Employment/CSU, Manchester.

Rousseau, D. (1995) *Psychological Contracts in Organizations: Understanding written and unwritten agreements,* Sage, Newbury Park, California.

Spera, S. and Lanto, S. (1995) *Beat Stress with Strength: Achieving wellness at work and in life,* DBM Publishing, New York.

Schein, E. (1988) *Organizational Psychology,* Prentice Hall, New Jersey.

Universum (1998) *The British Graduate Survey 1998: Monitoring the leaders of tomorrow,* Universum, Stockholm.

Warren, E. and Toll, C. (1993) *The Stress Work Book,* Nicholas Brealey, London.

Williams, R. (1999) *Prepare for Tests at Interview for Graduates and Managers,* NFER-Nelson, Windsor.

Woodruffe, C. (1993) *Assessment Centres: Identifying and developing competence* (2nd ed.), IPD, London.

# appendix: where to find information, help and advice

## CAREERS DECISIONS, JOBHUNTING SKILLS AND INFORMATION

### UNIVERSITY CAREERS ADVISORY SERVICES

Higher education careers advisory services are the main sources of information and advice about graduate careers and employers. My tip would be to visit your local careers office very early, preferably in your first year if you can. There is a wealth of information to help you find the right career direction and employer and plan for interesting and challenging ways to use your holidays.

The following is just a brief list of the main services and information available – you will find others:

▶ company directories – *Get, Prospects, Times 100*;
▶ careers publications;
▶ company files and feedback sheets from previous candidates;
▶ details about company presentations and recruitment fairs;
▶ videos – from careers advisory services' libraries;
▶ information from those who have been on work experience or placements or via contacts who work there;
▶ help with applications, CVs and interview skills;
▶ reference books – about employers, career planning, jobhunting skills;
▶ regular vacancy bulletins;
▶ links to local employers' mentoring schemes;
▶ personal advice and guidance;
▶ subject area and specialist advice, plus advice for women, ethnic minorities and disabled students;
▶ *Prospects* HE self-assessment careers guidance programme;
▶ Internet access.

## IF YOU HAVE ALREADY GRADUATED

Many of the above services are also available to recent graduates via your old university or whichever one is nearest to your home. Contact details are available in your telephone directory or at the national AgCAS web site, which provides regional and alphabetical indexes to higher education careers services:

www.agcas.csu.ac.uk/links/UK.htm

## GET ON-LINE

### For students and recent graduates

*General*
University careers services are closely connected with CSU and the *Prospects* directory. A helpful site, providing self-assessment opportunities, information about occupations and employers, plus on-line jobhunting, can be found at:

www.prospects.csu.ac.uk

Another key directory available on-line is *Get:*

www.get.hobsons.com

### For disabled students and graduates

**Cando** has:

▶ current vacancies;

▶ postgraduate study options;

▶ general advice and guidance;

▶ profiles of equal opportunities employers;

▶ related organizations and contacts;

▶ sources of financial support.

Find it at:

www.cando.lancs.ac.uk

**Hobsons** produces a casebook for disabled graduates annually, which contains personal case studies and company profiles.
Most local university careers services provide specialist help for disabled graduates, plus a mentoring or contact network of local employers.

Also visit:

▶ **Disability Net** at www.disabilitynet.co.uk

▶ **The Appointments Service** at www.taps.com

## Jobcentres

Branch offices advertise local jobs and a national Jobcentre database of vacancies is also available at:

www.employmentservice.gov.uk

## National newspapers

*The Guardian* is at:

www.jobsunlimited.co.uk

*The Independent* is at:

www.independent.co.uk

*The Times* is at:

www.the-times.co.uk

*The Daily Telegraph* is at:

www.appointments-plus.co.uk

## Regional newspapers

The London *Evening Standard* is at: www.thisislondon.com
*Manchester Evening News* is at: www.manchesteronline.co.uk/fish4jobs

# JOBHUNTING ON-LINE – SOME SITES TO CONSIDER

## KEY EUROPEAN GRADUATE EMPLOYMENT SITES

| Countries | Key directories | Internet addresses |
|---|---|---|
| UK | Prospects | www.prospects.csu.ac.uk |
| Belgium (and Luxembourg) | Move Up | www.moveup.be |
| Denmark | Karriere Vejviser | www.move-on.dk |
| France | Le Guide des Opportunités de Carrières | www.go.tm.fr |
| Germany | Absolventen Berufswahratgeber | www.az-online.de |
| Holland | Intermediaiar Jarrboek | www.bpa.nl/intermediair/ |
| Italy | (No directory equivalent) | www.mercurius.it www.careermosaic.it |
| Norway | (Check web sites for latest) | www.jobshop.no www.stepstone.no |
| Spain | Guia de las Empresas que Ofrecen Empleo | www.mad.servcom.es |

Here are some other useful sites.

http://www.taps.com
Recruitment site, including on-line CVs (UK, Ireland, international).

http://www.careermosaic.com
International job vacancy site, plus advice on CVs and electronic resumés.

http://www.westlake.co.uk
Includes further study, database of CVs and links to graduate recruiters' web pages (UK) – particularly in local government, engineering, medicine and computing.

http://www.diversitynow.net
Promotes diversity – links to employers plus conference calls.

http://www.kcl.ac.uk/kis/college/careers/links/vclmap.htm
Careers site based at King's College, London. It has a fairly comprehensive list of careers sites, plus lists of professional bodies and trade associations.

http://europa.eu.int
Links to national employment services across Europe – especially useful for jobs in European government.

http://www.worldnews.com and http://www.papers.com
Links to worldwide newspapers, including vacancies and current business news plus links.

http://www.eurograduate.com
Searchable database of employers and vacancies, and advice on planning a career in Europe.

www.overseasjobs.com
Jobs by keyword search, plus directory of over 4000 other job-related sites.

www.strath.ac.uk/Departments/Careers/guide
Good for contract researchers and using the Web for job searches.

http://www.jobhunter.co.uk
A link to most UK local and national papers' classified job adverts, including fish4jobs.

http://www.ifi.co.uk/
Information for industry site. Good for jobs concerning the environment.

# WORK EXPERIENCE OPPORTUNITIES

*Placement and Vacation Work Casebook 2000* has commonsense advice about a wide range of different types of holiday work experiences, including UK-based jobs with well-known employers of graduates. See more at:

www.get.hobsons.com

Local careers advisory services offer a range of information and link-up services for local, national and international opportunities for short and long holidays.

## WORK EXPERIENCE INFORMATION

**National Centre for Work Experience**
344-354 Grays Inn Road
London WCIX 8BP
*Tel:* 020 7833 9723
*Web site:* www.ncwe.com

A range of guides is produced by Vacation Work. Visit the web site for more information:
www.vacationwork.co.uk

# OVERSEAS AND HOLIDAY WORK

**AIESEC**
International Exchange Programme
29–31 Cowper Street
London EC2A 4AP
*Tel*: 020 7336 7939
*Web site*: www.uk.aiesec.org

**BUNAC Camp America**
16 Bowling Green Lane
London EC1R 0BD
*Tel*: 020 7251 3472
*Web site*: www.bunac.org.uk

**CIEE**
Council on International Educational Exchange
52 Poland Street
London W1V 4JQ
*Tel*: 020 7478 2000
*Web site*: www.ciee.org

**IAESTE**
The International Association for the Exchange of Students for Technical Experience
10 Spring Gardens
London SW1A 2BN
*Tel*: 020 7389 4774
*Web site*: www.iaeste.org.uk

**Raleigh International**
Raleigh House
27 Parsons Green Lane
London SW6 4HZ
*Tel*: 020 7371 8585
*Web site*: www.raleigh.org.uk

**Voluntary Service Overseas (VSO)**
317 Putney Bridge Road
London SW15 2PN
*Tel*: 020 8780 2266
*Web site*: www.oneworld.org

For a database of worldwide listings, visit the following site:
www.summerjobs.com

# EQUAL OPPORTUNITIES AND EMPLOYMENT RIGHTS

**Advisory, Conciliation and Arbitration Service (ACAS)**
National headquarters, tel: 020 7210 3642

Regional offices include:

- ► Birmingham     0121 456 5856
- ► Cardiff     029 2076 1126
- ► London     020 7396 5100
- ► Glasgow     0141 204 2677
- ► Manchester     0161 833 8585

Free leaflets available from:

ACAS Reader Ltd, tel: 01455 852225

Further details can be found at:
    www.acas.org.uk/advi_m.htm

**The Citizens Advice Bureau (CAB)**
For your nearest CAB, refer to your local telephone directory.

**Cando**
Provides specialist help and advice to disabled graduates on disability discrimination legislation. For details, visit Cando at:
    www.cando.lancs.ac.uk

**Commission for Racial Equality (CRE)**
Elliot House
10–12 Allington Street
London SW1E 5EH
*Tel*: 020 7828 7022
*Web site*: www.cre.gov.uk

**Department of Trade and Industry (DTI)**
Free national helpline: 0500 848489

**Equal Opportunities Commission (EOC)**
Overseas House
Quay Street
Manchester M3 3HN
*Tel*: 0161 833 9244
*Web site*: www.eoc.org.uk

### Health and Safety Executive (HSE)

Refer to your local telephone directory for the nearest HSE office.

Helpful HSE advice booklets are available free of charge. These can be obtained from your local government environmental health office.

### National Union of Students (NUS)

Nelson Mandela House
461 Holloway Road
London N7 6LJ
*Tel*: 020 7272 8900
*Web site*: www.nus.org.uk

### Trades Union Congress (TUC)

Congress House
Great Russell Street
London WC1B 3LS
*Tel*: 020 7636 4030
*Web site*: www.tuc.org.uk

# COUNSELLING AND PERSONAL PROBLEMS

## NATIONAL ORGANIZATIONS

### British Association of Counselling (BAC)

1 Regent Place
Rugby
Warwickshire CV21 2PJ
*Tel*: 01788 550899
*Web site*: www.counselling.co.uk

Can provide you with a list of trained and accredited counsellors in your area.

### MIND

Infoline (local call rate) *London tel*: 020 8522 1728; *outside London tel*: 0345 660 163
15–19 Broadway
London E15 4BQ
*Web site*: www.mind.org.uk

A leading mental health charity with a national information line and helpline. There are over 220 local MIND associations. Produces a comprehensive range of low-cost, issue-based booklets and practical information – how to cope with the stress of student life, loneliness, relationship breakdown and so on.

The web site has details, publications lists and so on.

**National AIDS helpline**
*Tel:* 0800 567123

**Gay and lesbian switchboard**
*London tel:* 020 7837 7324
*Web site:* www.llgs.org.uk
*Manchester tel:* 0161 274 3999
*Web site:* www.switchboard.mcmail.com

**Local health information point**
*Tel:* 0800 665544 (calls are free)
This service can give you phone numbers for local agencies or groups that can help you.

All health authorities now have a health information service called Health Point.

**Release**
388 Old Street
London EC1V 9LT
*Tel:* 020 7729 9904
*Web site:* www.release.org.uk
For drug-related problems.

**The Samaritans**
For local helpline numbers, look inside the front cover of your local telephone directory.
*National helplines, Tel:* 0345 90 90 90 in the *UK, Tel:* 1850 60 90 90 in the Republic of Ireland (calls charged at local rate).
*Web site:* www.samaritans.org.uk
Confidential support for anyone feeling depressed or suicidal.

**Local resources**
Information about most of the local services listed below will be available in your university prospectus, from the local students union office as well as on-line via your university intranet. Local branches of various national counselling agencies will be listed in the local telephone directory. If in doubt, seek advice from the university counselling service or your university welfare officer. They are there to help and advise you!

Many universities also allow recent graduates access to these facilities or can refer you to the right agency or person.

▶ Your student counselling service.

▶ Nightline telephone counselling and information.

▶ Your student union advice and information officer.

▶ Your student health centre.

▶ Your GP.

▶ Academic advisory or other learning support service.

- ► Your university chaplain.
- ► Your local church or other place of worship.
- ► Local branches of national counselling and advice agencies.

# CAREERS INTEREST, ABILITY AND PERSONALITY TESTING

The following services are available via your careers advisory service.

## PROSPECTS HE

*Prospects HE* is a user-friendly self-assessment system designed to help you match yourself to a suitable occupation. It enables you to

- ► find out about your skills, interests and motivation;
- ► find out about different jobs and occupations;
- ► find help and ideas to put your plans into action.

You can use the system in a number of different ways to suit the stage you have reached in the terms and years you use it. Your data is saved each time you use *Prospects HE* so you can work at your own pace and return to your investigations at any time.

You can access this system at your local careers office and via the campus network at many universities.

## PRACTICE TEST SESSIONS

Many careers services run practice test sessions covering verbal, numerical and logical reasoning. These usually run during the first and second term and are in great demand, so book early. There is usually a small charge made for administration and printing costs.

You can also practise the Civil Service familiarization test at many careers offices.

## TEST BOOKLETS

Available from most careers advisory services and Saville and Holdsworth Limited.

- ► SHL, 'Practice Tests'.
- ► SHL, 'Why are aptitude tests used?'.
- ► Information Technology Test Series 'Practice' Leaflet.

# TEST PUBLISHERS AND TESTS ON-LINE

The following list gives details of major UK test publishers. You will not be able to actually see or buy any of the ability tests they sell without the recognized British Psychological Society training and qualifications. However, publishers may be willing to send you a catalogue, which will contain useful information about their products. Some of these organizations offer an on-line career guidance and personal assessment service to graduates. Saville and Holdsworth Limited has a particularly good site for graduates.

**ASE**
Hanover House
2–4 Sheet Street
Windsor
Berkshire SL4 1BG
*Tel*: 01753 850333
*Web site*: www.ase-solutions.co.uk

In addition, the *ASE Career Expectations* survey (a short careers interest test) is available on-line at:
www.topjobs.co.uk/psychometrictest

**Oxford Psychologists Press**
Lambourne House
311–321 Banbury Road
Oxford OX2 7JH
*Tel*: 01865 510203
*Web site*: www.opp.co.uk

**The Psychological Corporation**
24–28 Oval Road
London NW1 7DX
*Tel*: 020 7424 4456
*Web site*: www.harcourt.com

**Saville and Holdsworth Limited (SHL)**
3 AC Court
High Street
Thames Ditton
Surrey KT7 0SR
*Tel*: 020 8339 2222
*Web site*: www.shlgroup.com

The SHL web site has a very useful interactive careers assessment service.

## REFERENCE BOOKS

Williams, Robert (1999) *Prepare for Tests at Interview for Graduates and Managers*, NFER-Nelson, Windsor.

Includes an opportunity to practise a comprehensive range of ability and personality tests. The sample ability and personality test questions used in Chapter 19 are taken from this book with the kind permission of NFER-Nelson.

Cohen, David (1993) *How to Succeed in Psychometric Tests*, Sheldon, London.

Kogan Page has produced a series of 'How to' books, including:

▶ *How to Master Personality Questionnaires: The Essential Guide* by Mark Parkinson, 1997
▶ *How to Pass Graduate Recruitment Tests* by Mike Bryon, 1994
▶ *How to Pass Technical Selection Tests* by Mike Bryon & Sanjay Modha, 1993
▶ *How to Pass Verbal Reasoning Tests* by Harry Tolley and Ken Thomas, 1996
▶ *How to Pass Computer Selection Tests* by Sanjay Modha, 1994
▶ *How to Pass Numeracy Tests* by Harry Tolley and Ken Thomas, 1996
▶ *How to Master Psychometric Tests* by Mark Parkinson, 1997

# index